Verge

STUDIES IN GLOBAL ASIAS

Volume 9, Issue 1
Spring 2023

Verge (ISSN 2373-5058) is published twice a year in the spring and fall by the University of Minnesota Press, 111 Third Avenue South, Suite 290, Minneapolis, MN 55401-2520. http://www.upress.umn.edu

Postmaster: Send address changes to *Verge*, University of Minnesota Press, 111 Third Avenue South, Suite 290, Minneapolis, MN 55401-2520.

Essays (between 6,000 and 10,000 words) should be prepared using parenthetical documentation with a list of works cited. Authors' names should not appear on manuscripts; instead, please include a separate document with the author's name and address and the title of the article with your electronic submission. Authors should not refer to themselves in the first person in the submitted text or notes if such references would identify them; any necessary references to the author's previous work, for example, should be in the third person. Submissions and editorial queries should be sent to verge@psu.edu.

Books for review should be addressed to

Verge: Studies in Global Asias
c/o Tina Chen, Editor
430 Burrowes
Penn State University
University Park, PA 16802

Address subscription orders, changes of address, and business correspondence (including requests for permission and advertising orders) to *Verge*, University of Minnesota Press, 111 Third Avenue South, Suite 290, Minneapolis, MN 55401-2520.

Subscriptions: For our current subscription rates, please see our website: https://www.upress.umn.edu. *Verge* is now available at the Project MUSE Hosted Journals Program at https://muse.jhu.edu. A subscription to *Verge* is a benefit of attending Penn State's biennial Global Asias symposium.

Verge Studies in Global Asias 9.1

SPRING 2023

Convergence

Essays

Editor's Introduction

TINA CHEN

Storying Global Asias

IN THEIR CONTRIBUTION to the *A&Q* feature on pedagogy in this issue, Nadine Attewell and Anushay Malik begin their collaboratively authored essay on teaching with the story of Faiz Ahmed Faiz, a Pakistani poet whose peregrinations connected him to a global network of writers and thinkers committed to realizing the unfulfilled dream of decolonization. Attewell and Malik suggest that Faiz's global itinerary produces "a Global Asia/s story" that we should recognize as such. We might understand labeling this a Global Asias story as a move that is primarily descriptive in nature, referring to Faiz's South Asian origins, his international collaboration with other leftist thinkers while living in Beirut and editing the quarterly *Lotus,* his long-standing relationships with readers and supporters in and beyond Asia, or some combination of these elements. But, as Attewell and Malik remind us, Global Asias stories are not always centered on the representational, important as that is. Indeed, while these stories can be about the figures and places constellating Asia and its multiple diasporas, they are also about how the "imaginable ageography" (Chen 2021) of Global Asias enables us to tell new stories about people, places, and the nature of the work we are doing as writers, thinkers, readers, and teachers. In other words, what if we expand our notion of what counts as a Global Asias story by exploring the ways in which such stories are platforms of invention, narratives that allow us to illuminate the possibilities and limits of the vast imaginable ageographies encompassed by Global Asias itself?

Inspired by this prospect, this editor's introduction synthesizes the diverse features and essays included here through the varied practices and uses of storying Global Asias. Although the topics, figures, issues, and problems examined in this open issue are widely varied, they collectively operate to make visible the conjectural opportunities generated by the Global Asias story, a narrative praxis that is never singular but rather proliferates across and between borders and boundaries. Storying Global Asias brings into visibility nodal points of collective interest and engagement, idiosyncratic constellations that nonetheless cast light on some of the questions and concerns animating the unruly nature of Global Asias as both epistemology and narrative.

As Louise Gwenneth Philips and Tracy Bunda (2018, 43) have demonstrated, "stories and storying are located," inextricably bound up with particular times and particular places even if they operate to expand the space and time of meaning-making. The importance of understanding the stories of Global Asias as located even as Global Asias is, itself, not always locatable is evidenced here. Beyond siting their work in particular locations—Okinawa, Brazil, Taiwan, the Philippines, Vietnam, Japan, Kashmir, mainland China, and Hawai'i, among other places—the contributors to this issue draw attention to the importance of locating themselves as writers, thinkers, researchers, and teachers, emphasizing the significance of storying Global Asias as a dual process of knowledge creation and situatedness. Accordingly, less geographically stable paradigms—the transpacific, diaspora, socialist Américas, Asian America, the oceanic, empire, and institution—operate in dynamic tension with the geohistorical sites listed above to make visible the paradox of location/unlocatability that marks Global Asias stories.

* * *

This issue's **Convergence** section opens with an *A&Q* feature titled "The Problems and Possibilities of Global Asias Pedagogy." Building on a series of Global Asias Cyber Chats in 2021–22 that *Verge* and the Global Asias Initiative cosponsored with the Global Asia program at Simon Fraser University and the Global Asian Studies Program at the University of Illinois Chicago, this feature invites colleagues to reflect on their experiences in the classroom, in their programs, and at their institutions in an effort to bring the theoretical and conceptual developments of Global Asias scholarship into dialogue with their role as educators. Working in varied institutional contexts and approaching the challenge of teaching Global Asias from different disciplinary vantage points, the feature's authors—Nadine Attewell, Anushay Malik, David Ludden, Michael R. Jin, and Mark Chiang—share a series of generative insights about Global Asias pedagogy. They collectively encourage us to "interrogate Asia as not just a place, a thing, or a collection of cultures to study but a set of global processes that is deeply shaped by lived experiences and struggles across those societies" (Jin), to "appreciate the very long histories of migration, mobility, and mingling that produced diverse composite cultures around the world" (Ludden), to "exploit the very fuzziness of the enormous conceptual field of 'Asia' as signifier as an entry point for the course to continually foreground the very contingency of Global Asia itself as an object of knowledge" (Chiang), and to "reproduce our training *queerly* so that students cultivate the skills and sensitivities needed to pursue Asia's global itineraries, across divides fundamental to twenty-first-century North American academic commonsense" (Attewell and Malik). They generously share the syllabi for their courses, making this entire feature a very useful dossier of materials for those of us interested in the pedagogical possibilities of Global Asias.

"Of Scrolls and Tears: Trinh Mai's Archival Art and Organic Ephemera" by H. J. Tam presents a *Portfolio* that illuminates how this Vietnamese American artist creates art that fuses public and private histories to enable a different way of recounting and remembering the complicated dynamics of the Vietnam War and its afterlives. Noting that the artist relies on two distinct types of materials—archival (identification cards, letters, photographs) and organic (tears, eggshells, feathers)—Tam argues that in combination, such "properties complement and transform each other: the organic materials lend their living aura to the historic documents, enabling these objects to conjure the specters of those who carried them through exile; at the same time, the archival materials fuse historicity into the ephemera, which symbolize refugees' precarious, embodied experiences often unacknowledged in history books."

Our final **Convergence** feature in this issue is a multiauthor *Field Trip* on "Left Internationalisms in Nationalist Times." Originally conceptualized as contributions to a series of linked panels on "Transpacific Socialisms" sponsored by *Verge* at the 2021 Association for Asian American Studies conference, these five short essays explore left internationalist imaginaries within Asia and in transpacific relation to the Americas. As the organizers of this conversation note, the stories included in this discussion do not so much reflect "the grand narrative ambition of 'transpacific socialisms'" as they explore "a structure of feeling in a minor key: a shared attention to instances of parasitic translation, reinvention, or reflective introjection of left internationalist imaginaries under conditions of extreme reaction and repression." In a diverse series of essays treating figures, histories, and events from internationalist practices and imaginaries from the 1930s to the 2020s, contributors Andrew Way Leong, Darwin H. Tsen, Paul Nadal, Roanne L. Kantor, Calvin Cheung-Miaw, and

Jason G. Coe engineer an exchange that "exemplifies the ethos of *Verge* as a forum for what lies on the edges of formations such as Asian area and Asian American ethnic studies." Rather than focusing on state socialisms (as might be expected in Asian studies) or (pan)-ethnic protest movements (as might be expected in Asian American studies), the authors instead bring together an eclectic group of figures and events—including Yamaga Taiji (1892–1970), Carlos Bulosan (1913–56), Agha Shahid Ali (1949–2001), the League of Revolutionary Struggle in the 1980s, and the 2016 trial of New York Police Department officer Peter Liang for the shooting death of Akai Gurley—to consider ways of building "infrastructures of translation toward future internationalisms."

This issue's first **Essay,** "Monuments of Culture: *Minzoku Taiwan* and the Search for Local History in Colonial Taiwan (1938–1950)" by Anne Ma Kuo-an, tells a fascinating Global Asias story about the development of the field of folklore studies or native ethnology (*minzokugaku*) in Taiwan. In making arguments about the diverse ways in which "culture" and "locality" were theorized by both Japanese and Taiwanese intellectuals during the mid-twentieth century, Ma narrates a story of how such scholars and community members navigated the complex dynamics of a colonial context that simultaneously encouraged Taiwanese assimilation into Japanese culture while also insisting on differentiating between locals and citizens. By analyzing *Minzoku Taiwan* (Taiwan folklore), a journal dedicated to "documenting, but not necessarily 'preserving,' the local customs and traditions of Taiwan," Ma highlights how focusing on defining and redefining "culture" created pathways for local responses to cultural assimilation.

Storying Global Asias entails revisiting history to find new stories and also speculating on the conditions required to imagine futural alternatives. In "Intimacies of the Future: Techno-Orientalism, All-under-Heaven (Tian-Xia 天下), and Afrofuturism," Lily W. Luo reads against the grain of genre and discipline to theorize the interconnective imaginative work required to counteract global systems of oppression. Drawing on Lisa Lowe's generative paradigm of "intimacy," Luo brings together the study of speculative fiction and the field of international relations (IR) and asks readers to read IR theory as speculative fiction and Afrofuturism and techno-Orientalism as IR theory. Luo argues that "techno-Orientalism, Afrofuturism, and All-under-Heaven (Tian-Xia 天下), a reemergent Chinese geopolitical philosophy, are all speculative theories of the future that can help us understand historically who has claimed a monopoly over modernity, who has been shut out, and who are trying to theorize their way into it today."

If Ma's research asks us to revisit the past, and Luo's **Essay** asks us to imagine the future, Elizabeth Wijaya's "Insomniac Nights and an Aesthetics of Passivity: On Tsai Ming-liang's Walker Series" encourages us to stay focused on the present. In carefully analyzing Tsai Ming-liang's films and exhibitions, Wijaya proposes that we understand the artist's focus on the perceptual and the experiential—through "the radical slowing down of character movements, the reduction of plot-based action, and the lengthening of shot duration to emphasize rather than cut away from quotidian acts like walking or sleeping"—as an exhortation to dwell in the moment, a dwelling that takes on renewed urgency in the context of a global pandemic that required all of us to slow down or stop what we were doing. Stripped of dramatic action, Tsai's focus on inaction creates opportunities for different kinds of Global Asias stories to emerge. As Wijaya demonstrates, the peculiarities of cinema and art in engendering passive cobelonging can "create experiential moments for alternative rhythms and shapes of collective existence."

As Shannon Welch illustrates in "Belonging beyond Borders: Japanese Brazilian Stories of Diasporic Return without a 'Homecoming,'" we understand the shapes of collective existence through the stories that we inherit. Although one popular tale concerns the dream of return for diasporic subjects, her analysis of two Japanese Brazilian texts authored by first-generation Japanese immigrant women—Arai Chisato's 1974 short story "Homecoming" and Tsuchida Machie's memoir-in-fragments, "I Cannot Sing the National Anthem" (2007)—highlights the impossibility of homecoming for these migrant subjects. Emphasizing how these texts counter existing narratives of diasporic return in a Japanese context and draw attention to the ways in which dominant historical narratives surrounding the Japanese diaspora in Brazil have largely been composed by male voices, Welch argues that "the dialogue between the[se] two texts renders visible the gendered, sexualized, racialized, and classed logics that underpin dominant imaginations of the Japanese national community and the Japanese diaspora in Brazil as putatively unified, stable entities."

The search for more elastic ways of theorizing and enacting the dynamic tension between the particularity of Global Asias sites and the ageographic imaginaries that map different Global Asias geoscapes is the subject of this issue's final **Essay**, "'Finding New Routes': Visualizing an Oceanic Okinawa in Laura Kina's *Holding On* (2019)" by Ryan Buyco. Buyco argues that mixed-race Okinawan American artist Laura Kina's 2019 exhibit of landscape paintings inspired by her visits to Okinawa challenges the view of Okinawa as a small island prefecture in southern Japan by looking toward the dynamic engagements of its diaspora in the

Pacific. In proposing the paradigm of an "oceanic Okinawa," Buyco shows how *Holding On* "can be read as a diasporic work that affiliates itself with the Pacific not only to articulate the collective agency of Okinawans and Indigenous peoples everywhere but also to disrupt the colonial processes that continue to marginalize Okinawans from their lands and waters."

As this issue demonstrates, storying Global Asias involves centering marginalized figures, recognizing forgotten or occluded voices, tracing journeys across vast geographical distances, transmitting important lessons, revisiting dominant historical narratives, and speculating about futural possibilities. The contributors included here show us that storying Global Asias is a collaborative endeavor. In company with others, we narrate the many stories that this imaginable ageography encompasses, and we invite you, dear reader, to listen.

Tina Chen is founding editor of *Verge: Studies in Global Asias* and director of the Global Asias Initiative at the Pennsylvania State University.

■ WORKS CITED

Chen, Tina. 2021. "Global Asias—On the Structural Incoherence of Imaginable Ageography." In Asian American Literature in Transition, 1996–2020, edited by Betsy Huang and Victor Román Mendoza, 311–30. Cambridge: Cambridge University Press.

Philips, Louise Gwenneth, and Tracy Bunda. 2018. *Research through, with and as Storying*. New York: Routledge.

Convergence

TINA CHEN

The Problems and Possibilities of Global Asias Pedagogy

IN 2021–22, *Verge* and the Global Asias Initiative (GAI) partnered with Simon Fraser University's Global Asia program and the University of Illinois Chicago's Global Asian Studies Program to sponsor a series of Cyber Chats on the pedagogies of Global Asias.[1] Those virtual conversations made clear that developing the conceptual horizons of Global Asias scholarship requires concomitant attention to issues of pedagogy, curriculum development, and program building within and beyond the university.

Unsurprisingly, Global Asias pedagogy generates more questions than answers. Although some of these questions are ontological (What is Global Asias? Who is included/excluded in this formulation?) and epistemological (How do Global Asias methods and praxes make self-evident and self-reflexive the ways in which academic knowledge is generated, disseminated, and authorized?), many of them are also institutional and bureaucratic in nature. More precisely, these questions involve the institutional challenges inherent in such a pedagogical mission, challenges that range from how to engage discrete knowledge formations (Asian studies, Asian American studies, and Asian diaspora studies, of course, but also Latin American studies, African American studies, and Indigenous studies) to the difficulties of creating team-based teaching approaches in an effort to tackle the capaciousness of the topic/field to the relative paucity of resources developed to explicitly support the teaching of Global Asias. Global Asias pedagogy requires a willingness to step outside of comfort zones given how its expansiveness exceeds any single scholar's research expertise. Additionally, the distinct pedagogical expectations and requirements for different programs and knowledge formations (e.g., language requirements in Asian studies and community engagement in

Asian American studies) are not easily integrated, which creates specific curricular challenges for programs and departments interested in moving in this direction.

Although there is clearly interest in how to teach Global Asias, the lack of existing resources (syllabi databanks, pedagogical volumes, crowd-sourced bibliographies) is, for many, a serious obstacle. In an effort to respond to the need for models, and reflecting the collaborative ethos of Global Asias pedagogy, this *A&Q* feature invites colleagues who are actively involved in Global Asia/s programs and centers, and actively teaching Global Asia/s courses, to discuss the problems and possibilities of Global Asias pedagogy and share their syllabi.[2]

This dossier of materials includes essays and syllabi by Nadine Attewell, Anushay Malik, David Ludden, Michael R. Jin, and Mark Chiang—all of whom were asked to use one or more of the following questions to jump-start their ruminations on the challenges and opportunities they have encountered in teaching these classes:

Why does your department/program offer a course on Global Asia/s?

What are some of the challenges of teaching a course on "Global Asia/s"?

For those who might be interested in teaching Global Asia/s courses, what critical pieces of advice would you offer on course conceptualization and syllabus design?

What are three key concepts that you want students to understand about Global Asia/s after taking your course?

Coming from a range of disciplinary and institutional backgrounds, the authors reflect on their experiences in the classroom, in their programs, and at their institutions in an effort to bring the theoretical and conceptual developments of Global Asias scholarship into dialogue with their role as educators. In taking up Global Asias pedagogy, we are all asked to revisit our scholarly training and areas of expertise, to be open to new intellectual configurations, and to be self-reflexive about what we choose to include/exclude from the conversations we engineer. As these essays and syllabi make clear, varying conditions of institutional labor inform the diverse approaches and outcomes possible. While we recognize that the practices outlined here respond to the legacies of a North American experience and are tailored to the needs of a North American classroom, we believe this feature does a wonderful job of beginning the processes of dialogue and collaboration that Global Asias pedagogy encourages, and we hope it inspires continued conversation about how such questions and practices might change in different global contexts.

Tina Chen is founding editor of *Verge: Studies in Global Asias* and director of the Global Asias Initiative at the Pennsylvania State University.

■ **NOTES**

1. https://sites.psu.edu/vergeglobalasias/2021/10/21/2021-2022-global-asias-cyber-chats-series/.

2. I use "Global Asia/s" to refer to a diverse set of transnationally oriented approaches to the study of Asia and "Global Asias" when discussing the specific iteration of such an approach promulgated by *Verge: Studies in Global Asias*.

Conversation, Collaboration, and the Work of Teaching Global Asia/s

NADINE ATTEWELL AND ANUSHAY MALIK

Faced with the task of introducing undergraduates to Global Asia/s as an object and framework of study, it can be difficult to know where to begin.[1] As other contributors to this *A&Q* feature note, the very concept of "Asia" poses questions that are impossible to answer definitively— what, where, and who is Asia?—even as it also elicits a sense of belonging, exclusion, or possibility, depending on who is telling the story and why. How, moreover, to trace the complexity of the processes through which Asia became global and contributed to "the world-making project of history and human life" in clear, compelling ways (Chen and Hayot 2015, vi)?

In our teaching as in our research, we are drawn to case studies and classroom strategies that foreground how individuals come to know, experience, and further such processes in their own messy lives. Thus, for example, we introduce students to the global itineraries of historical figures like South Asian poet Faiz Ahmed Faiz. In the 1970s, Faiz moved from Lahore to Beirut, where he edited *Lotus,* a quarterly magazine established by a group of like-minded leftists who were committed to realizing the unfulfilled dream of decolonization and had been mobilizing since 1958 as part of the Afro-Asian Writers Association.[2] This is a Global Asia/s story, but not just because *Lotus* published writers from across

Asia and Africa, was produced out of Beirut, and attracted funding from Egypt, Germany, and the Soviet Union. Through assembling a network of contributors, readers, and supporters in and beyond Asia, Faiz Ahmed Faiz and his colleagues also hoped to foster cross-cultural collaboration and translation as internationalist alternatives to empire as well as to the ethnonationalist, authoritarian statisms already then beginning to emerge across the decolonizing world, including in Asia.

In such histories, we recognize aspects of our own embodied experiences as racialized knowledge workers on complex itineraries to and from Asia, which shape how we labor in the classroom under institutional conditions largely not of our own making. Both Nadine and Anushay teach Global Asia 101 (Introduction to Global Asia) at Simon Fraser University (SFU), a public institution located on xʷməθkʷəy'əm, S̱ḵwx̱wú7mesh, səl'ilw'ətaʔɬ, q'ic'əy', and kʷikʷəƛ̓əm lands in suburban Vancouver. In its current form, Global Asia is a small, interdisciplinary undergraduate program in the Faculty of Arts and Social Sciences that began offering courses in 2018. However, the program has a history dating back to the mid-1990s, when SFU launched Asia-Canada studies. Asia-Canada was a pathbreaking initiative in at least two respects: it was the first Asian Canadian studies program in Canada, followed in 2013 and 2014 by programs at the Universities of Toronto and British Columbia, and it proposed to bring the study of Asian Canadian histories, struggles, and cultural formations together with the study of Asia in a global frame, anticipating more recent developments in the fields of Asian and Asian (North) American studies, including Global Asia/s. (It should be noted that, unlike the Universities of Toronto and British Columbia, SFU has no stand-alone area studies departments.) Reformulated as Global Asia, the program continues to afford students the opportunity to consider the heterogeneous experiences of Asian and Asian diasporic people as they navigate diverse and unequal societies. Through tracing the (post)colonial trajectories of categories like "Asian" as both homogenizing instruments of exclusion and grounds of relation, we enable students to grapple with their own implication in multiple formations of power and belonging.

Realizing Global Asia's potential as a framework for interdisciplinary, cross-contextual learning within a neoliberal institution is no walk in the park, however. For one thing, the institutionalization of Global Asia/s as a curricular formation at SFU reflects exigencies that aren't always easily reconciled. On one hand, Asia-Canada emerged during a period of significant Asian Canadian mobilization around redress for historical wrongs like internment and the head tax, a crucial legacy for understanding and addressing the anti-Asian and other racisms circulating in our own historical moment of pandemic and white populism. On the other hand, both programs have been cast as responses to Asia's importance as a site of investment, manufacturing, conflict, and political action. Meanwhile, students are drawn to Global Asia 101, whether as an elective or with the intention of minoring in Global Asia, for a mix of personal, professional, and political reasons. Many are of Asian origin or descent themselves—given the size and heterogeneity of Vancouver's Asian diasporic communities, it would be surprising if they were not—and take Global Asia 101 to learn more about who they are, where they come from, and how to negotiate the complexities of their positioning within overlapping Canadian, Asian, and Asian diasporic sociopolitical orders.[3] They may wish to flesh out their knowledge of Asian languages or popular cultural products, become better informed members of diverse communities, or gain an edge in competitive job markets. Complicating matters still further, they are trained in a range of (inter)disciplines from across the university, including education, molecular biology, integrated arts, political science, business, history, and gender, sexuality, and women's studies. Among the challenges—and joys—of teaching Global Asia 101, then, is figuring out how to ignite the curiosity of students with varying expectations and kinds of preparation.

This places special burdens on instructors, because, as Michael Jin observes in his contribution to this issue, we are unlikely to be trained in Global Asia/s approaches, possessing, rather, expertise in Asian or Asian diaspora studies, in South Asian history or Japanese American politics. In their introduction to the first issue of *Verge*, Tina Chen and Eric Hayot (2015, xv) suggest that Global Asia/s need not—and perhaps should not—"resolve into a singular, totalizing vision." Although we recognize the national(ist) exigencies that David Ludden invokes in his essay for this issue, we ask, rather, how we can reproduce our training *queerly* so that students cultivate the skills and sensitivities needed to pursue Asia's global itineraries, across divides fundamental to twenty-first-century North American academic commonsense. How, furthermore, can an underresourced program like Global Asia accomplish this ethically, when many of our instructors are on sessional or short-term contracts?

These problems, which will be familiar to readers at other institutions, cannot be solved once and for all but must be worked at, rather, from the positions we occupy as differently embodied, resourced, and knowledgeable subjects. In our case, for example, it matters that Nadine is a literary and cultural studies scholar of Chinese descent from Vancouver who holds a tenured faculty position at SFU, while Anushay is a labor historian from Lahore whose appointment at SFU is temporary, not continuing. At the same time, we share political projects and intellectual genealogies as leftist feminist scholars trained in postcolonial studies. These inform our focus on the active ways in which Asian and Asian diasporic people participate and intervene in the workings of global systems and phenomena as they intersect in particular places at particular times as well as our interest in "the actually existing mutual constitutions, intimacies, entanglements" that bind people and their struggles across differences of gender, sexuality, class, religion, caste, race, color, citizenship, and location.[4] In our heterogeneous classrooms, the challenges and affordances of working across difference are by no means only topics of discussion but shape the work of learning in company with others. In addition, they animate our own collaborative pedagogical practice as colleagues who regularly consult with one another about our syllabi, assignment design, and teaching strategies and share classroom experiences. Although our syllabi diverge in ways that testify to the particularities of our training, interests, and positionality, they also bear the marks of our ongoing conversations about the course and program. In the future, it seems likely that they will also reflect the conversations made possible by this feature on Global Asia/s pedagogy.

Among other things, we frequently discuss which and whose stories are centered or passed over by how program courses enact the "Asia" in Global Asia. As our professional journeys have taught us, Asia connotes differently in different parts of the world, surfacing distinctive geographies of interest shaped by histories of colonial-capitalist expansion and intervention: whereas "[North] America's Asia" has mostly meant China and Japan, "European knowledge about Asia evolved over centuries of mobility [and empire building] across the Indian Ocean, and as a result, European Asian Studies pay proportionately more attention to South and Southeast Asia" (Ludden 2003, 1059). Accordingly, academic organizations and university departments often (implicitly) silo "South Asia" and "Asia" as distinct areas of expertise. Through tracing the formation of the modern world in the colonial encounter and its reverberating afterlives, we encourage students to consider both how such divides have worked as well as how they have been bridged and contested through attempts to think the world—and Asia—differently. Thus, for example, Anushay introduces her students to the history of the 1915 Singapore Mutiny, featuring a heterogeneous Asian cast of anticolonial revolutionaries, police recruits, and others whose actions alternately defied and entrenched the taxonomies meant to contain them.

We also regularly reflect on what it means to teach Global Asia *here*, in the Vancouver region, to which Nadine, who grew up in Vancouver, has only just returned and where Anushay is a recent arrival. At Lahore

University of Management Sciences, where she worked for five years before moving to Canada, Anushay taught South Asian history as a local in a classroom in which students had been exposed to the same sorts of histories in school and shared lived experience of religion, terrorism, and scarcity. Because the SFU student body is much more international and consciousness of racialized difference is ever present in the classroom, here, Anushay must work to help students make sense of their individual experiences, which may be invisible to others in a settler colonial society but have real-life consequences for them. She therefore begins Global Asia 101 by drawing on the work of local artists and activists who identify as Asian to show students how Asian exclusion is historical and global even as it is lived in the local and apprehended through institutions like art galleries and museums. Drawing on research conducted as part of local public history projects, she also introduces students to digital materials in SFU's archival collections, including interviews with South Asian trade unionists and activists describing life in post–Second World War British Columbia. On one hand, their activism helped transform the Canadian political landscape, especially on the left; on the other hand, they were settlers who struggled to relate anticolonial struggles here and elsewhere. Through engaging with sources in local archives, Anushay and her students grapple with the fact that there have always been many Asias and ways of being Asian, forged in the interplay of local and global frameworks of meaning, and they reflect on the histories that haunt their relationships to this place.

Nadine's experiences at a range of kinds of universities across Canada and the United States have likewise shaped her pedagogy by instructing her in the value of meeting students where they are. Often, when teachers say this, we mean that we are committed to providing students, whatever their current capacity, with the supports they need to think critically and expansively about the world, a necessity in any introductory course. In addition, however, it might entail inviting students to take stock of where they are as learners, that is, to think carefully about the knowledges they bring to the course, where those knowledges come from, and how they shape students' conceptions of what it means to study Global Asia/s. In teaching Global Asia 101, Nadine draws on her own sense of responsibility and curiosity as a nonwhite Canadian citizen settler by asking students to consider how the place where we are learning, the southwestern coast of what is today called British Columbia, became a site of significance in Asia's global story, through transoceanic networks of travel, trade, and exchange as well as colonial and white supremacist projects of expropriation, exploitation, exclusion, and exaltation.

Discussing these histories requires that students reflect on the conditions of their arrivals in this place and the relationships and responsibilities in which they are enmeshed as a result; it also involves them in processes of unlearning by asking them to reassess the stories they have inherited about the world and their place in it. This is important work in and of itself, a call to center anticolonial, antiracist, and internationalist projects of transformation in our approaches to Global Asia/s. At the same time, the curiosity, humility, and compassion that students learn to exercise with regard to their own assumptions and limits make for better—more rigorous, more generative—learning in general. Throughout the course, Nadine assigns documentary films by Asian and Asian diasporic artists like Richard Fung, Ali Kazimi, and Baby Ruth Villarama, who model self-reflexive practices of knowing that are careful in the best way. Classroom conversations about topics in which students may feel personally invested or implicated, such as K-pop fandoms, inter-Asian and anti-Black racisms, or Chinese state counterinsurgency efforts in Xinjiang, are the better for such attention to how knowledge is produced and circulates.

The lives of revolutionary thinkers and activists like Faiz Ahmed Faiz, the migrant worker struggles featured in films like Kazimi's *Continuous Journey* and Villarama's *Sunday Beauty Queen,* and the stories of culinary improvisation and drift that fascinate Fung in films like *Dal Puri Diaspora* testify to the everyday ways and multiple scales at which different Global Asia/s are lived, imagined, and contested. Conversation and collaboration, the ongoing labor of making sense of the world collectively with others, are central to many such stories. We offer this essay and our syllabi as traces of their importance to our pedagogical practice as well. Rather than mitigate or excuse the academy's exploitation of precarious knowledge workers like Anushay, our collaboration underscores the need for transformed labor conditions within as well as beyond the university, so that *all* of the workers who make courses like Global Asia 101 possible are properly supported—including materially—to do so.

■ GLOBAL ASIA 101: INTRODUCTION TO GLOBAL ASIA SYLLABUS

NADINE ATTEWELL, GENDER, SEXUALITY, AND
WOMEN'S STUDIES AND GLOBAL ASIA

Course Description

This course offers an interdisciplinary approach to global Asian studies through four units designed to introduce students to different aspects of Asia's global story. Unit 1, "A Global Sense of Place," explores some of the specificities of British Columbia's history as a point of departure for encounters with Asia as well as a site of settlement by people of Asian descent from all over the globe. Unit 2, "Border Crossings," attends to the movement of Asian people both within and beyond Asia, both as part of and in response to translocal projects of nation building, empire, (settler) colonialism, war, and capitalism, with a focus on the experiences of migrant workers, refugees, and other marginalized subjects. Unit 3, "Relating through Difference," takes a closer look at how people from different racial, national, and religious backgrounds are brought together as a consequence of this movement: how do they experience and negotiate the tensions that often characterize relationships amongst Asian and Asian diasporic people as well as with people from other parts of the world? Finally, Unit 4, "Global Circulations," explores the global dimensions of two recent flashpoints in Asian political, social, and cultural history: Chinese state settler colonial and counterinsurgency projects in Xinjiang and the global ascendancy of South Korean popular culture. Throughout the course, students gain practice thinking with and writing about cultural texts, scholarship, and key concepts in the field; there are also opportunities to interact with thinkers in the field, who visit in person or virtually.

Weeks 1–3: A Global Sense of Place

Ludden, David. 2003. Excerpts from "Maps in the Mind and the Mobility of Asia." *Journal of Asian Studies* 62, no. 4: 1057–78.

Yu, Henry. 2009. "Global Migrants and the New Pacific Canada." *International Journal* 64: 1011–26.

Price, John. 2020. "Relocating Yuquot: The Indigenous Pacific and Transpacific Migrations." *BC Studies* 204: 21–44.

Kazimi, Ali, dir. 2004. *Continuous Journey*. Peripheral Visions.

Weeks 4–6: Border Crossings

Amrith, Sunil. 2011. Excerpts from *Migration and Diaspora in Modern Asia*. Cambridge: Cambridge University Press.

Espiritu, Yén Lê. 2003. Excerpts from *Home Bound: Filipino Lives across Cultures, Communities, and Countries.* Berkeley: University of California Press.

Mootoo, Shani. 1993. "Out on Main Street." In *Out on Main Street and Other Stories.* Vancouver: Press Gang.

Fung, Richard, dir. 2012. *Dal Puri Diaspora.* Vtape.

Weeks 7–9: Relating through Difference

Villarama, Baby Ruth, dir. 2016. *Sunday Beauty Queen.* Voyage Studios.

Constable, Nicole. 2009. "Migrant Workers and the Many States of Protest in Hong Kong." *Critical Asian Studies* 41, no. 1: 143–64.

Hui, Tiffany, and Xilan Liang. 2022. "Solidarity with Filipino Domestic Workers across the Fissures of Empire." In *Reorienting Hong Kong's Resistance: Leftism, Decoloniality, and Internationalism,* edited by Wen Liu, J. N. Chien, Christina Yuen Zi Chung, and Ellie Tse, 194–201. Singapore: Palgrave Macmillan.

Tang, Eric. 2011. "A Gulf Unites Us: The Vietnamese Americans of Black New Orleans East." *American Quarterly* 63, no. 1: 117–49.

Lan, Shanshan. 2019. "Reconstructing Blackness in Grassroots Interactions between Chinese and Africans in Guangzhou." *Anthropological Quarterly* 92, no. 2: 481–508.

Weeks 10–12: Global Circulations

Byler, Darren. 2019. "Preventative Policing as Community Detention in Northwest China." *Made in China Journal,* October 25. https://madeinchinajournal.com/2019/10/25/preventative-policing-as-community-detention-in-northwest-china/.

Salimjan, Guldana. 2021. "Camp Land: Settler Ecotourism and Kazakh Dispossession in Contemporary Xinjiang." *Lausan.* https://lausancollective.com/2021/camp-land/.

Appadurai, Arjun. 1996. Excerpts from *Modernity at Large: Cultural Dimensions of Globalization.* Minneapolis: University of Minnesota Press.

Kim, Youna. 2013. "Korean Media in a Digital Cosmopolitan World." In *The Korean Wave: Korean Media Go Global,* edited by Youna Kim, 1–27. New York: Routledge.

Anderson, Crystal. 2020. Excerpts from *Soul in Seoul.* Jackson: University Press of Mississippi.

Cho, Michelle. 2020. "Pandemic Media: Protest Repertoires and K-pop's Double Visions." In *Pandemic Media,* edited by Philipp Dominik Keidl and Laliv Mehamed, 333–40. Meson Press. https://pandemicmedia.meson.press/chapters/activism-sociability/pandemic-media-protest-repertoires-and-k-pops-double-visions/.

ANUSHAY MALIK, INTERNATIONAL STUDIES AND GLOBAL ASIA

Course Description
Introduces developments in Asia from a comparative and transregional perspective, focusing on economic interactions, cultural influences, and migrations. Surveys various issues, both historical and contemporary, including those involving diasporic Asian communities.

Week 1: Introductions
Jith, Atul, et al. 2021. *Dūje Pāse Toň: Arts across the Border, from the Two Punjabs.* Abbotsford, B.C.: The Reach Gallery.
Mochizuki, Cindy. 2021. *Autumn Strawberry.* Surrey, B.C.: Surrey Art Gallery.
Punjabi Market Collective. https://www.instagram.com/punjabimarketyvr.

Week 2: What Is "Asia"?
Chen, Kuan Hsing. 2010. Excerpts from *Asia as Method: Toward Deimperialization.* Durham, N.C.: Duke University Press.
Subrahmanyam, Sanjay. 2019. Excerpts from *Empires between Islam and Christianity, 1500–1800.* Albany: State University of New York Press.

Week 3: You and Your Passport
McKeown, Adam. 2008. Excerpts from *Melancholy Order: Asian Migration and the Globalization of Borders.* New York: Columbia University Press.
Ludden, David. 2003. "Maps in the Mind and the Mobility of Asia." *Journal of Asian Studies* 62, no. 4: 1057–78.

Week 4: Representations of "Asia" in the West
Hong, Won-Pyo. 2009. "Reading School Textbooks as a Cultural and Political Text: Representations of Asia in Geography Textbooks used in the United States." *Journal of Curriculum Theorizing* 25, no. 1 (2009).
Adachi, Jeff, dir. 2006. *Slanted Screen: Asian Men in Film and Television.* CAAM.

Week 5: 1907 and the Global Story of the Anti-Asian Riots
Tsang, Henry. 2019. *Riot Walk.* https://360riotwalk.ca.
Chang, Kornel. 2009. "Circulating Race and Empire: Transnational Labor Activism and the Politics of Anti-Asian Agitation in the Anglo-American Pacific World, 1880–1910." *Journal of American History* 96, no. 3: 678–701.

Week 6: Life Histories—Poets and Artists
Light, Allie, and Irving Saraf, dirs. 1981. *Mitsuye and Nellie: Asian American Poets.* WMM.

Week 7: Life Histories—Labor Activists
Miles, Miranda, and Jonathan Crush. 1993. "Personal Narratives as Interactive Texts: Collecting and Interpreting Migrant Life-Histories." *Professional Geographer* 45, no. 1: 84–94.
Mah, Roy. "Interview." https://www.veterans.gc.ca/eng/remembrance/those -who-served/chinese-canadian-veterans/profile/mahr.
Sangha, Darshan Singh. "Interview." https://digital.lib.sfu.ca/icohc-60/darshan -singh-sangha.
Miyazawa, Joe. "Interview." https://digital.lib.sfu.ca/johc-286/interview-joe -miyazawa.

Week 8: Labor, Gender, and Food
Fung, Richard, dir. 2012. *Dal Puri Diaspora.* Vtape.
Ray, Krishnendu. 2004. Excerpts from *The Migrant's Table: Meals and Memories in Bengali-American Households.* Philadelphia: Temple University Press.
Leong-Salobir, Cecilia. 2011. Excerpts from *Food Culture in Colonial Asia: A Taste of Empire.* London: Routledge.

Week 9: Asian Canadians in Two World Wars
Streets-Salter, Heather. 2013. Excerpts from "The Local Was Global: The Singapore Mutiny of 1915." *Journal of World History* 24, no. 3: 539–76.
Gray, David, dir. 2012. *Canadian Soldier Sikhs: A Little Story in a Big War.* OMNI TV.
Tashme Historical Project. "Life in a Japanese Canadian Internment Camp, 1942–1946." http://tashme.ca.

Week 10: Science Fiction and Imagining a Place in the World
Mathur, Suchitra. 2004. "Caught between the Goddess and the Cyborg." *Journal of Commonwealth Literature* 39, no. 3: 119–38.
Hossain, Rokeya Sakhawat. 1905. *Sultana's Dream.* https://digital.library.upenn .edu/women/sultana/dream/dream.html.
Ganesh, Chitra. 2021. *Sultana's Dream.* https://muse.union.edu/mandeville /project/chitra-ganesh-sultanas-dream/.

Week 11: Forming Networks, Making an Impact
Lipsitz, George. 2001. "To Tell the Truth and Not Get Trapped: Why Inter-ethnic Anti-racism Matters Now." In *Orientations: Mapping Studies in the*

Asian Diaspora, edited by Kandice Chuh and Karen Shimakawa, 296–309. Durham, N.C.: Duke University Press.

Week 12: Where We Are Now?

Coloma, Roland Sintos. 2013. "Too Asian? On Racism, Paradox and Ethno-nationalism." *Discourse: Studies in the Cultural Politics of Education* 34, no. 4: 579–98.

Ome, Morgan. 2021. "Why This Wave of Anti-Asian Racism Feels Different." *The Atlantic,* March 17. https://www.theatlantic.com/ideas/archive/2021/03/cathy-park-hong-anti-asian-racism/618310/.

Nadine Attewell is an associate professor in the Department of Gender, Sexuality, and Women's Studies at Simon Fraser University, where she directs the Global Asia program.

Anushay Malik is a limited-term lecturer at Simon Fraser University, where she teaches across the International Studies and Global Asia programs.

▪ NOTES

1. Whereas the interdisciplinary project that *Verge* helped initiate has always invoked Global Asia*s* as an importantly plural and pluralizing site of enquiry, we teach in the Global Asia undergraduate program at Simon Fraser University. Throughout our essay, we mobilize the "intervening slash" in Global Asia/s both as a practical way of navigating this discrepancy and in the spirit of Laura Hyun Yi Kang's (2002, 2) productively "awkward diacritical shorthand" Asian/American.

2. See Kassamali (2016) for more.

3. According to the 2016 household census, the population of Metro Vancouver, where all three SFU campuses are located, was nearly 50 percent nonwhite, predominantly people of Asian origin or descent.

4. Elsewhere, Nadine has argued that Global Asia/s curricular projects must center entangled struggles for global social justice within and beyond Asia (Attewell 2022).

▪ WORKS CITED

Attewell, Nadine. 2022. "(Un)learning at the Edge of Empires." *Verge: Studies in Global Asias* 8, no. 1: 82–88.

Chen, Tina, and Eric Hayot. 2015. "Introducing Verge: What Does It Mean to Study Global Asias?" *Verge: Studies in Global Asias* 1, no. 1: vi–xv.

Fung, Richard, dir. 2012. *Dal Puri Diaspora*. Vtape.

Kang, Laura Hyun Yi. 2002. *Compositional Subjects: Enfiguring Asian/American Women*. Durham, N.C.: Duke University Press.

Kassamali, Sumayya. 2016. "'You Had No Address': Faiz Ahmed Faiz in Beirut." *The Caravan,* May 31. https://caravanmagazine.in/reviews -essays/you-had-no-address-faiz-beirut.

Kazimi, Ali, dir. 2004. *Continuous Journey*. Peripheral Visions.

Ludden, David. 2003. "Presidential Address: Maps in the Mind and the Mobility of Asia." *Journal of Asian Studies* 62, no. 4: 1057–1078.

Villarama, Baby Ruth, dir. 2016. *Sunday Beauty Queen*. Voyage Studios.

Global Asia at New York University

DAVID LUDDEN

Responding to the prompt for this *Verge* essay, I will focus on challenges involved in teaching courses on Global Asia. I have a few critical pieces of advice for course conceptualization and syllabus design, based on key concepts for students to understand after taking our courses.

A pervasive challenge for teaching Global Asia is institutional inertia in higher education that locks pedagogy into the comfortable embrace of national sensibilities, disciplinary boundaries, and area studies. To overcome that inertia, faculty need to combine intellectual energies across disciplines, tap student interests, and take advantage of institutional opportunities that increase with Asia's accelerating globalization. Global Asia teaching opportunities seem to emerge most typically at intersections of Asian studies, global studies, and Asian American studies, in humanities disciplines.

At New York University (NYU), the globalization of Asian studies developed institutionally and pedagogically, at the same time, after the founding of the NYU Global Network, in 2007, when scholars of ancient, medieval, and modern West, South, and East Asia came together to develop Global Asia as a field of study. Humanities programs in Abu Dhabi and Shanghai are deeply embedded in Asian contexts, and students and faculty from New York travel and study in those contexts, making Global Asia an affective framing for Asian studies, which we elaborated after 2017 with support from the Henry Luce Foundation.

Our key Global Asia concept is Asia's mobility. We see Asia as being composed of mobility and connected spaces spanning areas all around the steppe and Indian Ocean, from ancient times, and extending around the globe, after 1500. Our faculty and courses have a strong historical component: our program is led by historians who approach history as an "interdiscipline" that embraces technology, religion, economics, migration, travel, climate and environment, language, literature, arts, politics, health, ideas, material culture, and more.

Global Asia at NYU embraces regions in Europe, Africa, and the Middle East, from ancient times; it also includes the Americas, after 1500, which presents the challenge of bringing faculty and students who do not identify "their regions" with Asia into our courses. A key concept in our pedagogy is that so-called civilizations are interwoven rather than being separately constructed and territorially enclosed. Global Asia is formed by the intellectual and personal mobility of students and faculty across boundaries among nations, civilizations, and disciplines, in a world of global interdependence, climate change, and pandemics. Our Global Asia teaching travels among three NYU campuses, weaving together insights, experience, and learning in these very different, distant, and deeply connected locations, spanning Global Asia. The pandemic environment has accelerated and deepened our internet connectivity.

In Abu Dhabi and Shanghai, Global Asia pedagogy is adapted to undergraduates studying in two new, innovative campuses, where the curriculum was built from scratch and where students come from all over the world and live in Asia. Their humanities curriculum weaves their local Asian environments into wider worlds of long-term global connectivity in the Gulf and China.

In New York, Global Asia pedagogy is evolving inside a stodgy old university curriculum, built by faculty with entrenched academic disciplines for students with U.S. job market priorities, inside America's self-centered imperial-nation culture and New York City's peculiar center-of-the-world parochialism. In that environment, Global Asia in New York has gathered support primarily from students and faculty with family backgrounds in East, West, and South Asia and/or with academic interests in various parts of Asia who are attracted to Global Asia because of NYU's relative academic weakness in Asian studies and Asian American studies (despite our large Asian student population and location on the fringe of Chinatown).

The syllabi attached represent two Global Asia survey courses. The first was launched in 2013 and covered ancient to modern times in one semester. It was a history course in the College Core Curriculum and served the Core's goal of teaching students about the world outside America, combining coverage of East, West, South, and Southeast Asia; East Africa; global migration; imperialism; and contemporary globalization. As such, it was a cheap way for NYU to introduce hundreds of students to world history in Asian perspective: it attracted many students with Asian backgrounds and enhanced the training of a dozen graduate teaching assistants.

After four years in the Core, that Global Asia survey moved into the history department, where it was divided into a two-semester premodern–modern sequence, in part to attract students who need to fulfill a pre-1800 history major requirement. That shift into history happened during pandemic teaching terms; enrollments were low, but student enthusiasm is encouraging.

My recommendation is to teach Global Asia courses in a variety of ways that do not all have Global Asia course titles. A successful new course on Pandemics in World History is a Global Asia course by another name. Attracting students and faculty who are not primarily interested in Asia as it is defined in the United States—which is mostly East Asia—is a big challenge for Global Asia. The Middle East is part of Asia, and the Mediterranean basin is part of Global Asia from ancient times, as Roman "plagues" and the Black Death clearly demonstrate. Following peoples from Asia around the world is a useful strategy. The second included syllabus is from that course.

Focusing on mobility is key for making Global Asia academically influential. That mobility includes many people who typically drop out of Asian studies, notably countless nomads who connect and influence peoples all around Afro-Eurasia. By teaching students to appreciate the very long histories of migration, mobility, and mingling that produced diverse composite cultures around the world, which have only recently been locked into national borders, Global Asia can make a major contribution to the pursuit of social justice, equity, and inclusion.

■ GLOBAL ASIA SYLLABUS

Course Description

Asia is a space of perpetual globalization shaping all regions, localities, cultures, economies, and polities from ancient times to the present. Global Asia is an exploration of Asia's very long history of globalization, and it thus provides a method for decolonizing History as a field of studies, which is traditionally focused on the West.

This course consists of two weekly lecture presentations and one weekly discussion section exploring in one semester the spatial expansion of human mobility and territorial order in Asia from ancient times to the present. Our readings, writing assignments, presentations, and discussions follow the travels of merchants, missionaries, nomads, armies, writers, and others who shape cultural, political, and economic systems around

Asia. We begin with ancient Greece, India, and China, where empires launched the long first millennium of Asia's circulatory system, connecting the Pacific and Mediterranean around Silk Roads and the Indian Ocean, shaping territories everywhere. We then see that in 1206, Genghis Khan launched a new phase of overland imperial expansion, which brought Russia, Europe, and Africa more firmly into Asian networks; and then, in 1492, Iberians launched centuries of seaborne spatial expansion, which made Asian port cities critical nodes in global networks of imperialism, capitalism, and nationalism. We end the term with a consideration of Asia's present-day globalization.

Part 1: Asia's Circulatory System—The Long First Millennium

Week 1: Introductions and Environments
Curtin, Philip D. *Cross-Cultural Trade in World History.* Cambridge: Cambridge University Press, 1984.
See map reference collection at https://prezi.com/mogyajxrdwj8/asias-circu latory-system/.

Week 2: Nomads, the Steppe, and Buddhism
Davis, Richard H. *Global India circa 100 CE: South Asia in Early World History.* Ann Arbor, Mich.: Association for Asian Studies, 2009.

Week 3: Agrarian Empires, Travels, and Moral Order
Sen, Tansen, and Victor H. Mair. *Traditional China in Asian and World History.* Ann Arbor, Mich.: Association for Asian Studies, 2012.

Week 4: Migration and Imperial Expansion after 600
Doak, Robin. *Empire of the Islamic World.* New York: Chelsea House, 2004. Pp. 7–58.
Doak, Robin. "Turk Empire." In *The Cambridge History of Early Inner Asia,* 285–31. Cambridge: Cambridge University Press, 1990.

Week 5: Tropics, Land, and Sea, 900–1200
Alpers, Edward A. *The Indian Ocean in World History.* Oxford: Oxford University Press, 2014.

Week 6: The Mongols
Weatherford, Jack. *Genghis Khan and the Making of the Modern World.* New York: Three Rivers Press, 2004. Pp. 1–132.

To Discuss
The Mongol Intervention

Part 2: Early Modern Asian Empires

Week 7: Turco-Mongol Militarism and Eurasian Commercial Expansion (1200–1500)

Weatherford, Jack. *Genghis Khan and the Making of the Modern World.* New York: Three Rivers Press, 2004. Pp. 1–132, 195–218.

"The Mongols in China," Columbia University's "The Mongols in World History" website, http://afe.easia.columbia.edu/mongols/index.htm.

BBC's documentary *Mongol: The Rise of Genghis Khan*

To Discuss

1200s: Mongol territory as mobility infrastructure: Marco Polo and Ibn Battuta

1300s: Il-Khans, Italians, Black Sea Routes, the Plague, and Timur

Week 8: Networks of Imperial Culture, Power, and Investment (1300–1700)

Dale, Stephen F. "The Rise of Muslim Empires." In *The Muslim Empires of the Ottomans, Safavids, and Mughals,* 48–76. Lewisburg, Pa.: Bucknell University Press, 2009.

Casale, Giancarlo. "The Islamic Empires of the Early Modern World." In *The Cambridge World History: Vol. VI. The Construction of a Global World, 1400–1800 CE,* 323–44. Cambridge: Cambridge University Press, 2015.

Romaniello, Matthew. "Transregional Trade in Early Modern Eurasia." In *Oxford Research Encyclopedia of Asian History.* Oxford: Oxford University Press, 2017.

To Discuss

Ottomans, Mughals, and Safavids. Visiting Lecture: Ayse Baltacioglu-Brammer

Networks of imperial culture, power, and investment

Week 9: Imperial Expansion—Technologies of Territorial Power (1300–1700)

"Asian Expansions: An Introduction" and "Why Do Empires Expand" from *Asian Expansions: The Historical Experiences of Polity Expansion in Asia,* edited by Geoff Wade, 1–51. New York: Routledge, 2015.

Levi, Scott. "Asia in the Gunpowder Revolution." In *Oxford Research Encyclopedia of Asian History.* Oxford: Oxford University Press, 2017.

Rieber, Alfred J. "Russia in Asia." In *Oxford Research Encyclopedia of Asian History.* Oxford: Oxford University Press, 2017.

Perdue, Peter. "The Expansion of the Qing Dynasty and the Zunghar Mongol State." In *Oxford Research Encyclopedia of Asian History*. Oxford: Oxford University Press, 2017.

Recommended

Lieberman, Victor. "The Qing Dynasty and Its Neighbors: Early Modern China in World History." *Social Science History* 32, no. 2 (2008): 281–304.

Wink, Andre. "Post-nomadic Empires: From Mongols to Mughals," in *Tributary Empires in Global History*, edited by Peter Fibiger Bang and C. A. Bayly, 121–31. New York: Palgrave Macmillan, 2011.

Ludden, David. "The Process of Empire: Frontiers and Borderlands," in *Tributary Empires in Global History*, edited by Peter Fibiger Bang and C. A. Bayly, 132–48. New York: Palgrave Macmillan, 2011.

To Discuss

The political economy of imperial territory: Asia's imperial engines of global connectivity

Port cities, coastal regions, and global networks: monetization, taxation, transportation, conquering Central Asia, the imperial integration of Asian coasts and imperial interior

Week 10: An Emerging Modern World—Commerce to Capitalism (1700–1900)

Alpers, Edward A. *The Indian Ocean in World History*. Oxford: Oxford University Press, 2014. Pp. 69–97.

Flynn, Dennis O., and Arturo Giráldez. "Born with a 'Silver Spoon': The Origin of World Trade in 1571." *Journal of World History* 6, no. 2 (1995): 201–21.

Perdue, Peter. "The Rise and Fall of the Canton Trade System—I: China in the World (1700–1860s)." https://visualizingcultures.mit.edu/rise_fall_canton _01/pdf/cw_essay.pdf.

Peacock, A. C. S. "The Ottoman Empire and the Indian Ocean." In *Oxford Research Encyclopedia of Asian History*. Oxford: Oxford University Press, 2017.

Allen, Richard B. "Asian Indentured Labor in the 19th and Early 20th Century Colonial Plantation World." In *Oxford Research Encyclopedia of Asian History*. Oxford: Oxford University Press, 2017.

Study

Caspian Report, "Fall of the British Empire," on YouTube, https://www.youtube .com/watch?v=CtHVoiiAwS8.

To Discuss

Transitions to imperialism: Portuguese, Dutch, French, and English

The British Empire: building the infrastructure for capitalist globalization

Week 11: Summary Part 2—Empire and Globalization

Part 3: Imperial Modernity—Nations and Globalization

Week 12: Modern History (since 1800) in Millennial Perspective

Alpers, Edward A. *The Indian Ocean in World History.* Oxford: Oxford University Press, 2014. Pp. 98–149.

Weatherford, Jack. *Genghis Khan and the Making of the Modern World.* New York: Three Rivers Press, 2004. Pp. 241–73.

Ludden, David. "Making Modern Societies." In *India and South Asia, a Short History.* London: Oneworld, 2004.

Perdue and Sebring, "The Boxer Uprising, I, II, II" and other readings in MIT's "Visualizing Cultures" online collection, https://visualizingcultures.mit .edu/home/vis_menu_02b.html.

To Discuss

Empire and nation

Hans Rosling, "200 Years That Changed the World," on YouTube, https:// www.youtube.com/watch?v=BPt8ElTQMIg.

Week 13: The End of Another Set of "Old Empires"

Huffman, James L. *Japan and Imperialism, 1853–1945.* New York: Columbia University Press, 2010.

To Discuss

"World wars" and imperial transitions

Week 14: The Inequity of Nations and Globalization

Ludden, David. "Imperial Modernity: History and Global Inequity in Rising Asia." *Third World Quarterly* 33, no. 4 (2012): 581–601.

To Discuss

Hans Rosling, "200 Years That Changed the World," on YouTube, https:// www.youtube.com/watch?v=BPt8ElTQMIg.

The Great Divergence, "moral inequality," and Global Asia today

Week 15: Summary—Empire, Nation, and Globalization

■ PANDEMICS IN WORLD HISTORY SYLLABUS

Course Description

Pandemics have traveled long distances to infect people in territories connected by routes of mobility since ancient times. Pandemic mortality and morbidity have provoked political, social, and cultural change; they have stimulated all kinds of intellectual activity, from medicine to philosophy, poetry, polemics, and folklore. This lecture and discussion course surveys the world history of pandemics and provides students opportunities for specialized research and creativity, including participation in the development of a course website. We focus primarily on the spatial, social, political, cultural, and economic aspects of pandemics; their Asian connections; and their entanglements with empire, capitalism, and globalization.

1. Introduction: The Space of Pandemics in World History

Ludden, David. "Maps in the Mind and the Mobility of Asia." *Journal of Asian Studies* 62, no. 4 (2003): 1057–78.

McKeown, Adam. "Periodizing Globalization." *History Workshop* 63, no. 1 (2007): 218–30.

Northrup, David. "Globalization and the Great Convergence: Rethinking World History in the Long Term." *Journal of World History* 16, no. 3 (2005): 249–67.

Part 1: The Long First Millennium

2. Ecology and Humanity

Gonzalez, Jean-Pau, Micheline Guiserix, Frank Sauvage, Jean-Sébastien Guitton, Pierre Vidal, Nargès Bahi-Jaber, Hechmi Louzir, and Dominique Pontier. "Pathocoenosis: A Holistic Approach to Disease Ecology." *EcoHealth* 7 (2010): 237–40.

McNeill, William. *Plagues and Peoples.* New York: Random House, 1998. Pp. 9–93.

3. The Ancient World of Mobility

Metropolitan Museum of Art, "Europe's Asia Trade in Antiquity," https://www.metmuseum.org/toah/hd/trade/hd_trade.htm.

Di Cosmo, Nicola. *Ancient China and Its Enemies: The Rise of Nomadic Power in East Asian History.* Cambridge: Cambridge University Press, 2002. Chapter 5, on imperial Han and Hsiung-nu, pp. 161–206.

McLaughlin, Raoul. *Rome and the Distant East: Trade Routes to the Ancient Lands of Arabia, India and China.* London: Bloomsbury, 2010. Pp. 83–111 (and whatever else you like).

4. Ancient "Plagues" and the First Plague Pandemic

Aberth, John. *Plagues in World History*. New York: Rowman and Littlefield, 2011. Chapter 1, pp. 19–33.

Little, Lester K. "Life and Afterlife of the First Plague Pandemic." In *Plague and the End of Antiquity: The Pandemic of 541–750*, 3–32. Cambridge: Cambridge University Press, 2006.

Gourevitch, Danielle. "The Galenic Plague: A Breakdown of the Imperial Pathocoenosis: Pathocoenosis and Longue Durée." *History and Philosophy of the Life Sciences* 27, no. 1 (2005): 57–69.

Wazer, Caroline. "Between Public Health and Popular Medicine: Senatorial and Popular Responses to Epidemic Disease in the Roman Republic." In *Popular Medicine in Graeco-Roman Antiquity: Explorations*, edited by William V. Harris, 126–46. Leiden, Netherlands: Brill, 2016.

Hays, J. N., and J. Hays. "The Western Inheritance: Greek and Roman Ideas about Disease." In *The Burdens of Disease: Epidemics and Human Response in Western History*, 9–18. New Brunswick, N.J.: Rutgers University Press, 2009.

5. Expanding Eurasian Connectivity, by Land and Sea, 600–1200

McNeill, William. *Plagues and Peoples*. New York: Random House, 1998. Pp. 94–160.

Drompp, Michael R. "The Kök Türk Empires." In *Oxford Research Encyclopedia of Asian History*. Oxford: Oxford University Press, 2018.

HistoryMarche, video on Abbasid-Tang conflict, "Battle of Talas, 751AD," on YouTube, https://www.youtube.com/watch?v=cQiFY5x_DrY.

Shaffer, Lynda. "Southernization." *Journal of World History* 5, no. 1 (1994): 1–21.

Recommended

Beaujard, Philippe. "Islam: The Conquest of Lands and Oceans." In *The Worlds of the Indian Ocean: A Global History*, 42–71. Cambridge: Cambridge University Press, 2019.

6. The Black Death

McNeill, William H. *Plagues and Peoples*. New York: Anchor Random House, 1998. Pp. 161–207.

Aberth, John. *Plagues in World History*. New York: Rowman and Littlefield, 2011. Chapter 1, pp. 34–61.

Biran, Michal. "The Mongol Empire and Inter-civilizational Exchange." In *The Cambridge World History*, edited by Jerry H. Bentley, Sanjay Subrahmanyam, and Merry E. Wiesner-Hanks, 534–58. Cambridge: Cambridge University Press, 2015.

BBC article, "Dubrovnik: The Medieval City Designed around Quarantine,"

https://www.bbc.com/travel/article/20200421-dubrovnik-the-medieval
-city-designed-around-quarantine.

Recommended

Arvide Cambra, Luisa Maria. "The Causes of the Black Death Described by Ibn Khatima in the World of Tahsil al-Garad." *Annals of Reviews and Research* 4, no. 1 (2018): 1–2.

Watts, Sheldon. "The Human Responses to Plague in Western Europe and the Middle East, 1347–1844." In *Epidemics and History*, 1–39. New Haven, Conn.: Yale University Press, 1997.

Hays, J. N., and J. Hays. *The Burdens of Disease: Epidemics and Human Response in Western History*. New Brunswick, N.J.: Rutgers University Press, 2009. Chapters 2 and 3, pp. 19–61.

Part 2: Empire and Globalization

7. The Globalization of Disease

Webb, James L. A. "Globalization of Disease, 1300 to 1900." In *The Cambridge World History*, edited by Jerry H. Bentley, Sanjay Subrahmanyam, and Merry E. Wiesner-Hanks, 54–75. Cambridge: Cambridge University Press, 2015.

McNeill, William H. *Plagues and Peoples*. New York: Random House, 1998. Pp. 208–42.

Web page "Visualizing the History of Pandemics," https://www.visualcapitalist .com/history-of-pandemics-deadliest/.

Hays, J. N., and J. Hays. *The Burdens of Disease: Epidemics and Human Response in Western History*. New Brunswick, N.J.: Rutgers University Press, 2009. Chapter 4, pp. 62–76.

Recommended

Watts, Sheldon. "Smallpox in the New World and in the Old: From Holocaust to Eradication, 1518–1977." In *Epidemics and History*, 84–121. New Haven, Conn.: Yale University Press, 1997.

Aberth, John. *Plagues in World History*. New York: Rowman and Littlefield, 2011. Pp. 34–61.

8. Pandemic Empire: Cholera

Watts, Sheldon. "Cholera and Civilization: Great Britain and India, 1817–1920." In *Epidemics and History*, 167–212. New Haven, Conn.: Yale University Press, 1997.

Aberth, John. *Plagues in World History*. New York: Rowman and Littlefield, 2011. Chapter 1, pp. 101–11.

Hays, J. N., and J. Hays. *The Burdens of Disease: Epidemics and Human Response in Western History*. New Brunswick, N.J.: Rutgers University Press, 2009. Chapter 7, pp. 135–54.

Blog post by Sagaree Jain, "Anti-Asian Racism in the 1817 Cholera Pandemic," https://daily.jstor.org/anti-asian-racism-in-the-1817-cholera-pandemic/.

Recommended

Echenberg, Myron. *Africa in the Time of Cholera: A History of Pandemics from 1817 to the Present*. Cambridge: Cambridge University Press, 2011. Pp. 13–86.

Wellcome Collection article, "The Colonist Who Faced the Blue Terror," https://wellcomecollection.org/articles/WsT4Ex8AAHruGfWj.

Dr. John Bell (1796–1872), "All the material facts in the history of epidemic cholera: being a report of the College of physicians of Philadelphia, to the Board of health: and a full account of the causes, post mortem appearances, and treatment of the disease." Philadelphia: T. Desilver, June 1832.

9. Empire, Disease, and Terror

Hays, J. N., and J. Hays. *The Burdens of Disease: Epidemics and Human Response in Western History*. New Brunswick, N.J.: Rutgers University Press, 2009. Chapter 9, pp. 179–213, and chapter 12, pp. 283–314.

Polu, Sandhya. *Infectious Disease in India, 1892–1940: Policy-Making and the Perception of Risk*. New York: Palgrave Macmillan, 2012. Chapter 5, pp. 140–57.

Fatima, Anjuli, and Raza Kolb. *Epidemic Empire: Colonialism, Contagion, and Terror, 1817–2020*. Chicago: University of Chicago Press, 2021. Chapter 2, pp. 55–82.

Recommended

Kramm, Robert. *Sanitized Sex: Regulating Prostitution, Venereal Disease, and Intimacy in Occupied Japan, 1945–1952*. Berkeley: University of California Press, 2017.

Webel, Mari K. *The Politics of Disease Control: Sleeping Sickness in Eastern Africa, 1890–1920*. Athens: Ohio University Press, 2019.

10. Imperial War and the Great Flu Pandemic

Aberth, John. *Plagues in World History*. New York: Rowman and Littlefield, 2011. Chapter 1, pp. 111–35.

Tomes, Nancy. "'Destroyer and Teacher': Managing the Masses during the 1918–1919 Flu Pandemic." *Public Health Reports* 125 (2010): 48–62.

Farmer, Paul. "Ebola, Spanish Flu and the Memory of Disease." *Critical Inquiry* 46 (2019): 56–71.

Chhun, Maura. "1918 Flu Pandemic Killed 12 Million Indians, and British

Overlords' Indifference Strengthened the Anti-colonial Movement." *The Conversation*, April 17, 2020.

Patterson, David, and Gerald Pyle. "The Diffusion of Influenza in Sub-Saharan Africa during the 1918–1919 Pandemic." *Social Science and Medicine* 17, no. 1 (1983): 1299–1307.

Recommended

Crosby, Alfred W. *America's Forgotten Pandemic: The Influenza of 1918*. Cambridge: Cambridge University Press, 2003.

Fisher, J. *Envisioning Disease, Gender, and War: Women's Narratives of the 1918 Influenza Pandemic*. New York: Palgrave Macmillan, 2016.

Part 3: A Pandemic World of Nations

11. *Creating Global Public Health, and the Case of HIV/AIDS*

Mackenbach, J. P. "Politics Is Nothing but Medicine at a Larger Scale: Reflections on Public Health's Biggest Idea." *Journal of Epidemiology and Community Health* 3 (December 2008): 181–84 (good Wikipedia page on Rudolph Virchow).

White, Franklin. "History, Aims, and Methods of Public Health." In *Global Public Health: Ecological Foundations*, 1–26. Oxford: Oxford University Press, 2013.

Aberth, John. *Plagues in World History*. New York: Rowman and Littlefield, 2011. Chapter 1, pp. 135–79 (see AIDS mortality map, 2017: https://our worldindata.org/hiv-aids#death-rates-are-high-across-sub-saharan-africa).

Siplon, Patricia. "The Troubled Path to HIV/AIDS Universal Treatment Access: Snatching Defeat from the Jaws of Victory?" In *Global HIV/AIDS Politics, Policy, and Activism: Persistent Challenges and Emerging Issues*, edited by Raymond A. Smith, 3–26. Santa Barbara, Calif.: ABC-CLIO, 2013.

12. *Pandemic Inequity*

Farmer, Paul. *Pathologies of Power: Health, Human Rights, and the New War on the Poor*. Berkeley: University of California Press, 2004. Pp. 1–22, 213–46.

Brookings Institution, "Pandemics and the Poor," 2017, https://www .brookings.edu/blog/future-development/2017/06/19/pandemics-and -the-poor/.

Chauduri, Anis, and Jomo Sundaram. "Privatized Healthcare Worsens Pandemic," IPS News, http://www.ipsnews.net/2021/08/privatised-health -services-worsen-pandemic/.

Human Rights Watch, "United States: Pandemic Impact on People in Poverty," 2021, https://www.hrw.org/news/2021/03/02/united-states-pandemic -impact-people-poverty.

Gravel Institute, "David Cross: Why America Sucks at Everything" (especially health), on YouTube, https://www.youtube.com/watch?v=aNghg1Y-WIc.

Kaufman, Jay S. "Science Alone Can't Heal a Sick Society." *New York Times,* September 12, 2021.

13. *The First Truly Global Pandemic*

GlobalUnion, "Covid-19: An Occupational Disease. Where Frontline Workers Are Best Protected," 2013, https://uniglobalunion.org/report/covid-19-an-occupational-disease-where-frontline-workers-are-best-protected/.

Dahir, Abdi Latif. "Booster Shots 'Make a Mockery of Vaccine Equity,' the WHO's Africa Director Says," *New York Times,* August 19, 2021.

Oxfam report, *The Inequality Virus,* https://www.oxfam.org/en/research/inequality-virus.

Das, Koustav. "How Covid-19 Crisis Has Exposed India's Growing Wealth Gap," *India Today,* https://www.indiatoday.in/business/story/explained-how-covid-19-crisis-has-exposed-india-s-growing-wealth-gap-1795932-2021-04-28.

Viewing

David Ludden, "Global Pandemic in National Territory," October 5, 2020, https://wp.nyu.edu/globalasiacourses/pandemic-history-sources/.

"Global Asia Webinar on Migration, Globalization, and Covid-19," October 23, 2020, https://wp.nyu.edu/cga/2020/10/19/oct-23-immigration-and-covid-19-in-the-gulf/.

Final Discussion Prompt

How does historical perspective influence your understanding of our latest pandemic?

David Ludden is a professor of political economy and globalization and former chair in the Department of History at New York University. His research has focused primarily on southern India, Bangladesh, and northeast India. His publications include four edited volumes, three monographs, and dozens of articles and chapters exploring various dimensions of capitalist economic development and long-term histories of globalization. He served as president of the Association for Asian Studies and is the founding director of the NYU Global Asia program, based in New York, Abu Dhabi, and Shanghai.

Introduction to Global Asian Studies and Pedagogical Practice: Part 1

MICHAEL R. JIN

I joined the University of Illinois Chicago (UIC) Global Asian Studies Program (GLAS) in fall 2016, tasked with teaching the program's new course, Introduction to Global Asian Studies (GLAS 100), in my first semester. GLAS launched that same year, after Asian studies and Asian American studies merged. The rationale for this merger of the two programs, which had existed as separate academic units for more than a decade, was both intellectual and practical. Over the years, there had emerged a consensus among faculty that the institutional division had become an obstacle for sustaining the cross-fertilization of the two programs. Many among the core faculty members in both disciplines had been actively engaging in transnational research and teaching that emphasized linkages and intersections between ethnic and area studies. Equally important, there had emerged a shared understanding that combining the faculty and resources of the two units would facilitate our goal of creating a major-granting program with a robust list of course offerings and programming opportunities for both students and scholars.

What does it mean to teach Introduction to Global Asian Studies in this North American institutional context? For the past six years, I have wrestled with what it means for me to claim my stake in this pedagogical project as a practitioner of the emerging Global Asias framework. Teaching GLAS 100 has involved constant self-reflection and reevaluation of my own positionality as an Asian American historian with multiple disciplinary identities. The project of designing (and redesigning) this course has been a test of my training and experience accumulated over time, as well as my continued intellectual exploration. I went through a graduate program that exposed me to theoretical and methodological conventions across the established boundaries of national and regional histories. In addition to the standard coursework for U.S. history, I built my secondary teaching field in "global" history through my department's world history program. I also studied the historiography of modern East Asia and undertook rigorous language training to equip myself for conducting archival and field research in Asia. In addition to my "eclectic graduate training"—in the words of Eiichiro Azuma (2021)—my first full-time teaching job at a small regional state university in South Texas demanded that I teach all things related to Asia as well as multiple sections of U.S. history survey every semester. Since the start of my academic career, I have straddled the boundaries of national histories, area studies, and ethnic studies every day.

However, although my training and daunting teaching assignments gave me lots of pedagogical strengths, what has sustained me as a scholar with global consciousness and prepared me for teaching GLAS 100 is my political identity as an Asian Americanist. I am deeply influenced by the internationalist and global roots of my primary discipline—in particular, the anticolonial and antiracist movement that had given birth to the Third World curriculum of the early 1970s, the progenitor of the ethnic studies programs that soon followed. Asian American studies—and ethnic studies more broadly—emerged from that movement's connection to the Cold War–era global unrest and the longer history of anticolonial struggles throughout Asia and elsewhere. The young students who led the Third World Liberation Front movement in North America had found their inspiration in the anticolonial works of Frantz Fanon, Albert Memmi, and countless other intellectuals from afar, who had drawn their own inspiration from the anti-imperialist struggles of everyday folks throughout West Asia, Southeast Asia, the Americas, and beyond. As Gary Y. Okihiro (2016) has noted, the Third World curriculum reflected those activists' emphasis on antiracist, anticolonial, and internationalist solidarity, through a critical eye toward the impact of U.S. imperialist projects on those global struggles. In the words of Nadine Attewell and Anushay Malik, this is a "Global Asias story." My scholarship, and my identity as a historian of both Asian America and Asia, is a product of that intellectual movement.

I have approached GLAS 100 as an opportunity to revitalize that fundamentally internationalist framework to help students understand how intimately their lives are connected to the histories and lived experiences of peoples across borders. Like Nadine Attewell and Anushay Malik, I often turn to materials that demonstrate the complex, bizarre, messy, and remarkably rich "processes through which how Asia became global." Attewell and Malik's discussion of Faiz Ahmed Faiz's Lotus serves as a powerful example that can transform the pedagogies of Global Asias. What makes this story of writers and readers from different corners of Eurasia and Africa compelling is not simply its geographical and cultural expansiveness that defies a singular "Asia." More than that, as the authors articulate, what makes it a truly "Global Asias story" is the collective vision of a decolonized world expressed and sustained by folks across multiple geographical, linguistic, national, and diasporic boundaries beyond the Eurocentric constructions of Asia that have dominated academia.

Exploring these multifaceted processes of how Asia has become global has been one of the core strategies in my own approach to teaching

GLAS 100 at a public university in Chicago, home to many communities of migrants and refugees from around the world. This diasporic lens to interrogating Global Asias has allowed me and my students to examine the historical legacies of imperialism, war, human migration, global capitalism, and other complex geopolitical and socioeconomic developments that have converged in the experiences of Chicago's diasporic communities from Myanmar, Palestine, Syria, and elsewhere. Learning the processes of how different representations of "Asia" in their own communities attribute meanings to those historical issues serves as a critical exercise in my students' broader engagement with the settler colonialism, militarism, and ongoing "war on terrorism" that have affected communities across colonial outposts, such as Dededo, Honolulu, Jeju, Chagos, Kabul, and Okinawa. One of the critical objectives of such intellectual exploration is for students to interrogate Asia as not just a place, a thing, or a collection of cultures to study but a set of global processes that is deeply shaped by lived experiences and struggles across those societies.

What has buttressed this approach is that many of our students at UIC, as I have learned, come to the university with diverse conceptualizations of Asia that already defy the rigid, artificial, and Eurocentric geographic orientation of Asia that dominates academic disciplines. On day 1 of my first semester at UIC, I started my class lecture by asking students "what is 'Asia?'" to gauge their perceptions, assumptions, and previous knowledge of Asia. I was curious to learn how much they took this term for granted and what might have influenced their views. Although a number of students described Asia as a continent and a region, as I had expected, I was surprised to learn that many students already conceptualized Asia as a cultural and intellectual product, rather than simply a geographical unit. Many students also understood Asia as a primarily racial concept, especially in the U.S. context (as in "Asian American"). I see GLAS 100 as an opportunity not only to help students unlearn their assumptions about Asia but also to allow them to critically examine their own perceptions of culture, race, and history as a way to understand the shifting meanings and representations of Asia over time.

Given this context and the broad conceptual and geographical sweep of the subject matter, I have had to clearly establish what the course does not and cannot do. From the outset, it was clear to me that I could not design this course as just a survey of "Asian" histories, cultures, or peoples. The course does not rely on the established geographical boundaries and state-centered narrative practices common in my own discipline of history and in other scholarly fields in the humanities, arts, and social sciences. Instead, focusing on the evolution of various representations of Asia has been one of the fundamental questions that serves as the core organizing principle for the course. By introducing the concept of Asia as a European construct, the course problematizes the common geographical, cultural, and even racial assumptions about Asia. Edward Said's (1978) formulation of Orientalism as a mix of fact and fiction in the Western intellectual project to define, locate, structure, and dominate non-European peoples serves as a foundational framework for understanding the historical implications of European colonial projects that have disrupted societies in the non-European world and forced displacement of many Asian peoples. Simultaneously, we introduce how colonized peoples' rejection of Western imperial dominance, their struggles for sovereignty, and their claim to agency have shaped history and redefined ideas about and representations of Asia.

As my colleague Mark Chiang articulates, our case studies and reading assignments reflect the various historical representations of Asia since antiquity and how resistance to the Western construct of Asia in the multiple contexts of trade, migration, imperialism, and global capitalism have wrought the making of Global Asias. For instance, one of the intellectual exercises in the early part of the semester is the active unlearning of Eurocentric, land-based geographical constructs like continents, regions, and nations. Okihiro's (2016) conceptualization of the "ocean worlds" is a useful and accessible way to challenge students to rethink the representation of the oceans as barriers that have separated societies and human experiences. By examining the dynamic transformations of the Indian Ocean world, the Mediterranean world, and the Island world of the Pacific over centuries, students learn that the oceans and other bodies of water were important connecting forces that allowed circulation of peoples, commodities, and ideas across multiple "Asias" long before the age of Western imperialism. The work of Henry Yu and others on the impact of Orientalism on shaping Asian American history allows students to explore the experiences of Asians in North America and other settler colonial societies around the world in that broader global context. Students then explore how peoples and ideas from Asia and across transoceanic and transnational diasporas have influenced a globalized world and continue to inform our contemporary understanding of many "Asias" around the world.

Furthermore, the framework for Introduction to Global Asian Studies serves as an important program-building strategy to foster cross-disciplinary and "collaborative knowledge production" among our faculty (Chen 2021). One of the important guiding principles I have employed in designing GLAS 100 is attention to specific ways that this course would facilitate the growth of our young program and our students' pathway to the new major in Global Asian Studies (GLAS) at UIC.[1] Because GLAS 100 serves as the foundational core course for the GLAS major, I want students to get exposure to topics and readings that would help them develop interests in other courses in our program or the cross-listed courses offered in other departments in the humanities, arts, social sciences, and beyond. For the same reason, I have added material that reflects the diverse research and teaching fields in which our core and affiliated faculty members specialize. The strategic rationale for this approach is to help ensure that if a student taking GLAS 100 develops an interest in pursuing a research project or taking a course in a specific GLAS-related topic in the future, we would be able to connect that student to one of our colleagues.

For a small start-up academic unit with an ambitious goal of thriving as a degree-granting interdisciplinary department, this and other introductory courses would always play a critical role in building that pipeline for future majors and minors. Over time, we have added to the course reading list material from fields like critical refugee studies, history of science, and Asian diasporas in Latin America, as our growing program has welcomed new colleagues specializing in those subject areas. For example, the reading assignments on the displacement of Chagos people from Diego Garcia, Chamorros from Guam, and Rohingya refugees from Myanmar employ critical refugee studies, Indigenous studies, and diaspora studies to place recent global events in the historical contexts of imperialism and human migration. The reading assignment for the topic "The War on Terror and Global Asia" further demonstrates the longer historical legacies of Western imperialism, the Cold War in Asia, Asian diasporas, and the global refugee crisis on the ongoing U.S. war on terrorism. In this unit, students engage with an Afghan American writer's account of post-9/11 Islamophobia that traces its origins far back to British imperialism, the Soviet–Afghan War, the ensuing Afghan refugee crisis, and the longer history of anti-Muslim sentiment in the United States and the Western world. Through their examination of these materials, students are encouraged to think of Global Asias as a conceptual tool to connect those complex historical legacies to the contemporary issues that shape the world around them.

Course Description

What is Global Asian studies? This interdisciplinary course invites students to critically examine and rethink historical, cultural, and political representations of Asia and Asians in the world. In addition to surveying Asian histories and cultures, students will examine how peoples and ideas from Asia and across transoceanic and transnational diasporas have influenced a globalized world and continue to inform our contemporary understanding of Asia and Asian America. We will use conversation, intensive reading, and writing to establish, clarify, communicate, and revise our views on how historical issues such as colonialism, war, global capitalism, and migration have shaped the experiences and representations of Asians, Asian Americans, and peoples in Asian diasporas.

Conceptual and Contextual Matters

Week 1: Locating (Global) Asia
Philip Bowring, "What Is 'Asia?'"
Gary Y. Okihiro, "Ocean Worlds" and "The World System"

Week 2: Orientalism and Asia
Edward Said, "Introduction" from *Orientalism*
Hippocrates, "Airs, Waters, Places"

Week 3: Orientalism and Asian America
Henry Yu, "Asian Americans"
Moon-Ho Jung, "Worlds Empire Made"

Week 4: History of Global Asia and Asian Diasporas—Multiple Crossings
Kenneth R. Hall, "Multi-Dimensional Networking"
John Chaffee, "Diasporic Identities in the Historical Development of the Maritime Muslim Communities of Song-Yuan China"

Week 5: Charting the Ocean Worlds
Gary Y. Okihiro, "Oceania's Expanse"
K. N. Chaudhuri, "Trade and Civilization in the Indian Ocean"

The Making of Global Asia

Week 6: The Islamic World and the Making of Global Asia

K. N. Chaudhuri, "The Rise of Islam and the Pattern of Pre-Emporia Trade in Early Asia"

Ibn Battuta, "North Africa," "Egypt," and "Syria"

Week 7: The First "World System" and the Making of Global Asia

Ibn Battuta, "Persia," "Central Asian Steppes," "Byzantium-Afghanistan," "India," "India to the Indonesian Archipelago," and "To China"

Week 8: Early Modern Conjunctures and Global Asia

Robert B. Marks, "The Rise of the West?" and "The Material and Trading World, circa 1400"

Week 9: Global Asia in the Age of Imperialism

Robert B. Marks, "Empires, States, and the New World"

Timothy H. Parsons, "The Imperial Century"

Week 10: Between Two Empires

Susan A. Brewer, "Selling Empire: American Propaganda and War in the Philippines"

John W. Dower, "Japan's Beautiful Modern War"

Hot and Cold Wars

Week 11: Memories of War in Asia-Pacific

John W. Dower, "Triumphal and Tragic Narratives of the War in Asia"

Vicente M. Diaz, "Deliberating 'Liberation Day'"

Week 12: Global Asia and the Cold War

Naoko Shibusawa, "Channeling Atomic Guilt"

David Vine and Laura Jeffery, "Give Us Back Diego Garcia"

Rethinking Diasporas and Borders in Global Asia

Week 13: Legacies of War and Colonialism

Ronan Lee, "Bamboo, Tarpaulin and Mud" and "We Are Rohingya"

Week 14: Migration, Exile, and Global Border Regime
Catherine Ceniza Choy, "A Transnational History of Filipino Nurse Migration"
Reece Jones, "The Global Border Regime"

Week 15: The War on Terror and the Making of Global Asia
Maryam Qudrat Aseel, "Prologue," "The Real Islam," "Between Two Friends,"
    and "As the Smoke Clears"

Michael R. Jin is an associate professor of Global Asian studies and history at the University of Illinois Chicago. He is the author of *Citizens, Immigrants, and the Stateless: A Japanese American Diaspora in the Pacific* (2021).

■ **NOTE**

1. The thirty years of student, faculty, and community activism at the University of Illinois Chicago have led to the creation of the bachelor of arts in Global Asian Studies (GLAS) in fall 2022. GLAS is the first degree program in the Midwest offering curricular content from both Asian studies and Asian American studies.

■ **WORKS CITED**

Azuma, Eiichiro. 2021. "The Challenge of Studying the Pacific as a 'Global Asia': Problematizing Deep-Rooted Institutional Hindrances for Bringing Asian Studies and Asian American Studies." *Journal of Asian Studies* 80, no. 4: 1023–31.

Chen, Tina. 2021. "Global Asias: Method, Architecture, Praxis." *Journal of Asian Studies* 80, no. 4: 997–1009.

Okihiro, Gary Y. 2016. *Third World Studies: Theorizing Liberation.* Durham, N.C.: Duke University Press.

Said, Edward W. 1978. *Orientalism.* New York: Vintage Books.

Introduction to Global Asian Studies and Pedagogical Practice: Part 2

MARK CHIANG

As the contributions to this *A&Q* feature amply demonstrate, teaching Introduction to Global Asian Studies immediately poses numerous questions regarding what the course is supposed to introduce. One fundamental commonality here is to exploit the very fuzziness of the enormous conceptual field of "Asia" as signifier as an entry point for the course to continually foreground the very contingency of Global Asia itself as an object of knowledge, whether as a project of ideological mastery, as world-making, or as a space of perpetual globalization or mobility, just to name a few of its iterations. All introductory courses are constructed out of a balance of priorities and compromises, but the examples here illustrate the daunting number of permutations that an introduction to Global Asian studies might encompass, for having once traveled beyond the safety of disciplinary boundaries, one is confronted with a bewildering array of possibilities. There are not only questions of content, knowledge, and disciplinarity to consider but also ones of temporal and geographical parameters, institutional location, programmatic histories, curricular fit, and multiple levels of personal and political commitments. Perhaps this applies to all courses, but given the nascent state of Global Asian studies institutionally, instructors must prioritize aims and methods from within their own personal and professional perspectives and limitations. Tina Chen has advocated a vision of Global Asias scholarship in terms of structural incoherence and relational nonalignment, which are theoretically provocative paradigms yet not necessarily easy to implement within the more delimited and structured context of a course, especially an introductory one. As Nadine Attewell and Anushay Malik observe in their own case, "the institutionalization of Global Asia/s as a curricular formation at SFU reflects exigencies that aren't always easily reconciled."

Even the few syllabi included here exemplify the wide spectrum of possible answers to these questions, ranging from those that emphasize history and Asian studies to ones that focus on more contemporary issues of geopolitics, globalization, migration, and racialization. The essays here all provide fascinating instances of how these variations are motivated to a great degree by the particular institutional histories of the courses and their instructors. At University of Illinois Chicago (UIC), for example, the Global Asian Studies Program (GLAS) was formed from the merger of Asian American studies and Asian studies, but unlike in many other schools, the former was institutionally stronger because it had its own faculty lines, whereas Asian studies had always existed only as a stand-alone minor with no academic unit. Consequently, when the two programs merged, the only faculty with actual appointments in GLAS were the Asian American studies faculty. This history had a major impact on the development of the program at UIC, as can be seen in its emphases on diaspora and migration, comparative racialization, and community-engaged research and teaching. Again, the syllabi include samples that feature more of an Asian American, ethnic, and cultural studies approach, and those that are much more rooted in Asian studies and history, with one ending prior to modernity, while others begin with that periodization. Given the aim of overcoming political and intellectual divisions between ethnic and area studies, each instructor will necessarily be forced to chart his or her own paths between them.

In his essay, my colleague Michael Jin narrates some of his intellectual journey to developing Introduction to Global Asian Studies, a course whose name expresses its dual purpose of introducing students to both the field and the program. I was fortunate to be the second instructor to teach the course because I had the benefit of Michael's template to follow, which I have subsequently modified and adapted to my own interests and purposes over several iterations. As a scholar primarily of nineteenth- and twentieth-century Asian American and American literature, film, race, and cultural studies, teaching the course prompted me to learn the Asian historical components of it, an experience that perhaps all instructors will need to undergo because to teach only within the areas of our expertise is necessarily to reproduce the limitations of our own training, as David Ludden observes. One common starting point is to approach Asia as a question: What is Asia? What does Asia mean, and to whom? In practice, this entails a mode of relational, conjunctural, and contextualizing analysis that seeks to provoke questions of borders and networks, whether geographical, historical, ethnoracial, economic, cultural, or epistemological. The course is heavily oriented toward history as a necessary foundation, yet the aim is not to construct a cohesive, unified historical timeline but rather to present multiple perspectives and iterations of particular historical conjunctures, and it seeks to unfold the multiple dimensions of particular historical and local moments by enveloping them within concentric theoretical frames while at the same time attending to the specific dynamics of difference and change.

Given the long timelines and expansive (a)geographies of the course (to use Chen's term), our course favors broad, synthetic paradigms and focuses more on the historical development of political and economic relations that connect and integrate multiple regions of the globe. We have found the concept of ocean worlds to be especially useful in this context, as it offers a fundamental restructuring of many of the categories and assumptions that undergird conventional territorial and state-based histories, displacing the emphasis on territorial states, military conquest, and empire, with another history of migration, merchants, commerce, and the development of trade and exchange routes. Of course, the decision to relegate the histories of states to the margins of the course in favor of migration and trade brings with it a number of implications. One is that it treats war and imperial conquest primarily in terms of territorial expansion as a precondition for the establishment of long-distance trade routes. Given the very broad overview of trade relations, however, it is difficult to impart a more finely grained sense of how trade routes evolved, the goods that traveled along each, and the various social and political circumstances that travelers would encounter on different stages of the journey. In this context, Ibn Battuta's account of his travels across the Islamic world of the fourteenth century offers more immediate descriptions of various regions of the world, while his journeys as a religious pilgrim can also be contrasted with the more commercially motivated travels of Marco Polo, for example.

Students have asked why Islam occupies such a central place in the course, but this very question betrays so much about contemporary discourses concerning Islam in the West and is indeed one of the major reasons for that attention. Certainly, in the period between the seventh and the fifteenth centuries, the history of Asia in general can in many ways be traced through relations between West Asia and East Asia. Again, the choice to focus on transcontinental dynamics means that the complex histories of states in South Asia and Southeast Asia are largely left out, while there is the barest outline, for example, of the Abbasid and Ummayyad Islamic dynasties and the Song and Tang Dynasties. Emphasizing the Islamic world in this period highlights its role as intermediary between Europe and China, and its control over the major land routes between them, but it also provides an opportunity to address the relations between religion, military conquest, economic processes, and cultural exchanges. Moreover, centering Islam, at least provisionally, for a brief period of the course functions to dislocate students from the deeply embedded ideological imaginaries of Eurocentrism. At the same time, Islam itself is situated as the central node in transcontinental trade routes spanning Afro-Eurasia, and it serves to link topics like Indian Ocean trade, diasporic Muslim communities, and Southeast Asian riverine states, material that demonstrates trade's impact on the formation of diaspora, culture, community, and polity. After the sixteenth century, the work of undoing Eurocentrism necessarily takes the form of teaching the history of Europe and its settler colonies as global history within the context of the ways that Europe has sought to construct itself as the Subject of Asia. Similarly, global labor migration in the nineteenth century and the rise of U.S. global hegemony in the twentieth century are crucial mediating contexts that link the histories of Asia and of Asian Americans. In this manner, Asian American panethnicity is introduced from the beginning in the larger global contexts that reflect its origins in the Third World and decolonizing movements of the mid-twentieth century and how these arose from the cross-fertilizing connections between liberation struggles both inside and outside the West.

While the initial iteration of the course leaned heavily in the direction of historical material, given Michael's disciplinary training, we have each adapted the course to include a greater range of topics and diverse approaches across the social sciences and humanities, in large part to reflect the particular interests and methods of faculty members in GLAS and to introduce students to its courses. Another locus of gravity is the effort to trace the impact of Global Asia on local Chicago Asian American communities; this has the effect of skewing the course toward the United States somewhat, but it also creates greater possibilities for students to explore how the course material connects to their own lives and those of their families and communities. The course ends with some reflection on the histories of Asian and Asian American studies and of ethnic and area studies as the theoretical paradigms that have most directly shaped the course and that also frame the political and intellectual projects of GLAS.

■ GLAS 100: INTRODUCTION TO GLOBAL ASIAN STUDIES SYLLABUS

Course Description
What is Global Asia? This introductory and interdisciplinary course will provide a broad survey of Asian histories and cultures over the last two millennia, examining how peoples and ideas from Asia and across transoceanic and transnational diasporas have influenced a globalized world and continue to inform our contemporary understanding of Asia and Asian America. Rather than focusing on particular nations or regions, the course will emphasize the historical trajectories and interrelations between states and regions within Asia, and between Asia and other parts of the world. We will examine Asia's role in the development of the world

system and the global capitalist economy, and we will also explore the impact of European imperialism and modernization on Asians around the globe. Given our location, the course will focus especially on the impact of the United States on Asia and Asian peoples in the twentieth century, and we will conclude by exploring how phenomena such as militarism, immigration, adoption, labor struggles, gender and sexuality, and popular culture have shaped the contemporary world.

Week 1: Introduction—What Is "Asia"?
Hippocrates. "Airs, Waters, Places."
Said, Edward W. 1979. "Introduction." In *Orientalism*. New York: Vintage Books.

Week 2: The Origins of the World-System
Okihiro, Gary Y. 2015. "Ocean Worlds" and "The World-System." In *American History Unbound: Asians and Pacific Islanders*. Oakland: University of California Press.
Excerpts from *The Travels of Ibn Battuta* and *The Travels of Marco Polo*

Week 3: The Indian Ocean and Muslim China
Chaudhuri, K. N. 1985. "Trade and Civilisation in the Indian Ocean" and "The Rise of Islam and the Pattern of Pre-Emporia Trade in Early Asia." In *Trade and Civilisation in the Indian Ocean: An Economic History from the Rise of Islam to 1750*. Cambridge: Cambridge University Press.
Chaffee, John. 2006. "Diasporic Identities in the Historical Development of the Maritime Muslim Communities of Song-Yuan China." *Journal of the Economic and Social History of the Orient* 49, no. 4: 395–420.

Week 4: Southeast Asia as Crossroads of Trade
Hall, Kenneth R. 2006. "Multi-dimensional Networking: Fifteenth-Century Indian Ocean Maritime Diaspora in Southeast Asian Perspective." *Journal of the Economic and Social History of the Orient* 49, no. 4: 454–81.
Hall, Kenneth R. 2011. "Trade and Statecraft in Early Southeast Asia." In *A History of Early Southeast Asia Maritime Trade and Societal Development, 100–1500*. Lanham, Md.: Rowman and Littlefield.

Week 5: The Story of "the West"
Marks, Robert. 2020. "The Rise of the West?," "The Material and Trading Worlds, circa 1400," and "Empires, States, and the New World." In *The Origins of the Modern World: A Global and Environmental Narrative from the Fifteenth to the Twenty-First Century*. Lanham, Md.: Rowman and Littlefield.

Week 6: European and U.S. Imperialism

Parsons, Timothy. 2019. "The Imperial Century." In *The British Imperial Century, 1815-1914: A World History Perspective*. Lanham, Md.: Rowman and Littlefield.

Brewer, Susan A. 2013. "Selling Empire: American Propaganda and War in the Philippines." *The Asia-Pacific Journal* 11, no. 40.

Week 7: U.S. Borders and the Immigration Regime

Fujita-Rony, Dorothy B. 2003. "Empire and Migration." In *American Workers, Colonial Power: Philippine Seattle and the Transpacific West, 1919–1941*. Berkeley: University of California Press.

Lee, Erika, and Judy Yung. 2010. "'A People without a Country': Korean Refugee Students and Picture Brides" and "In Search of Freedom and Opportunity: Russians and Jews in the Promised Land." In *Angel Island: Immigrant Gateway to America*. Oxford: Oxford University Press.

Week 8: Settlers and Natives—Pacific Islanders and Asian Americans

Okihiro, Gary Y. 2015. "Regions of Fire" and "Oceania's Expanse." In *American History Unbound: Asians and Pacific Islanders*. Oakland: University of California Press.

Hau'ofa, Epeli. 1994. "Our Sea of Islands." *The Contemporary Pacific* 6, no. 1: 147–60.

Lee, Erika. 2003. "The Chinese Are Coming." In *At America's Gates: Chinese Immigration during the Exclusion Era, 1882–1943*. Chapel Hill: University of North Carolina Press.

Week 9: The Pacific War between the United States and Japan

Dower, John W. 1995. "Triumphal and Tragic Narratives of the War in Asia." *Journal of American History* 82, no. 3: 1124–35.

Yui, Daizaburo. 2015. "Between Pearl Harbor and Hiroshima/Nagasaki: Nationalism and Memory in Japan and the United States." In *Living with the Bomb: American and Japanese Cultural Conflicts in the Nuclear Age*, edited by Laura E. Hein and Mark Selden. New York: Routledge.

Cook, Haruko Taya, and Theodore Cook. 1993. Excerpts from *Japan at War: An Oral History*. New York: New Press.

Sodei, Rinjirō. 1998. "From Hiroshima, Back to Hiroshima." In *Were We the Enemy? American Survivors of Hiroshima*. Boulder, Colo.: Westview Press.

Week 10: Humanitarian Aid and the International Adoption Industry

Shibusawa, Naoko. 2006. "Channeling Atomic Guilt." In *America's Geisha Ally: Reimagining the Japanese Enemy*. Cambridge, Mass.: Harvard University Press.

Choy, Catherine Ceniza. 2013. "Race and Rescue in Early Asian International Adoption History." In *Global Families: A History of Asian International Adoption in America.* New York: New York University Press.

Week 11: U.S. Military Occupation in Asia

Vine, David, and Laura Jeffery. 2009. "Give Us Back Diego Garcia: Unity and Division among Activists in the Indian Ocean." In *The Bases of Empire: The Global Struggle against U.S. Military Posts,* edited by Catherine Lutz. New York: New York University Press.

Akibayashi, Kozue, and Suzuyo Takazato. 2009. "Okinawa: Women's Struggle for Demilitarization." In *The Bases of Empire: The Global Struggle against U.S. Military Posts,* edited by Catherine Lutz. New York: New York University Press.

Tremblay, Regis, dir. 2013. *The Ghosts of Jeju.*

Week 12: Asian Labor Migration in Contemporary American Society

Choy, Catherine Ceniza. 2016. "A Transnational History of Filipino Nurse Migration." In *Major Problems in Asian American History: Documents and Essays,* edited by Lon Kurashige and Alice Yang Murray. Boston: Cengage Learning.

Quan, Katie. 2004. "Global Strategies for Workers: How Class Analysis Clarifies Us and Them and What We Need to Do." In *What's Class Got to Do with It? American Society in the Twenty-First Century,* edited by Michael Zweig. Ithaca, N.Y.: ILR Press.

Pinsker, Joe. 2016. "Why Some Cuisines Are More Expensive than Others: A Theory." *The Atlantic,* July 13. https://www.theatlantic.com/business/archive/2016/07/the-future-is-expensive-chinese-food/491015/.

Hilgers, Lauren. 2014. "The Kitchen Network: America's Underground Chinese Restaurant Workers." *New Yorker,* October 6. https://www.newyorker.com/magazine/2014/10/13/cookas-tale.

Week 13: Sexuality and Queer Asia

Masequesmay, Gina. 2003. "Emergence of Queer Vietnamese America." *Amerasia Journal* 29, no. 1: 116–34.

Nanda, Serena. 1992. "The Third Gender: Hijra Community in India." *Manushi* 72: 9–16.

Davies, Sharyn Graham. 2018. "The West Can Learn from Southeast Asia's Transgender Heritage." *Aeon.* https://aeon.co/essays/the-west-can-learn-from-southeast-asias-transgender-heritage.

Han, C. Winter. 2013. "Darker Shades of Queer: Race and Sexuality at the Margins." In *Men Speak Out: Views on Gender, Sex and Power,* edited by Shira Tarrant and Jackson Katz. New York: Routledge.

Week 14: Cultural Politics and Cross-Racial Coalitions

Prashad, Vijay. 2003. "Bruce Lee and the Anti-imperialism of Kung Fu: A Polycultural Adventure." *Positions: East Asia Cultures Critique* 11, no. 1: 51–90.

Tang, Eric. 2013. "How the Refugees Stopped the Bronx from Burning." *Race and Class* 54, no. 4: 48–66.

Week 15: Ethnic Studies and Area Studies: Reconceptualizing "Asia"

Mark Chiang is an associate professor of Global Asian studies and English at the University of Illinois Chicago. He is the author of *The Cultural Capital of Asian American Studies: Autonomy and Representation in the University* (2009).

CURATED BY **H. J. TAM**

Of Scrolls and Tears: Trinh Mai's Archival Art and Organic Ephemera

Titled *Ba Ơi (Dear Father),* Vietnamese American artist Trinh Mai's 2017 mixed media portrait reproduces an enlarged photograph of the artist's father-in-law, a former high-ranking official in the Army of the Republic of Vietnam (South Vietnam) named Phơủ Vân Thạch,[1] holding a sign of his name at a reeducation camp after the Communist takeover of the country in 1975 (Figure 1). We see Phơủ with a deep frown, his mouth half open as if in mid-speech, defiant despite the abjection imposed by the state. In Trinh Mai's depiction, this photograph from a haunting past becomes a memorial: carved onto the artwork's surface are seventeen punctures representing the bullet wounds Phơủ sustained through the war, and the hand-painted Sanskrit words "dear father" cascade around the subject. The incisions reveal the thick texture of materials underneath: swatches from mourning bands worn in Vietnamese funerals and copies of Phơủ's camp release papers. Less visible materials used in the artwork include rainwater from Vietnam, the tears Trinh Mai shed for her father-in-law, and the natural oils left on the canvas from her fingertips. In *Dear Father,* as in her other works introduced in this *Portfolio* feature, Trinh Mai combines the tangible and the imperceptible, discarded objects and living things, official documents and bodily secretions, to give form to the interstitial: between public and private, alive and demised. This critical interstitiality holds the diasporic Vietnamese consciousness that exists outside of dominant national histories in the United States and contemporary Vietnam; as such, the artworks grapple with "the sad and violent history that exists between Vietnam and the United States, and the politics of translocated race, gender, and class that springs from this past" (Espiritu 2010, 200).

Two prominent types of materials appear throughout Trinh Mai's oeuvre: those that could be considered archival in nature (identification cards, letters, photographs) and organic elements (tears, eggshells, feathers). Combined in each work, their properties complement and transform each other: the organic materials lend their living aura to the historic documents, enabling these objects to conjure the specters of those who carried them through exile; at the same time, the archival materials fuse historicity into the ephemera, which symbolize refugees' precarious, embodied experiences often unacknowledged in history books. In her use of photographic and written materials, Trinh Mai evinces what art critic Hal Foster (2004, 3) calls "an archival impulse." Diverse in their subjects and media, Foster writes, archival artists share "a will to relate—to probe a misplaced past, to collate its different signs . . . to ascertain what might remain for the present" (21). For Trinh Mai, the "misplaced past" is the ill-understood story of Vietnamese refugees like her family after the fall of Saigon. Moreover, Trinh Mai's mixing of organic substances recalls the influence of bioart, which, as Robert Mitchell (2010, 26) explains, couples artistic goals with biological technologies to make statements about the problematic of biotechnology. While Trinh Mai shares with bioartists the desire to solicit a moral response to the living beings and biological processes manipulated into art, her focus and intent in integrating organic materials in her work are different: instead of commenting theoretically on the state of biotechnology and its industries, Trinh Mai situates her work historically and politically in the legacy of the Vietnam War and mourns through her art those deemed disposable by regimes of power, in Vietnam and the United States.

Without Trinh Mai's artistic treatment, Phổủ, the reeducation camp inmate in Mai's *Dear Father,* would otherwise have no public recognition: he is disavowed in Vietnam, where the government continues to suppress critiques of its postwar treatment of South Vietnamese, and in the United States, where the American soldier/veteran retains discursive primacy. Neither is Phổủ a "boat person" figure, with its representational burden of helplessness and proof of the West's humanitarian gift of freedom, as Mimi Nguyen (2012) has suggested. The artist's father-in-law appears here only through reproduced state documents, that is, his mug shot and his release papers. These archival materials carry political significance. As Jacques Derrida (1995, 9) explains, the word *archive* comes from the Greek *arkheion,* "the residence of the superior magistrates, the *archons,* those who commanded." The *archons* have the power to make the law, and their authority makes them guardians of official documents. That is to say, the archive is traditionally put in service of the state, and in

Figure 1. *Ba Ơi (Dear Father)*, 2017. Gouache, living plants, papyrus, rainwater from Việt Nam, copies of Bác Phươl's release papers from reeducation camp, scripture from the book of James, tears shed in mourning for his suffering, textile, and tree bark on digital image printed on Arches watercolor paper, 44 × 60 in. Image courtesy of the artist.

Figure 2. Detail of *Ba Ơi (Dear Father)*. Image courtesy of the artist.

turn, the state polices what it admits into the archive. Trinh Mai's art-work not only critiques that power dynamic by laying bare how the state forces criminality onto her father-in-law but also subverts that state logic by turning the evidence of his political persecution into a dignified portrait. Mitigating the camera lens's accusatory gaze, Trinh Mai's tears and Sanskrit chant transform this image of injustice into a part of the grief process. Grief does not harden into grievance in Trinh Mai's work, as the sprouting plants from one of the punctures on the canvas indicate life and growth from historical wounds (Figure 2). Trinh Mai thus invites the viewer to witness the brutality of authoritarianism, meet the subject's frowning gaze, and acknowledge his dignity and courage. The artist conjures a shroud of protection with her repeated chants of "dear father," invoking a prayer that sacralizes remembrance and gestures toward consolation.

Two other artworks, *That We Should Be Heirs* (2019) and *Seed* (2022), bear the hallmark of Trinh Mai's amalgamation of the archival and the ephemeral. The first work asks spectators to write their fears on paper scrolls, tie them up with red strings, and leave them in holes bored out of a gallery wall (Figure 3). These miniature vaults also contain pieces of cotton that have been doused in holy water and Pacific Ocean water, and a stone is placed in each hole, seemingly to guard the scrolls entrust-ed to the work by gallerygoers (Figure 4). The personal divulgences lie

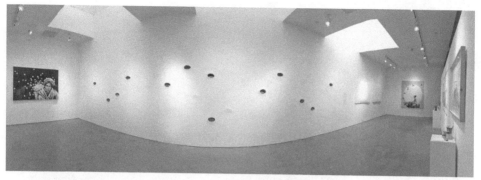

Figure 3. *That We Should Be Heirs,* 2019. Acrylic, unread letters inherited from the artist's grandmother, cotton grown at the farm from which the artist's husband and his family harvested when they first arrived in America, hand embroidery, holy water, stones collected from the Pacific Coast, raw canvas, personal handwritten scrolls as contributed by community members, thread, Pacific Ocean water, and wool, dimensions variable. Image courtesy of the artist.

Figure 4. Detail of *That We Should Be Heirs.* Image courtesy of the artist.

vulnerable to prying eyes and fingers, yet many participants take that risk and entomb their fears, a gesture at once confessional and triumphal. This archive exists only for the duration of the exhibit, but while it lasts, its form changes and grows with new submissions. The willing participant turns a blank piece of paper into a record of fear, and the confided

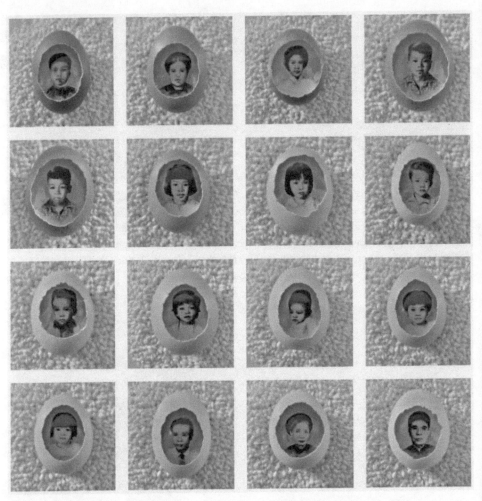

Figure 5. *Seed,* 2022. Acrylic, ink, charcoal, and resin encapsulated in heirloom chicken eggs, resting upon mounds of sweet rice, dimensions variable. Image courtesy of the artist.

words that make up *That We Should Be Heirs* recall the sweat and tears featured in Trinh Mai's other artworks. Compared to traditional files shelved in dusting collections, these scrolls do not bear the evidentiary weight of history; nonetheless, Trinh Mai's creative archive tracks more undisciplined, private temporalities: those of traumas and nightmares, of dashed dreams and thwarted hopes.

The same aesthetic idea runs through *Seed,* in which we see hollowed chicken eggs whose shells have been meticulously chipped away to reveal

Figure 6. Detail of *Seed*. Image courtesy of the artist.

what the artist has tucked inside: black-and-white portrait photographs of her family—her mother, the mother's nine siblings, their parents and grandparents (Figure 5). The sixteen eggshells, each of which rests on a mound of uncooked sweet rice, together transform a multimedia family album into a solemn altar (Figure 6). Varying in colors, shapes, and specks, the shells represent unique individuals belonging to a family. With its mixed use of organic ephemera (eggshells and rice grains) and photographs from the family archive, *Seed* encapsulates Trinh Mai's fine balance between an archival impulse and the magnetic aura of the organic. The delicate eggshells become membranes protecting the family presences summoned by the photographs. Though different in subject matter and materials, *That We Should Be Heirs* and *Seed* both exemplify Trinh Mai's aesthetic play with diverse textures and symbolic meanings, mediating between the perishable, ephemeral, and fragile, on one hand, and the archival traces of history and memory, on the other.

Harking back to the use of a male subject in *Dear Father,* Trinh Mai's 2020 mixed media installation portrait *Flesh of My Flesh* centers on her husband, Hiền. Standing at almost eight feet tall and three and a half feet wide, Trinh Mai's charcoal drawing of the man, stripped down to boxer shorts and staring straight ahead, is adorned with three colorfully painted birds perching on his head, shoulder, and left arm. Breaking the

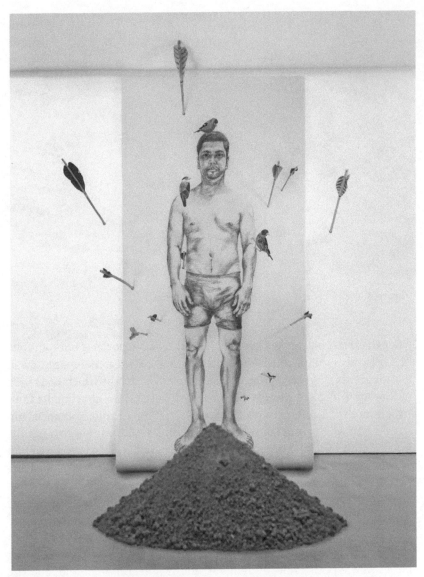

Figure 7. *Flesh of My Flesh,* 2020. Commissioned by MCLA Arts and Culture, North Adams, Massachusetts. Belle's acrylic; charcoal; dirt collected from the almond orchards in which the artist's husband, Hiên, and his family labored with other immigrant families after arriving in America; holy water; ink; Pacific Ocean water collected from the harbor of San Pedro, where Hiên served time in the immigration detention center; and tears shed for him as the artist considered the hardships that he endured, on paper; arrows crafted with indigenous methods using found branches, found feathers, found string, and wax, drawing 42 × 94 1/2 in., installation dimensions variable. Image courtesy of the artist.

Figure 8. Detail of *Flesh of My Flesh*. Image courtesy of the artist.

two-dimensionality of the painting's surface, Trinh Mai places in front of the portrait a pile of dirt collected from the garlic fields where Hiền harvested for a dollar a bucket (Figure 7). The subject seems to emerge amid a field of arrows hitting the canvas and the gallery wall around it. Though targeted, he is unharmed and undaunted. The work does not explicitly reference Vietnam, but war manifests in the symbolic form of arrows. Like *Dear Father*, this artwork features suffused and indiscernible elements: tears Trinh Mai shed for her husband, holy water, and ocean water from the harbor in San Pedro where Hiền served time in an immigration detention center. Situating a legally and economically precarious body in the basic elements of water, earth, and air, *Flesh of My Flesh* reaches for the elemental and eternal without compromising its intersectional concerns about class and state violence.

Catholic sources, tropes, and iconographies—liberally altered and adapted—profoundly inform Trinh Mai's diasporic art. The title *Flesh of My Flesh* comes from the Book of Genesis, where Adam accepts God's creation of Eve from his rib. Here Trinh Mai subverts the originary gender dynamic by asserting her position as a woman creating an image of her husband. Moreover, the near-naked male subject as an archer's target recalls the iconic image of St. Sebastian, with its long history in the visual arts, from the seven attempts by Baroque artist Guido Reni to numerous gay male cultural works, including Derek Jarman's controversial film *Sebastiane* (1976) and covers of popular magazines. In an influential essay, art historian Richard Kaye has traced Sebastian's multiple reinvents from the Renaissance through the AIDS crisis. A "beleaguered, existential hero," Sebastian's erotic power comes from his utter vulnerability, silent receptivity to arrows, and ecstatic submission—qualities that render him "a prototypical portrait of tortured closet case" (Kaye 1996, 87). Trinh Mai is no doubt aware of this Catholic icon with a deep artistic legacy, and her diasporic Vietnamese Adam cum Sebastian refuses to be a self-absorbed eroticized object: whereas the saintly Sebastian looks to the heavens, Hiên defiantly locks eyes with the viewer; he bares his body but rejects any apartness from the world (Figure 8). The pile of dirt, the ground of Hiên's labor, asserts his earthly presence, and the arrows miraculously cannot touch him. If martyrdom and refugeehood are both to be narrowly understood in terms of salvation, *Flesh of My Flesh* demands an alternative way to understand precarity, one not predicated on submission to a higher order.

Indeed, Trinh Mai goes far in "illuminating the cross-border operations of power and its abuse, greed and its operations" (Viet Nguyen 2016, 216). *Flesh of My Flesh* belongs to a larger series called *We Who Seek Refuge*, which also includes a work titled *Black Đeath* (2020). Created in May 2020, this work commemorates the ground-shattering death of George Floyd as well as those who lost their lives due to Covid-19. Measured at two feet in height and nineteen inches in width, *Black Đeath* comprises ten thousand fingerprints black-inked by the artist on paper (Figure 9). The fingerprints radiate in a centrifugal manner, the pitch-black center losing density as it moves outward to more isolated imprints. In this way, Trinh Mai gives form to an existentially challenged moment of

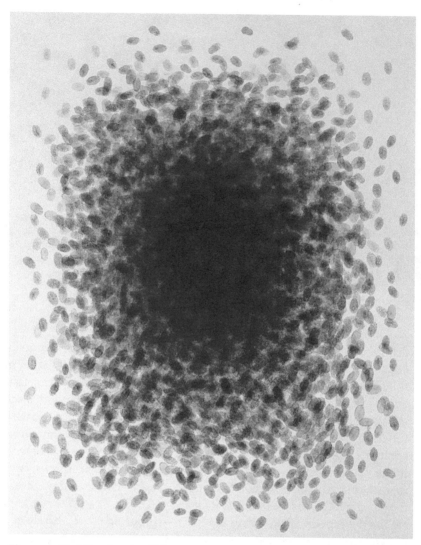

Figure 9. *Black Đeath,* 2020. Holy water, tears shed for George Floyd and the Black community, and ink (the artist's fingerprints), on paper, 19 × 24 in. Image courtesy of the artist.

national and global pain, grief, anger, and dark distrust. Yeats's oft-quoted line from "The Second Coming" intones through this apocalyptic work: "Things fall apart; the center cannot hold." Yet even the depthless hollow of *Black Đeath* fails to extinguish an intrinsic hope that shines throughout Trinh Mai's oeuvre. With a perspectival shift, the centrifugal force that

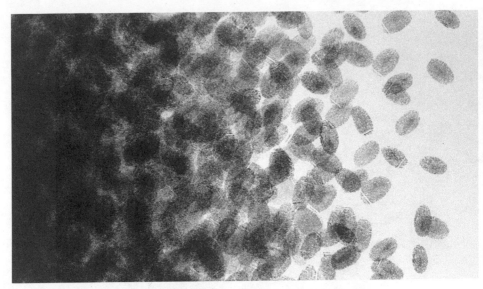

Figure 10. Detail of *Black Ðeath*. Image courtesy of the artist.

disintegrates the fingerprints could also be seen as its opposite, centripetal: the fingerprints are not coming apart; they are coming together in solidarity. Like a Rothko, *Black Ðeath* becomes a color field painting that opens a space of deep reflection for its viewer: the artist's play with black ink on white paper yields shades of gray, and each fingerprint joins with others to generate new forms, like smoke, clouds, blossoms, ocean waves, or the strange figures in our dreams (Figure 10). If we were to give time to the work and let it wash over us, perhaps we could even see faces, ones we recognize and ones we don't. Trinh Mai suggests here that we owe it to them, and to ourselves, not to look away.

The delicate details in Trinh Mai's art—sprouting plants, barely visible words from official documents, eggshells, fingerprints, and invisible tears—sustain amazing gravitas. Though family is a major motif in her work, Trinh Mai's archive does not end with family photographs and documents. Whereas *Dear Father* and *Seed* focus on the artist's family, *That We Should Be Heirs* encourages the community of the exhibit to find solace in the collective act of archiving their fears. Trinh Mai's representations of vulnerable figures also point to pressing social and cultural issues. *Flesh of My Flesh* relies on the thoroughly queered visual life of St. Sebastian, the "go-to saint for the homoerotic imaginary" (Parker 2018, 87). Flirting with Sebastian's symbolic deviance, Trinh Mai offers her husband up for public viewing, not to heroize him, but to demand a response to precarious life marked by war, refugeehood, and racialized labor. That goal finds urgency in *Black Đeath,* where the artist moves from the figurative to the abstract to throw open the monochromatic painting as an ambitious site for national and global solidarity. Margo Machida (2008, 131) opines in her study of Asian American visual arts, "What is socially meaningful about art is its capacity to bridge very different spheres of memory: private and public, vernacular and historical." In her deft experiments with archival and ephemeral matters, Trinh Mai arrives at compelling visions that foreground Vietnamese refugees, low-wage workers, and the world's millions jointly confronting political oppression, racism, and pandemic devastation.

H. J. Tam is the Florence Levy Kay Fellow in Anglophone Literature and Film of the East Asian Diaspora at Brandeis University. He earned a PhD in English from the University of Pennsylvania and held postdoctoral fellowships at Dartmouth College and Harvard University. Tam is working on a book on diasporic Vietnamese literature published in France and the United States. His essays have appeared in *American Literature* and the *Journal of Vietnamese Studies.*

■ NOTE

1. Readers of Vietnamese will notice that Phơủl is not a conventional Vietnamese last name. A more likely spelling is Phước. Because I do not intend to correct the artist's language, I am following the spelling in Trinh Mai's description of the work.

■ WORKS CITED

Derrida, Jacques. 1995. "Archive Fever: A Freudian Impression." Translated by Eric Prenowitz. *Diacritics* 25, no. 2: 9–63.

Espiritu, Yen Le. 2010. "Negotiating Memories of War: Arts in Vietnamese American Communities." In *Art in the Lives of Immigrant Communities in the United States,* edited by Paul DiMaggio and Patricia Fernández-Kelly, 197–213. New Brunswick, N.J.: Rutgers University Press.

Foster, Hal. 2004. "An Archival Impulse." *October* 110: 3–22.

Kaye, Richard A. 1996. "Losing His Religion: Saint Sebastian as Contemporary Gay Martyr." In *Outlooks: Lesbian and Gay Sexualities and Visual Cultures,* edited by Peter Horne and Reina Lewis, 86–105. London: Routledge.

Machida, Margo. 2008. *Unsettled Visions: Contemporary Asian American*

Artists and the Social Imaginary. Durham, N.C.: Duke University Press.

Mitchell, Robert. 2010. *Bioart and the Vitality of Media.* Seattle: University of Washington Press.

Nguyen, Mimi. 2012. *The Gift of Freedom: War, Debt, and Other Refugee Passages.* Durham, N.C.: Duke University Press.

Nguyen, Viet Thanh. 2016. *Nothing Ever Dies: Vietnam and the Memory of War.* Cambridge, M.A.: Harvard University Press.

Parker, Sarah. 2018. "The Male Wound in *Fin-de-siècle* Poetry." In *The Male Body in Medicine and Literature,* edited by Andrew Mangham and Daniel Lee, 87–102. Liverpool, U.K.: Liverpool University Press.

Field Trip

ANDREW WAY LEONG AND DARWIN H. TSEN

Left Internationalisms in Nationalist Times

This *Field Trip* consists of five essays written by scholars studying left internationalist imaginaries within Asia and in transpacific relation to the Americas. Our impetus for collaboration was a series of *Verge*-sponsored panels on "Transpacific Socialisms" at the 2021 Association for Asian American Studies conference. In our call, we asked, "What might happen if we stop assigning sole determinative force to the imperial imaginaries of capitalist powers, and viewed socialist labor networks and revolutionary itineraries as integral to the formation of the 'transpacific'?"

While assembling our *Field Trip*, we found the grand narrative ambition of "transpacific socialisms" to be less salient as a description for our shared concerns. None of our essays turned to triumphalist imaginaries of the transpacific under conditions of plausible left unity or ascendancy (e.g., the 1920s Third International or 1960s global Maoism/Third Worldism). Instead, we found a structure of feeling in a minor key: a shared attention to instances of parasitic translation, reinvention, or reflective introjection of left internationalist imaginaries under conditions of extreme reaction and repression. This structure of feeling is an understandable response to our present, where ascendant ultranationalisms make the prospects for left internationalist visions of global Asias seem increasingly dire.

Like the *Asias* of "Global Asias," our left *internationalisms* are "deliberately plural/pluralizing" (Chen 2021, 1002).[1] We build on the insights of Shuang Shen (2009, 65), whose study of "Chinese writers in left-oriented internationalist journals" has encouraged us to shift away from "conventional histories of internationalism" that "tend to focus on major political organizations such as the Communist International" and instead approach internationalisms "from the point of view of translation and cultural circulation." From the vantages of translation and circulation, left internationalisms can never be singular because they are constantly embedded within negotiations of "difference and disjunction" (65). As such, left internationalisms are simultaneously explicit programs of "political alliance forged on the basis of the common goal of world revolution among oppressed peoples" *and* the positive cultural mediations—"literary exchange, critical reading, and imaginative identification"—that make such programs legible and realizable among different languages, cultures, and peoples (73).[2]

By turning to left internationalisms in the midst of translations and incipient re-formations, our *Field Trip* exemplifies the ethos of *Verge* as a forum for what lies on the edges of formations like Asian area and Asian American ethnic studies. We have not focused, as one might in Asian area studies, on direct analyses of the state socialisms of China, North Korea, or Vietnam. We also do not focus, as one might in Asian American studies, on how writers or protest movements conform to U.S.-based modes of ethnic or pan-ethnic identification.

The five essays proceed chronologically through internationalist practices and imaginaries from the 1930s to the 2020s. Darwin H. Tsen's essay, on the travels of Japanese anarcho-socialist Yamaga Taiji (1892–1970), interprets his activities as a publisher and translator in Taiwan and the Philippines as a "parasitic" strategy of building structures for internationalist solidarity while negotiating the infrastructures of Japanese empire at its apex. Paul Nadal's essay prompts us to consider how negotiation of another "empire at its apex" might be at play in the works and reception of Carlos Bulosan (1913–56). Nadal argues that the retroactive categorization of Bulosan as a "Filipino American" writer has obscured how his long prose works, when read in concert, project an internationalist horizon of Asian socialist futurity. Roanne L. Kantor makes a parallel argument about Kashmiri American poet Agha Shahid Ali (1949–2001), arguing, through the trope of the "rearview mirror," that standard readings of Ali's post-1980s poetry in terms of his Kashmiri diasporic identity have failed to consider how closely his persona of "witness" not only reflects Pablo Neruda's vision of a "unified socialist Américas" but also introjects this vision following the counterrevolutions of the 1970s and 1980s. Calvin Cheung-Miaw asks us to reassess the 1980s, seeing this decade not only as a period of "socialist crisis" defined by counterrevolution in the Americas and market reforms in China but as what the U.S.-based League of Revolutionary Struggle understood as a period of "socialist re-invention." Cheung-Miaw's provocative question—"what [does it] mean to maintain a commitment to revolutionary transformation during counterrevolutionary times"—looms large over the final essay of the series. Jason G. Coe brings us to the 2010s, when the 2016 trial of New York Police Department officer Peter Liang for the shooting death of Akai Gurley laid bare a schism between Third Worldist concepts of "Asian American" political identity and a Han Chinese ethnonationalism facilitated by WeChat, a social media "super-app" whose "CCP-monitored posts are . . . maintained in mainland China for all accounts." Read in a full circle with Tsen's essay, Coe prompts us to consider how renewed work in media like multilingual documentary film could provide tactics for challenging state/corporate-abetted media to build infrastructures of translation toward future internationalisms.

In sum, the essays ask us to look for the building blocks of left internationalisms in unlikely times and places, from Japanese and American Empire in the 1930s–1950s through the counterrevolutions of the 1980s and 2010s. While these essays may—given the nature of the times they address and our own—be fragments gesturing to greater wholes, we hope their assembly inspires further work toward envisioning the internationalist possibilities of global Asias.

Andrew Way Leong is an assistant professor of English at the University of California, Berkeley.

Darwin Tsen is an assistant teaching professor and coordinator of Chinese at Syracuse University.

■ **NOTES**

In addition to extending thanks to the authors included within this *Field Trip,* we wish to acknowledge the contributions and feedback of the three other presenters in the "Transpacific Socialisms" panels: Christopher Fan, Steven Lee, and Hiroaki Matsusaka.

1. For contrast, see the singular assertions in political theorist Michael Walzer's (2018) "What Is Left Internationalism?," which employs the definitional *is* to espouse a set of normative/prescriptive claims about what Walzer believes *ought* to be left internationalism: a "practical post-Marxist" (38) foreign policy for the left that "is not, either now or in the foreseeable future, a revolutionary politics" (48).

2. For an account of "mediation" as a "positive process" inherent within "social reality," as opposed to a "process added to it by way of projection, disguise, or interpretation," see Williams ([1977] 2009, 98–99).

■ WORKS CITED

Chen, Tina. 2021. "Global Asias: Method, Architecture, Praxis." *Journal of Asian Studies* 80, no. 4 (2021): 997–1009.

Shen, Shuang. 2009. "Lu Xun, Cultural Internationalism, Leftist Periodicals, and Literary Translation in the 1930s." In *China Abroad: Travels, Subjects, Spaces,* edited by Elaine Yee Lin Ho and Julia Kuehn, 63–81. Hong Kong: Hong Kong University Press.

Walzer, Michael. 2018. "What Is Left Internationalism?" In *A Foreign Policy for the Left,* 35–52. New Haven, Conn.: Yale University Press.

Williams, Raymond. (1977) 2009. *Marxism and Literature.* New York: Oxford University Press.

Yamaga Taiji's Parasitic Internationalism

DARWIN H. TSEN

During Japan's transformation into an imperial power in the early twentieth century, its domestic political struggles quickly synchronized with contemporary developments in global right- and left-political formations (see Hoston 1987; Crump 1983). Although the empire is remembered as part of the fascist Axis, the extent to which the Japanese left contributed to early twentieth-century internationalism remains relatively unexplored. Throughout this period, Japanese anarchism gave rise to many internationalist figures, such as Kōtoku Denjiro (1871–1911) and Ōsugi Sakae (1885–1923), who engaged with fellow anarcho-socialists in the United States, Korea, Europe, and China. This short essay focuses on one of Ōsugi's protégés, Yamaga Taiji 山鹿泰治 (1892–1970), a printer and Esperanto activist who traveled to China, Taiwan, and the Philippines from 1914 to 1946.

A polyglot known for his mastery of Mandarin, English, and Esperanto—a world language used by anarchists[1]—Yamaga was not just an inheritor of the internationalism cultivated by his predecessors.[2] He instead fostered what I call a "parasitic internationalism": a praxis that relies on an empire's infrastructure while subverting it for other ends. Yamaga's travels in Japan's imperial peripheries eschewed direct confrontation with the state in favor of organizing under it; his was an anarcho-internationalism that advocated for building communication and solidarity toward the future, even if such work did not directly confront the present. This was the prefigurative core of Yamaga's parasitic internationalism.

Yamaga Taiji was born in Kyoto in 1872. In 1907, Yamaga traveled to

Tokyo as a typesetting apprentice and became interested in Esperanto. In December 1910, he encountered Ōsugi Sakae, who invited him to work for the Esperanto Association of Japan, later entrusting Yamaga to establish connections with overseas Esperantists. Yamaga's parasitic internationalism burgeoned after the repression that followed the 1923 Great Kanto Earthquake. Military police used the earthquake as cover to murder Ōsugi and his feminist partner, Itoh Noe 伊藤野枝 (Kurihara 2013, 91). While Yamaga hid in Tokyo and moonlighted as a carpenter, he informed international networks about Japan's situation. Yamaga's linguistic prowess and pragmatic caution later culminated into a knack for working with comrades in colonial and semicolonial spaces ruled by a militaristic Japan.

Although many Japanese socialists emigrated to Shanghai after 1923,[3] Yamaga's trajectory differed. He chose two locales entwined with the empire: Taiwan and the Philippines. Yamaga's engagements in Taiwan and the Philippines are chronicled in his *Twilight Diaries*, a collection born from a sense of impending mortality. In December 1961, after a two-year trip to India for the tenth War Resister's International (WRI) Conference in Gandhigram, a cerebral hemorrhage paralyzed Yamaga's left side. At the behest of his biographer, Mukai Kou 向井孝 (1920–2003), he began serializing *Twilight Diaries* between June 1962 and August 1968, before passing in 1970. These diaries appeared in *Yuu* magazine but were never compiled into books. Organized into four parts, eight sections, and ninety-one entries, the diaries consist of essays reflecting on topics including anarchism, politics, food, culture, and Yamaga's Asian friends and comrades.

Twilight Diaries matter-of-factly accepts Japan's imperial infrastructure as a precondition for Yamaga's parasitic internationalism. According to part 1, chapter 5, "Life in Taiwan and the Philippines," Yamaga relocated to Kaoshiung, Taiwan, in September 1939 in the hope of escaping the potential devastation of the Japanese archipelago, avoiding the colder Manchurian climate, and providing for his family while meeting Esperantists based in Taiwan (Yamaga 1965, 12).[4] Yamaga explains how the impetus for his trip was meeting an unsuspecting imperial army officer at a dinner; the officer disclosed the government's impending Southern Offensive to Yamaga and revealed that they would need printers for propaganda efforts (11). Yamaga's employer refused to send him to Taiwan, so he bribed a psychiatrist to prove his "need" to recuperate in the warmer south (12).

In the same chapter, Yamaga reminisces about other forms of work and solidarity in both Taiwan and the Philippines. In December 1941, after

Pearl Harbor, Yamaga was drafted into the Taiwanese army alongside his printing partners and relocated to the Philippines with invading Japanese forces (14). In 1943, after two years of reintegrating into civilian life and working as the editor of Manila Shimbun マニラ新聞, Yamaga copublished *The Japanese-Tagalog Small Dictionary* with Paul Rodriguez Verzosa of Centro Escobar University in Manila. At the time, only the Philippine government could access offset printers, so Yamaga had to painstakingly enter each Japanese and Tagalog word by hand on a linotype machine and let Verzosa proofread them (19–20).

In 1945, prior to the war's end, Yamaga returned to Taiwan and raised the banner of the Taiwan Freedom Society (Taiwan Jiyu Sha 台湾自由社) with local comrades. He taught English, Mandarin, and Esperanto there until returning to Japan in 1946. According to Shijie Qiu 丘世杰 (2012), Yamaga was in frequent contact with the Taiwanese Esperantist Lian Wenqing 連溫卿. Reflecting on his time at Lian's rice chaffing factory in Zhongli 中壢, Yamaga (1965, 24) observes an organically "communist" way of sharing that originates from Chinese agricultural family structures and contrasts it with the property-centered habits of the Japanese. His example? When one is asked to share a cigarette in Taiwan, no one ever refuses (24). This episode demonstrates in Yamaga both a naïveté colored by the anthropological lens of empire and a utopian impulse that senses a doorway to another world in a gesture as small as cigarette sharing.

While Yamaga Taiji's actions in Taiwan and the Philippines could be understood as the work of a lifelong anarchist internationalist, the conditions of his travel raise the question of how even networks that oppose empire and capital are entangled with them. Richard So (2016, xxxvi) recommends thinking about power in the transpacific and its networks "beyond a binary frame" to "rediscover this space as animated by exploits." Yamaga's adventures expand the concept of the exploit: his ability to pursue collaborations, ethnographies, and publications in Taiwan and the Philippines hinged on the spatial access provided via imperial Japan. Yet instead of striking the empire from the periphery, Yamaga focused on maximizing solidarity and communication in his present and planting seeds for the future—an expression of his anarchist emphasis on prefigurative politics, "the deliberate experimental implementation of desired future social relations and practices in the here-and-now" (Raekstad and Gradin 2020, 10). There were compromises—but it is with these complexities that the lives and works of figures like Yamaga help us understand the dialectic between complicities and solidarities formed in internationalist networks, no matter how tight or frayed they appear. Within this *Field Trip* feature, I see this dialectic both in Nadal's discussion of Carlos Bulosan's remittances from the idea of "America" and in Coe's exposition of how a multilingual documentary form engages Asian American communities' entanglements with and oppositions to police power.

If Yamaga's story sounds familiar, it is because the necessity of working through, and sometimes *with,* an imperial formation is a nigh-universal condition of activism and intellectual production today. Yamaga Taiji's tale provide us with a picture of these conditions in a different era, with its risks, rewards, and lessons for those of us toiling as parasites of empires.

Darwin H. Tsen is an assistant teaching professor and coordinator of Chinese at Syracuse University.

■ NOTES

1. For Esperanto's history, see Schor (2016).

2. For English sources on Ōsugi and Kotoku, see Ōsugi (1992). Additionally, see Tierney (2015).

3. Linkhoeva (2017) shows that the deaths of Ōsugi and Itoh in 1923 partly prompted the Japanese Communist Party to disband and regroup in Shanghai.

4. My citations of the diaries come from the Japanese manuscripts photographed at the CIRA-JAPANA (2015) anarchist library in Fujinomiya, Shizuoka, not from its serialized edition in *Yuu.*

■ WORKS CITED

CIRA-JAPANA. 2015. *Anarchism Calendar 2015: Yamaga Taiji.* Shinjuku, Japan: CIRA-JAPANA.

Crump, John D. 1983. *The Origins of Socialist Thought in Japan.* London: Routledge.

Hoston, Germaine A. 1987. *Marxism and the Crisis of Development in Prewar Japan.* Princeton, N.J.: Princeton University Press.

Kurihara, Yasushi 栗原康. 2013. *Ōsugi Sakae: Anarchism Is Forever* [大杉栄伝：永遠の アナキズム]. Tokyo: 夜光社.

Linkhoeva, Tatiana. 2017. "New Revolutionary Agenda: The Interwar Japanese Left on the 'Chinese Revolution.'" *Cross-Currents: East Asian History and Culture Review,* no. 24: 83–103.

Ōsugi Sakae. 1992. *The Autobiography of Ōsugi Sakae.* Translated by Byron K. Marshall. Oakland: University of California Press.

Qiu, Shijie. 2012. "A Mirror for Social Movements: Taiwan's Anarchist 'Seediq.'" *The Observer,* October 9. https://www.guancha.cn/QiuShiJie /2012_10_09_102401.shtml.

Raekstad, Paul, and Sofia Gradin. 2020. *Prefigurative Politics: Building Tomorrow Today.* Cambridge: Polity Press.

Schor, Esther. 2016. *Bridge of Words: Esperanto and the Dream of a Universal Language.* New York: Metropolitan Books.

So, Richard Jean. 2016. *Transpacific Community: The Rise and Fall of a Cultural Network.* New York: Columbia University Press.

Tierney, Robert Thomas. 2015. *Monster of the Twentieth Century: Kotoku Shusui and Japan's First Anti-Imperialist Movement.* Oakland: University of California Press.

Yamaga, Taiji 山鹿泰治. 1965. *Tasogare Nikki.* Fujinomiya, Japan: CIRA-JAPANA.

Carlos Bulosan, Socialist?

PAUL NADAL

And then there is Carlos Bulosan (1914–56). Filipino American, journalist, poet, migrant worker. But also, socialist? Some have insisted that Bulosan is "a proletarian novelist of a decidedly Marxist cast" (Feria 2016, 197). Yet the post-1970s recovery of his writings in the United States has tended to reduce his literary radicalism into an expression of a specifically ethnic, rather than an international, Filipino American consciousness. Bulosan's prominence in U.S. multiethnic literature today owes much to the Asian Americanist recuperation of his writings as a critique of U.S. nationalism. This recovery, however, has obfuscated the more expansive Asian orientation of Bulosan's socialist outlook, hence the ambivalence within Bulosan scholarship around the idealization of liberal democracy in his fictional autobiography *America Is in the Heart* (1946) and the continued obscurity of *The Cry and the Dedication* (1952–54), Bulosan's only novel—unfinished, posthumously published, and, in contrast to *America,* set entirely in the Philippines.

I do not mean to suggest that *The Cry* stands as the radical "Asian" antonym to the liberal "Asian American" or "Filipino American" idealism of *America.* I wish rather to ask what horizons come into view when we shift our reference point from the United States to the Philippines. For one, Bulosan would have seen "Filipino American literature" as an anachronism, because he envisioned his writings as a contribution to Philippine letters primarily and only secondarily to American literature. The ideological corollary to Bulosan's interest in Philippine letters was his commitment to connect his U.S.-based writing to the peasant-led struggles back home for socialism, a commitment encapsulated in *The Cry*'s fictionalization of the agrarian militant uprising known as the Hukbalahap rebellion (1942–54). That Bulosan turned to novel writing to narrow the distance between writing overseas and the fight for socialism at home means that his was a transpacific creative practice, a literary remittance, that is at the same time a theory of aesthetics and politics (Nadal 2021).

The contents of this theory are linked to Bulosan's prognostication in an undated letter to Philippine literature scholar Florentino B. Valeros that "imperialism is doomed; it has doomed itself; something else will take its place. Another cataclysm will make most of the Orient [*sic*] a world of socialism" (Bulosan, n.d.; see Figure 1). We gain a new understanding of Bulosan if we read his radicalism in terms of this rather stunning world-historical conviction, which, in this same letter, crescendos into his claim that—in a telling reversal of the title "America Is in the Heart"—"the future of the Philippines is bound with *the future of Asia*" (emphasis added).

To pursue Bulosan's vision of Asian socialist futurity, we might turn to narrative beginnings and endings. In Bulosan's fiction, beginnings and endings are engendered through manipulations of horizons, or literary-visual boundaries, which are susceptible, as the experience of migration attests, to indefinite extensions resulting from shifts in standpoint. We will take as our representative example the threshold marked by the intervals of his two long prose works: the "outer" interval separating the 1946 publication of *America* and the early 1950s composition of *The Cry* and the "inner" interval distinguishing the note of optimism with which *America* concludes against the more tentative mood of *The Cry*'s opening lines.

These intervals, formal and biographical, afford a doubling perspective for examining the distances between the Philippines and the United States, art and politics. It also invites us to consider more dialectically how the apparent difference in genre and subject matter marked by *The Cry*'s turn to the Philippine peasant revolt represents a *return to*—rather than, as is often thought, a departure from—*America* (San Juan 1995). My claim is that *America Is in the Heart* and *The Cry and the Dedication* are united by an abiding compositional principle that I call "future work," or the imaginative projection of socialist possibilities into the present. The future work woven into the composition was propelled by Bulosan's belief that the war for liberation—even with formal independence in 1946—was far from over.

First, *America Is in the Heart*: "I knew that no man could destroy my faith in America that had sprung from all our hopes and aspirations, *ever*" (327, emphasis original). This final sentence has raised the question of what to make of its manifest affirmation of American liberal democracy in view of the autobiography's otherwise unsparing indictment of U.S. racial violence. Critics interpret the optimism of the last line in terms of authorial reclamation, wherein Bulosan, it is said, "makes [America] his own" (Isaac 2006, 124). But neither the self nor reclamation is quite figured by the text as punctually discrete. With *ever*—meaning "at any time," "constant," "perpetual"—Bulosan bends the declarative to the dynamism of an asymptote. The rhetorical weight of "ever," as closural device, spirals a recursively circular form: a *forward movement toward* an (as yet unrealized) political ideal of freedom, which is at the same time a *recessive movement away* from "America" itself. The reader would be forgiven for assuming a linearity if they took "America" here to be a fixed territorial referent rather than something already transformed by Bulosan's fugitive transvaluation, in the sentence prior, into a chimeric summation of "the sacrifices and loneliness of my friends, of my brothers in America and my family in the Philippines." Like the shared enunciative acts of Agha Shahid Ali's socialist poetics (see Kantor's essay), Bulosan's "America" proffers an affiliative practice, one that amplifies U.S. Popular Front laborism with the "hopes and aspirations" of the Filipino peasantry. Thus whatever polemic we might deduce from *America*'s ambiguous ending would be leveled by this magnification of the individual into a cross-oceanic expression of solidarity.

Consider, by contrast, the opening sentences of *The Cry*:

> Now long shadows were falling upon the hushed silence of the great forest. Dancing violent streaks of the dying sun penetrated the trees, revealing flitting butterflies and crawling insects. (1)

Now vis-à-vis *ever*: adverbs differently poised toward their respective political horizons—*ever* Bulosan's adverbial adjunct to his interminable belief in the ongoing revolution he vexingly calls "America," *now* a nontemporal "now" that indicates a narrative discourse in media res, revealing a fictional world descending from a state of suspension. Although this *now* thrusts readers into the warren of Philippine tropicality, the whole scene takes on a shadowy unreality. For this *now*, like *America*'s closing *ever*, bespeaks a suprasensuous present. It narrates continuity and rupture simultaneously: rupture, a break between the present that the novel will

Figure 1. "Imperialism is doomed. . . . Another cataclysm will make most of the Orient a world of socialism." Carlos Bulosan to Florentino Valeros, n.d., box 4, folder 8, Carlos Bulosan Papers, accession no. 0581-012, University of Washington Libraries.

You asked for ten poems to illustrate my socio-economic ideas. I intimated in my first letter that I could borrow from a person here who has in her possession numberless pieces written by me. Unfortunately, however, those poems are not what your wife needs for her thesis. Going over my mass of papers lately I found the attached unfinished abstraction of Rizal's life, work and times which should be sufficient for your wife's needs. The tentative plan calls for three scenes, but I will perhaps change the present form to a narrative one, somewhat in the style of Edwin Arlington Robinson or Robinson Jeffers, two poets whose fertility won my early admirationx for poetry. (Here I forgot to mention that my poem "If You Want To Know What We Are" is the only poem included in Literature Under The Commonwealth, which was published by the Philippine Writers' League under the sponsorship of the government in 1940, I believe, but the same piexe was republished in Philippine Prose & Poetry, Volume IV, two years ago. There is so much to write about today, but the day to day struggle for a living is a great harrassment, especially now that terror is let loose upon the world by the mad dogs again. There is really no peace for those who understand the nature of society in any form; there is only the vigilant and perpetual fight for a better world. In America, where big names in literature and science hide behind a conspiracy of silence, the fascists and warmongers are bent on throwing the grownups into the cesspool of war and death, while their robotization of the young is so incredibly subtle that even thinking people are taken by it. They use mass media for this work of animalizing the young such as the movies, schools, radio, TV, comic magazines, etc. Where is that master of style Hemingway? In Cuba and Africa with his rum and big guns. What Steinbeck doing now? Making and advocating an imaginary war against the USSR. And Carl Sandburg? Singing his folk songs now that the American bourgeoisie has made him a public institution. And Caldwell? Still trying to cash on Tobacco Road, where sex seems to be the only occupation of the people. Dos Passos? Bitter and angry; disgusted with every idea that he ever espoused, he has turned brutally against the first that gave him his original inspiration to study society. Faulkner? Lost in the childhood decay of a fabled county of the south. Saroyan? Richard Wright? Both safe with their fabulous wealth. Steinbeck said when he was informed by his publishers that his latest book, Tortilla Flat, would be a best-seller: "A writer should not have plenty of money!" It is the early Steinbeck, poor, a field laborer, living in a mountain cabin in Salinas, that counts in American literature, minus his mysticism which is abundant in To A God Unknown, The Cup of Gold, The Long Valley, and several of the stories. The same goes with the writers of his generation: Caldwell, James T. Farrell. You or one among you should make a study of American writers of our time in three groups: a) Mencken, Dreiser, Sherwood Anderson, Ring Lardner, Sr.; b) Hemingway, Thomas Wolfe, Dos Passos, F. Scott Fitzgerald, Hart Crane; c) Caldwell, James T. Farrell, Steinbeck, Thomas Wolfe, Richard Wright, Saroyan. And fourth, the young writers today, should be included: Norman Mailer, Irwin Shaw, John Horne Burns, Paul Bowles, Gore Vidal, Truman Capote, Alfred Hayes, Merle Miller, Frederick Buechner, and Vance Bourjaily. The last are the products of the second world war; the second are the products of the first world war; the first are the products of the complete industrialization and cartelization of the United States and the beginning of American imperialism; the second to the last are the products, more or less, of the depression and the last days of prosperity. We can go beyond Mencken and his group, but they are the last of the provincials who opened up an avenue of re-examining the American Dream. In doing here you would be pointing out to our writers arx the path followed by the great thinkers in this country who were unafraid to expose the false and the rotten in American life, and whose affinity with the democratic tradition was unquestioned and the strength of latter day writers, not only in this country but in many countries in thexx world especially South America, France, Spain, Italy, etc. It seems to me that a country like the Philippines a state publishing house is the solution for mass production and distribution, and which should publish books cheap enough to be accessible to the masses of people.Japan and India have solved that problem. Also Argentina and Brazil. While the present administration has appropriated fabulous sums for arms and war machines, the mental and physical health of the people is sadly neglected, as though the ruling class in the Philippines and their American cabals were thinking of a future imperialist Philippines. Imperialiaam is doomed; it has doomed itself; something else will take its place. Another cataclysm will make most of the Orient a world of socialism; there is no doubt about it. And there is no hope for imperialism to rise again, to dominate the world again, because it has become a destructive force, an enemy of civilization and progress. And the future of the Philippines is bound with the future of Asia; the next thousand years will witnes the emergence of Asia, the resurgence of Asiatic power and genius. It is unfortunate to dissociate the Philippines from the destiny of Asia; it is suicide actually, definitely. What are the barbarian rulers of the Philippines thinking about? In reading the fragment attached to this letter you will tell and everything that came before the telling, and continuity, a feeling of ongoingness, of picking up the thread.

All this is prelude to the introduction of the leader of the revolutionaries, Hassim, the central intelligence of the novel, whose name resounds with regional history: an Indonesian, Malay, Arabic, and Urdu surname that means "crusher" or "breaker." Bulosan has chosen for his novel's protagonist a figure plucked from the crucible of intra-Asian encounters. The name, transplanted in revolutionary context, melds plurally dispersed struggles in syntony with socialist energies in the decolonizing Philippines.

The paradoxical movement of continuity and rupture sparked by the word *now*, and henceforth dramatized by the novel's revolution plot, will sustain itself in the ambient prose. The subsequent sentences unfold according to a rhythmic play of opposites: "dancing"/"dying," "flitting"/"crawling" (1). Read the opening paragraph out loud and you will hear the repetition of the cadences in "long shadows," "hushed silence," and "old forest"—two stressed syllables followed by an unstressed syllable. This repeated figure hymns a falling rhythm, a walking pace we shall follow into the great forest. As the paragraph concludes, Bulosan unites the play of opposites by striking yet another double movement. The falling cadences meet their vertical counterpoint in the ascent to a nonearthly, utopian horizon: "the whole forest seemed to float away with its thrilling beauty" (1).

To close the circles we've been threading through the outer interval that separates *America* and *The Cry* and the inner one that binds them in tone, time, and theme, consider the final line of *The Cry*: "Hassim and his companions departed, and walked into the new morning" (304). The near-symmetrical shape of that sentence alone suggests a synthesis achieved, a horizon momentarily surpassed. The "new morning" summoned in the novel's last page corresponds to the first paragraph's "long shadows," which are also an echo of those of "my brothers" in *America*. As in *The Cry*'s beginning, we hear the same cadence: two stressed syllables and an unstressed syllable. Are the revolutionaries walking into a folktale, into a liberated future, into death?

Carlos Bulosan was ineligible for U.S. citizenship, and he never returned to the Philippines. Martin Joseph Ponce (2012, 90) has remarked that the Philippine setting of *The Cry* "enact[s] a kind of symbolic return to the homeland." By reading the threshold delineated by how one text ends and another begins, we appreciate how *The Cry* enacts, too, a reverse homecoming of *America*. Bulosan achieved these recursive returns by composing literary remittances impelled by his conviction that the future of the

Filipino people is aligned with "the destiny of Asia," an internationalism earlier invoked in *America,* albeit in covert, displaced form. *The Cry and the Dedication* is Bulosan's first and only novel, written under Cold War conditions of FBI surveillance (Baldoz 2014). Unfinished, the novel is aptly bookended by an opening *now* and this closing *new,* suggesting that even beyond the present, that is, beyond the self-enclosing horizons of postindependence nationalism, there remains future work. The revolutionaries do not walk into the evening; they walk into the morning, into the possibilities of a new day.

Paul Nadal is an assistant professor of English and American studies at Princeton University.

■ **WORKS CITED**

Baldoz, Rick. 2014. "'Comrade Carlos Bulosan': US State Surveillance and the Cold War Suppression of Filipino Radicals." *The Asia-Pacific Journal* 11, no. 33: 1–18.

Bulosan, Carlos. 1995. *The Cry and the Dedication.* Philadelphia: Temple University Press.

Bulosan, Carlos. 2019. *America Is in the Heart.* New York: Penguin.

Bulosan, Carlos, to Florentino Valeros. n.d. Box 4, folder 8, Bulosan Papers, accession no. 0581-012, University of Washington Libraries.

Feria, Dolores Stephens. 2016. "Bulosan's Power, Bulosan's People." In *Writer in Exile/Writer in Revolt,* edited by Jeffrey Cabusao, 197–99. Lanham, Md.: University Press of America.

Isaac, Allan Punzalan. 2006. *American Tropics: Articulating Filipino America.* Minneapolis: University of Minnesota Press.

Nadal, Paul. 2021. "Cold War Remittance Economy: US Creative Writing and the Importation of New Criticism into the Philippines." *American Quarterly* 73, no. 3: 557–95.

Ponce, Martin Joseph. 2012. *Beyond the Nation: Diasporic Filipino Literature and Queer Reading.* New York: NYU Press.

San Juan, E., Jr. 1995. Introduction to *The Cry and the Dedication,* by Carlos Bulosan, ix–xxxvi. Philadelphia: Temple University Press.

"I See Chile in My Rearview Mirror": Agha Shahid Ali's Reflections on Pan-American Socialism

ROANNE L. KANTOR

This essay explores the pan-American socialist internationalism of the Kashmiri American writer Agha Shahid Ali (1949–2001) in the 1980s and early 1990s, a moment of widespread antisocialist violence in the Americas. Ali grew up in India and moved to the United States in the 1970s to complete a PhD and teach creative writing. Ali uses the motif of the rearview mirror to reanimate past poetic resistances to political violence so their legacies can be recognized in the present. The rearview mirror echoes the politics of solidarity, which require the negotiation of difference (reflection as opposition) alongside the recognition of shared goals (reflection as relation).

Ali is best known for his later work: *The Country without a Post Office* (1997), *Ravishing DisUnities: Real Ghazals in English* (2000), *Rooms Are Never Finished* (2001). These three works, along with his free translation of the poetry of the Urdu socialist writer Faiz Ahmed Faiz in *The Rebel's Silhouette* (1995), share an engagement with the political situation of occupied Kashmir. They also reflect a greater willingness to thematize the most politically legible aspects of his "own" culture as South Asian (through locations like Delhi and Srinagar) and Muslim (through poetic forms like the *ghazal, marsiya,* and *muwashshah*). As a result, critics frequently discuss Ali as a popular Anglophone or postcolonial Asian writer, as opposed to an Asian American writer. In this sense, his reception inverts the problem Paul Nadal identifies in the creation of Carlos Bulosan as a canonical "Asian American" writer. In both cases, an attention to their socialist commitments illuminates new, transnational communities for their work. Ali's earlier poetry demonstrates that he developed a more capacious sense of Americanness through an engagement with pan-American socialism.

As Ali's political project as a speaker for Kashmir came into focus in the later 1990s, it reshaped the meaning of "Shahid," his *takhallus*—a name that operates as an internal signature within oral poetry in South Asia. In one of his most famous poems, the ghazal "In Arabic," he writes, "They ask me to tell them what Shahid means: Listen, listen: / it means 'The Belovéd' in Persian, 'witness' in Arabic" (Ali 2009, 226). "Beloved Witness" lives on as the title of one of his poetry anthologies, the title of a forthcoming book of critical essays, and the name of his online archive.

Figure 2. Vivan Sundaram, *Portrait of Pablo Neruda*, from *The Heights of Macchu Picchu*, 1972. Asia Art Archive.

But the idea of poet-witness was already apparent in Ali's early collections, *The Half-Inch Himalayas* (1987) and *A Nostalgist's Map of America* (1991). Both focus on his emerging American identity, as opposed to his Kashmiri and Muslim roots. Ali's poetic identity as (hemispheric) American and witness emerges in part through his reflection on Pablo Neruda's epic poem *Canto general* (1950) and its hopeful projection of unified socialist Américas. In the wake of right-wing dictatorships that swept through Chile and many other South American nations in the 1970s and 1980s, Ali used key elements of Neruda's poetics to mourn the betrayal of that earlier socialist futurity.

In *The Half-Inch Himalayas,* Ali includes a poem called "The Previous Occupant." Ali opens up his own body to the "previous occupant" of his apartment, a man who has been "disappeared" in the antisocialist political violence in Chile. The poem begins with a survey of the emptied space, whose ghostly, missing contents include books of poetry by Neruda whose lines he knows "by heart."

Even while Ali was still in Delhi, Neruda's poetry circulated in several Indian languages. The Chilean's 1971 Nobel Prize in Literature and subsequent death amid the coup in 1973 were deeply felt among India's Anglophone poets. They often used a gesture of affiliation to signal a desire for South–South solidarity (Gabriel 1973; Sahni 1974). Among these remembrances was a portrait of Neruda by the Indian artist Vivan Sundaram (1972), part of a pen and ink series titled *The Heights of Macchu Picchu,* after the most famous section of *Canto general.*

In Figure 2, the form of the poet dissolves into minute patterns of stonework, textiles, vegetation, and bodies. These details recall the lines in which Neruda commands the buried laborers at Machu Picchu to "tell me everything, tell chain by chain, / link by link, and step by step" (Neruda, quoted in Sahni 1974). They illustrate Neruda's concept of political witnessing, one that is not primarily visual or vocal but embodied, pulling subjectivities from the past into the present of his figure. By opening Neruda not as a text but as a shared enunciative act known "by heart," Ali introduces this same logic of introjection that progressively overtakes the other Chilean, the "disappeared" political dissident at the center of "The Previous Occupant."

Ali then draws on the mirror motif to emphasize his identification with the Chilean despite their spatial and cultural distance. Imagining the other as a blinded political prisoner, Ali imagines his own body and gaze sliding into the place before a mirror previously held by his Chilean predecessor (Ali 2009, 65). The repeated refrain "some country as far as Chile" suggests the portability of antisocialist violence across political contexts. In the final lines, Ali offers up his body (and his poem) to safeguard the absent one: "my body casts his shadow everywhere. / He'll never, never move out of here" (Ali 2009, 65). The mirror-work images of one's body willingly bearing another's reflection echo lines of the final section of Neruda's "Alturas de Macchu Picchu" (The Heights of Macchu Picchu; 1949), in which the poet introjects the dead laborers who constructed the temple complex so that he can "speak through your [dead] mouth[s]" (Neruda, quoted in Sahni 1974, 39). By placing this reflection on workers' plight in the deep past within a prophetic poem about the socialist horizon of the mid-twentieth century, Neruda offers a model for how failed struggles of the past can still shape the present. When Ali reanimates Neruda decades after the Chilean's death, he does a version of the same.

These themes come further into focus in "I See Chile in My Rearview Mirror," from Ali's subsequent collection, *A Nostalgist's Map of America.* The poem's conceit is that as the speaker drives north toward Utah, he looks southward and sees the hemisphere's inverted image in his rearview mirror. From the perspective of the early 1990s, Ali gazes on a continent riven by civil war and right-wing dictatorship. Whereas the mirror in "The Previous Occupant" offered a space of self-recognition, here mirroring operates as an inversion. The speaker is driving through a summer landscape while looking at winter in South America. At the same time, the poem's focus on dictatorial violence constitutes the dark reflection of earlier expansionism in the American West.

Ali's attention settles on a single figure—a witness to the concentration camp established after the coup at the Estadio Nacional in Santiago, Chile. "Those about to die are looking at him, / his eyes a ledger of the disappeared" (Ali 2009, 162). It is easy to imagine this figure as the same disappeared Chilean in "The Previous Occupant." Yet this section of the poem was written much earlier, first published as "A Dream of Buenos Aires" in 1984! Certainly Argentina was also controlled by a dictatorship that "disappeared" leftists. Why, then, change the location to Chile, and why add to it these other reflections about driving through the United States?

Neruda suggests an answer. By adding the motif of the rearview mirror, Ali holds together two continents otherwise separated by language and political violence. He thus contributes to the project of Neruda's *Canto general*: willing a hemispheric Américas into being. The "ledger of the disappeared" redeploys the witnessing function that Neruda employs throughout *Canto general*, the same energy Sundaram recognized and redeployed in his portrait. Neruda commands, "Rush into my veins and to my mouth / . . . speak through my words and in my blood" (Neruda, quoted in Sahni 1974, 39). The poet shelters and reanimates those killed by political violence. This is precisely what Ali aims to do.

But in 1991, seeming to invoke Neruda via Chile, Ali also names the violence during which he died. That same dictatorial wave foreclosed Neruda's vision for Chile, and for the Americas. For Ali, too, the dream of *Canto general*, of inter-American socialist solidarity, of continental identification, fades to black. The poet continues north, while in the rearview mirror, "the continent vanishes." Negotiating across gulfs of time, space, and identity, Ali's mirror-work reveals a past that is immediately recognizable but radically inaccessible to the speaker. Ali's Neruda-inspired poet-witness acknowledges that division while still preserving the past for future reflection.

Roanne Kantor is an assistant professor of English at Stanford University. She is the author of *South Asian Writers, Latin American Literature, and the Rise of Global English* (2022).

■ **WORKS CITED**

Ali, Agha Shahid. 2009. *The Veiled Suite: The Collected Poems*. New York: W. W. Norton.
Gabriel, M. C. 1973. "Pablo Neruda." *Vrishchik*.
Sahni, Bhishm, ed. 1974. *Dedicated to the Memory of Pablo Neruda*. Delhi: Indian National Committee of Afro-Asian Writers.
Sundaram, Vivan. 1972. *The Heights of Macchu Picchu*. Asia Art Archive. https://aaa.org.hk/en/collection/search/archive/geeta-kapur-and-vivan-sundaram-archive-the-heights-of-macchu-picchu-1972.

Reinventing Socialism in the 1980s: The League of Revolutionary Struggle and China

CALVIN CHEUNG-MIAW

In November 1984, cadres of the League of Revolutionary Struggle received their copy of the *Communist,* the organization's internal bulletin. Each of the hundreds of League members maintained a frantic pace of work as community organizers in cities across the United States. But they were also expected to thoroughly digest the reports contained in the *Communist.* Among the reports in the November issue was "China at 35," authored by a PhD student in history at Stanford, Gordon H. Chang. One of the group's leading intellectuals, Chang had just coordinated a delegation of League members to China, where the group had visited Shanghai, Wuhan, Guangzhou, and Shenzhen and stood beneath the massive display of fireworks in the Beijing sky on the thirty-fifth anniversary of the founding of the People's Republic (Chang 1984; Mark Prudowsky, interview with the author, March 10, 2020).

"China at 35" crackled with excitement. "Something profound is happening in China," Chang (1984) began his report. "Changes are taking place there that are actually altering the complexion of Marxist-Leninist socialism in the world" (A1). The movement away from highly centralized planning and the introduction of economic incentives and small enterprise had achieved "widespread popularity," relegating earlier ideas about socialist economics to the dustbin of history. Equally significant was progress toward socialist democracy. "No longer will the party have the virtually complete formal and informal authority it once had," Chang predicted (A2).

Mark Prudowsky, a Chicago-based labor activist, was part of the 1984 delegation. But just a year earlier, he had been immersed in the campaign to elect Harold Washington as the first Black mayor of Chicago. As Prudowsky later recalled, the Washington campaign "revitalized us in a way that I can't even begin to describe because we felt relevant. . . . It was so visceral in Chicago to see, especially in the Black community but even in the Latino community . . . what a truly broad movement looked like" (Mark Prudowsky, interview with the author, March 10, 2020). Prudowsky's experience in Chicago was part of a larger political reorientation. In the aftermath of Reagan's election, the League sought to reconcile a new, more serious approach to electoral politics with its Marxist–Leninist roots. This contribution explores the League's left internationalist imaginary to argue that its understanding of Chinese socialism mediated the organization's own reinvention of socialist politics.

The League of Revolutionary Struggle formed in October 1978 from the merger of the Asian American group I Wor Kuen and the Chicana/o group August Twenty-Ninth Movement. A year later, the Revolutionary Communist League, a Black organization led by Amiri Baraka, joined. The organization expanded steadily until its dissolution in 1990, but its membership remained predominantly Asian American, Latinx, and Black—what the group termed "oppressed nationalities." Though many League members took Mao and the Cultural Revolution as a source of inspiration, the League rejected the idea that socialists in the United States ought to mimic the strategies and tactics of socialists in other countries, including China. Yet China loomed large in the League's political imaginary. In the Sino-Soviet split, the group aligned itself with China and argued that the Soviet Union had restored capitalism and become an imperialist superpower. China, by contrast, stood at the head of the Third World struggle against domination by both the United States and the USSR (Elbaum 2002, 234–35).

The League's founding occurred at nearly the same time that the Chinese Communist Party (CCP), in pursuit of socialist modernization, began to espouse a favorable view of small-scale entrepreneurship, wage incentives, and other market mechanisms. In 1979, the CCP established special economic zones to attract foreign investment. The same year, the party issued a reevaluation of the Cultural Revolution, describing it as a catastrophic setback to socialism. As Chang later recalled, the pace of developments in China led him and others in the League to wonder, "Was it [China] really revolutionary? Was it socialist? Was it something to emulate or to support?" (Gordon H. Chang, interview with the author, March 3, 2020).

In the 1979 issue of the League's theoretical journal, *Forward,* Chang attempted an initial explanation. In line with the organization's belief in the importance of upholding the Marxist–Leninist tradition, Chang argued that the CCP's policies, including the importation of foreign technology, the acceptance of capitalist investments, and the implementation of productivity incentives, adhered to "basic Marxist-Leninist tenets" (Chang 1979, 22).

By 1984, however, what excited Chang about China was the way its practice challenged Marxist–Leninist orthodoxy. Chang's new perspective on Chinese socialism emerged, in part, from his frequent travels to China. The League's leadership had already organized at least six delegations prior to the 1984 tour. In general, these travels did not lead League cadres to a romanticized view of Chinese socialism or the CCP. One report on a 1980 trip in the *Communist* noted that the Cultural Revolution had bred "disillusionment and cynicism" among Chinese in their twenties. A later report expressed frustration that CCP leaders did not grasp the significance of the oppressed nationality movements and still "tend to see the U.S. as mainly a 'white' country" (*Communist* 1982).

Despite this, the impact of the post-Mao reforms was striking. Chang had first visited China in 1971. During his trips in the 1980s, "the change . . . was palpable," Chang recalled. "People's housing changed, almost overnight, and at least in some of the villages . . . farmers were making money, they were very entrepreneurial. You see the change in the . . . food quality, . . . the clothes, everything" (Gordon H. Chang, interview with the author, March 3, 2020).

With Ronald Reagan's election in 1980, the League confronted the question of what it meant to maintain a commitment to revolutionary transformation during counterrevolutionary times. This confrontation catalyzed a rethinking of the organization's assumptions about elections and Marxist–Leninist politics. In 1980, the organization denounced both Carter and Reagan as candidates of bourgeois parties. The ferocity of Reaganism's onslaught against the working class and oppressed nationalities served as a wake-up call. Then, Jesse Jackson's 1984 presidential campaign provided an opportunity to reach millions of voters with an unabashedly progressive political message. Jackson's Rainbow Coalition also gained momentum and offered a way to unite oppressed nationality movements. All this, as well as experiences like those Prudowsky had in the Harold Washington campaign, made the organization's prior attitude toward electoral politics untenable. By 1984, the League wholeheartedly embraced the Jackson insurgency, and leaders like Amiri Baraka began to argue that the path to political empowerment of oppressed nationalities ran through, not around, the electoral arena (Elbaum 2002, 275–81; Baraka 1985).

The League's imagination of Chinese socialism mediated its efforts to develop a Marxism–Leninism adequate to the exigencies of U.S. politics. Richard Fleming, who oversaw the League's international support work, penned an essay in the 1989 issue of *Forward* about the development of Lenin's thought from 1917 to 1924. An editorial note framed the article as a contribution to questions about the meaning of socialism, questions that had arisen in part due to the "momentous changes" (21) occurring in China. Fleming's portrait was of a Lenin whose socialism was flexible, constantly adapting to a shifting reality. This Lenin rejected orthodoxy and blueprints as hindrances to the socialist project, and, in a subtle reference to the CCP, battled the assumption that socialism always demanded higher levels of collectivization.

But Fleming's article was not only a response to the far-ranging interrogation among socialists provoked by China. Fleming later recalled that part of his motivation for reconstructing a Marxist–Leninist sensibility of reinvention was to support the League's new political strategy and counter the ingrained dismissal of engagement in electoral politics among Marxist–Leninists (Richard Fleming, interview with the author, March 16, 2021). For Fleming, the League, like the CCP or Lenin, was remaking the meaning of socialist politics as it gained a deeper understanding of the objective conditions it confronted. For the League's leading members, the 1980s was a decade of socialist reinvention.

As a multiracial organization, the League suggests the fruitfulness of extending Global Asias beyond the imagined boundaries of Asian America. Doing so, in this instance, allows us to recover the global and radical dimensions of what was ostensibly a nation-state-based project of defending multiracial democracy in an era of white revanchism, an era that continues to the present.

Calvin Cheung-Miaw is an assistant professor of history at Duke University.

■ **NOTE**

I thank the following individuals who supported this project through conversations and research assistance: Gordon H. Chang, Richard Fleming, Alex Hing, Steven Hom, Jon Marienthal, Don Misumi, Mark Prudowsky, Peter Shapiro, Karen Wing, Fay Wong, and Judy Wu.

■ **WORKS CITED**

Baraka, Amiri. 1985. "¡¡@*#!! Reagan!!" *Forward* 4, 1–11.

Chang, Gordon H. 1979. "China Is Vigorously Building Socialism." *Forward* 1, no. 1: 19–46.

Chang, Gordon H. 1984. "China at 35." *The Communist* 6, no. 4: A1–A3.

Communist. 1980. "A Report on the July, 1980 Central Committee Delegation to China." 2, no. 3: B2–B8.

Communist. 1982. "Report on 1982 LRS Trip to China." 4, no. 2: F1–F2.

Elbaum, Max. 2002. *Revolution in the Air: Sixties Radicals Turn to Lenin, Mao, and Che.* New York: Verso.

Fleming, Richard. 1989. "Lenin's Conception of Socialism." *Forward* 9, no. 1: 21–38.

Divergent Movements: Asian American Politics with Chinese Characteristics in *Down a Dark Stairwell*

JASON G. COE

As Calvin Cheung-Miaw has argued, the PRC's "socialist reinvention" in the 1980s provided justifications for U.S.-based socialists to support the Rainbow Coalition, an initiative that, without a global perspective, might look like a "nation-state-based project of defending multiracial democracy." However, the PRC's reinvention, with its emphasis on a socialism "with Chinese characteristics," also portended the rise of Han Chinese nationalism in Asian American politics today. Instead of building on the left internationalist legacies of the Asian American movement, some Chinese American activist organizations have reframed Asian American identity as an avenue for "racial victimology" (Liu 2018, 429). This movement made its national debut on February 20, 2016, when hundreds of thousands demonstrated in major cities across the United States and Canada to protest the conviction of Chinese American New York Police Department (NYPD) officer Peter Liang for the killing of Akai Gurley (Feng and Tseng-Putterman 2019, 238–39). Other Asian American activist organizations protested in solidarity with Gurley's family and Black Lives Matter (BLM) (Fu et al. 2019, 254–55).

Ursula Liang's (no relation) documentary feature *Down a Dark Stairwell* (2020) recounts how these coalitions defined their political stances in response to the Liang–Gurley case. Through footage of community discussions, courtroom proceedings, and demonstrations, the documentary offers multiple perspectives of what Liang's conviction signifies about racial justice in the United States, illustrates the divergent processes by which Asian Americans imagine themselves within different national and international communities, and offers tactics for developing mutual understanding despite those differences.

Although the term *Asian American* emerged from a pan-ethnic movement aligned with the Third World Liberation Front, that tradition does not inform this new wave of Asian American activists, who neither align themselves with leftist politics nor see themselves in solidarity with other racial minorities. The Liang–Gurley case epitomizes this divergence, which Wen Liu (2018, 444) argues "is only a symptom of the larger process of transformation of Asian American subjectivity, ... driven by ... competing paradigms of U.S. racial relations and multiple forms of nationalism at a transnational scale." Made up mostly of post-1965 Chinese American immigrants, the pro-Liang coalition framed his conviction as a failure of color-blind meritocracy wherein one of their co-ethnics was not treated like his white peers. By contrast, Asian American BLM supporters saw justice for Akai Gurley as a necessary step toward ending police brutality, imagining community as pan-ethnic solidarity.

Down a Dark Stairwell offers tactics for mediating polarization in Asian America by defamiliarizing simple conclusions regarding the Liang–Gurley case. The title references both the circumstances of Gurley's death and the difficulty of disentangling the outcome of an individual trial from the systematic oppression of U.S. white supremacy. The film presents two sets of facts, one about Liang's individual actions, the other about a legal system unwilling to prosecute white police officers who kill Black people. Through intertitles, the film shares the first set of facts: Liang entered a pitch-black stairwell with his gun drawn in one hand and a flashlight in the other; he was startled; the gun discharged, and the bullet ricocheted off a wall and struck Gurley in the chest; Liang and his partner did not give medical assistance, and Gurley died minutes later. The jury ruled out accidental discharge and convicted Liang of manslaughter and official misconduct. This conviction galvanized Chinese American community members to protest in his defense. The film concludes with the second set of facts: that as of the film's 2020 release, Liang was the only NYPD officer convicted of a police-involved killing in fifteen years, during which New York City police killed 117 Black men.

This distinction between individual and systemic culpability also divided those protesting for and against leniency in Liang's sentencing. To the organizations that raised funds for Liang's defense, he was a victim of a racist justice system that let off white officers who had committed more heinous crimes. To the Gurley family and their supporters, Liang was yet another police officer who would get away with killing an innocent Black man.

Although both sides of the divide recognized the racism of the U.S. justice system, what emerged from the protests was a Chinese American ethnonationalist movement formed through transnational social media. State-abetted social media facilitated the massive protests in Liang's defense, many of which were organized through WeChat—the Tencent-owned super-app whose Chinese Communist Party–monitored posts are censored and maintained on servers in mainland China for all accounts (Knockel et al. 2020).[1] While local organizations led the groundwork of protests, WeChat reduced the cost of organizing, distributed protest information to millions, and amplified a growing sense of Chinese American political identity (Fang 2016). As a "counterpublic enclave" mediated in Simplified Chinese, WeChat provided a platform for internal debates among right-leaning Chinese Americans, thereby allowing a heterogeneous counterpublic to unite around "the colorblind rhetoric of American equality and liberty" (Feng and Tseng-Putterman 2019, 246–47).

To understand how this counterpublic melded color-blind rhetoric with ethnonationalism, we must consider how pro-Liang activists encouraged dynamics of Chinese identification. Through footage of speeches at pro-Liang demonstrations, *Down a Dark Stairwell* captures how protestors identified with Liang and his family—as kin in need of saving. By placing Liang's conviction alongside the history of "Chinese Exclusion and victims of state and vigilante violence such as Danny Chen and Vincent Chin," activists channeled an "affective sense of identification" that positions Chinese Americans as a marginalized community whose "basic rights have been damaged" (Zhang 2017, 248). The documentary contrasts that victim discourse by also featuring outnumbered BLM activists at the demonstration, who lament the incongruity of pro-Liang activists invoking civil rights icon Martin Luther King Jr. in their protest slogans to protect a cop who killed a Black man.

By detailing these perspectives, *Down a Dark Stairwell* illustrates how leftist internationalism—a social imaginary beyond nation-state formations—requires what the director calls "long-term storytelling" (Trahan 2021). While nation-state and corporate media apparatuses encourage racial, linguistic, and national siloing, the documentary brokers space and time for difficult interactions across and within cultural communities. By filming civil debates between antagonists, including English subtitles for all Mandarin and Cantonese dialogue, and releasing a version with Chinese-language subtitles, the filmmaker creates opportunities for seeing others and listening to their stories. The film documents how Black and Chinese American communities both experienced grief and injustice without diminishing the suffering of either. Moreover, the film portrays the heterogeneity within movements, including disagreements within camps, such as when Justice for Akai activists debate problematic language that portrays Asians as a "model minority" and when pro-Liang coalition leaders shame protestors for celebrating his light sentencing in front of Gurley's grieving family. Even if the film does not position itself as leftist or socialist, it provides left internationalist media with a model for deeper interlingual, intergenerational, and intercommunal engagement.

Jason G. Coe is an assistant professor in the Academy of Film at Hong Kong Baptist University. His research has been published in *Journal of Cinema and Media Studies, Canadian Literature, Journal of Chinese Cinemas,* and *Asian Cinema.* He is currently writing a monograph on the films of director Ang Lee.

■ **NOTES**

I thank Xin Shani and the School of Communication and Film at Hong Kong Baptist University for providing research assistance. I am grateful to Darwin Tsen and Andrew Way Leong for their leadership, support, and editorial guidance.

1. WeChat is not popular with communities from Taiwan, Hong Kong, and Southeast Asia, of whom few participated in the demonstrations (Zhang 2016).

■ WORKS CITED

Fang, K. 2016. "The 'Supporting Peter Liang' Parade: A Collective Action Based on WeChat?" [方可成.华人声援梁彼得大游行:一场依靠微信动员的集体行动?.新闻春秋]. Translated by Xin Shani. *Journalism Evolution* 4: 47–51.

Feng, Yuanyuan, and Mark Tseng-Putterman. 2019. "'Scattered Like Sand': WeChat Warriors in the Trial of Peter Liang." *Amerasia Journal* 45, no. 2: 238–52.

Fu, May, Simmy Makhijani, Anh-Thu Pham, Meejin Richart, Joanne Tien, and Diane Wong. 2019. "#Asians4BlackLives: Notes from the Ground." *Amerasia Journal* 45, no. 2: 253–70.

Knockel, Jeffrey, Christopher Parsons, Lotus Ruan, Ruohan Xiong, Jedidiah Crandall, and Ron Deibert. 2020. "We Chat, They Watch: How International Users Unwittingly Build Up WeChat's Chinese Censorship Apparatus." *Citizen Lab Research Report,* no. 127.

Liu, Wen. 2018. "Complicity and Resistance: Asian American Body Politics in Black Lives Matter." *Journal of Asian American Studies* 21, no. 3: 444.

Trahan, Erin. 2021. "Documentary 'Down a Dark Stairwell' Examines Divergent Responses to Racism in Policing." WBUR, February 4. https://www.wbur.org/news/2021/02/04/documentary-down-a-dark-stairwell.

Zhang Gehao. 2016. "The Materiality of Digital Diaspora: Cultural Techniques in the Use of WeChat during the 'Supporting Peter Liang Demonstration.'" *Journalism Evolution* 4: 47–51. [章戈浩.数字流散的物质性:声援梁彼得游行微信使用中的文化技术. 新闻春秋, 2016(04): 52–56. Translated Xin Shani]

Zhang Jiawei. 2017. "An Analysis of Mobilization Mechanism in Overseas Chinese Society: A Case Study of 'Peter Liang Event'" [张家祎. 海外华人社会中的动员机制分析——以"梁彼得事件"为例. 厦门大学]. PhD diss., University of Xiamen.

Essays

ANNE MA KUO-AN

Monuments of Culture: *Minzoku Taiwan* and the Search for Local History in Colonial Taiwan (1938–1950)

The term "monument" derived from the word "memory" in its verbal form. Inscriptions on bronze, stones or any other material media are merely meant to simplify the process for memorization. A true "monument" should be able to travel from one's heart to another's in the form of memory without any medium. A group which keeps inheritance for generations, namely a people of one nationality 民族, is of itself a great monument.

—Kanaseki Takeo, 1941

IN 1941, readers from Japan's island colony of Taiwan would have been confounded by this statement by Kanaseki Takeo (1897–1983). Using expressions like "people of one nationality" and "monument for generations," this poignant statement reflected the complicated cultural milieu of a colony that was turning into a battleground in multiple aspects during the 1940s. On one hand, an escalating "assimilation" (or *dōka*) movement called for colonial citizens' unreserved identification with Japan, as the empire's increasingly heavy investment in the war against China required a much more fully fledged propaganda campaign in its colonies. Working in line with stricter rules for censorship on public speech, official propaganda began to establish reasons and methods for people to "culturally" identify with their ruling nation, forsaking customs or traditions passed on for generations. On the other hand, the actual process of such identification was never simple or straightforward. It was necessary, in other words, first to recognize and define the customs, lifestyles, and even "spirits" of the local people, thus establishing the "authenticity" of

84

"local culture" that could then be articulated, studied, categorized, and, finally, assimilated—or at least, this was the process that the Taiwan government-general claimed to have accomplished.

For Kanaseki Takeo, however, what should have been much more crucial than the propaganda on assimilating culture was really the problem— or, to be more precise, the lack of definition—of "culture" in this world of intensifying propaganda discourses. A professor of physical anthropology at the School of Medicine, Taipei Imperial University, Kanaseki was not satisfied with the governmental or official definitions of "local culture" and/or its authenticity. In 1941, together with a group of Taiwanese and Japanese scholar-intellectuals, some of whom also worked at Taipei Imperial University, he founded *Minzoku Taiwan* (Taiwan folklore), a journal dedicated to documenting, but not necessarily "preserving," the local customs and traditions of Taiwan. The passage that opens this essay is from the foreword he wrote for the first issue of *Minzoku Taiwan*. After introducing the metaphor of "monument" (original as モニュメント), he then touched upon the ways in which "monument" not only served as a form of memory but could even be a synonym for a "people" of one nationality. As the official agenda for cultural assimilation necessarily entailed the repudiation of colonial subjects' "monuments of culture," Kanaseki's statement could be interpreted as a subtle critique of the assimilation policy. And Kanaseki and his friends' thinking was indeed not exactly in line with the intent of the colonial government. The rest of the foreword was narrated in a half-nostalgic, half-repentant tone, as Kanaseki went on to confess that "when the Romans destroyed Carthage, . . . it is most detestable that the Romans did not keep a record of the customs and traditions of the Carthaginians" (Kanaseki 1941, 1). The "monument" Kanaseki proposed, then, is apparently the Taiwanese, the people waiting to be fully assimilated.

Kanaseki's statement, in other words, evoked the dilemma that lay at the heart of Japan's assimilation propaganda: how do you give history meaning but disavow its value at the same time? Also, how do you both deny and grant "nationality" to a people? The answer, as officials involved in the assimilation propaganda would have suggested, has everything to do with "culture," a term that had already been proven to function well as a tool for the transformation and construction of new value systems in Japan. Theorizing the concept of "culture" that evolved with the discourses of *minzoku* (folklore) as structured mainly by Yanagita Kunio (1875–1962) in early twentieth-century Japan, Harry Harootunian (1990, 120–25) concludes that early Japanese "folklorists" came to pose "culture" as a kind of "nature" that was basically constituted by the "folk." For these folklorists, Japan's culture existed as a "primal given" that had "prevailed prior to the organization of contemporary society" (Harootunian 1990). Ultimately, it would have been "culture" that came to challenge established narratives of history—in Japan and globally, thus becoming the "great antagonist of history" (Harootunian 1990, 125). Harootunian argues that Japan's folklorists deliberately created a new framework for "native ethnology" and social science for twentieth-century Japan, refashioning ideas about cultural authenticity and modernity. And beyond the framework of Japan's social science academies, the idea of culture also entered the capitalistic discourses of the late 1920s and began to permeate popular media. In his study on domestic space and architecture in early twentieth-century Japan, Jordan Sand (2003, 229–75) demonstrates how the promotion of "culture life" *(bunka seikatsu)* by a group of social scientists (mainly economists) was successfully fused into discourses for reforming or westernizing Japanese households. As exemplified by the case of "Culture Village" and "Culture House," "culture" in Japan's popular conception after the 1930s quickly came to be associated with universal, cosmopolitan, and modern values. Utilized as a trendy selling point in an increasingly commercial society, it promised a better/new future for the yet-to-be "middle class," and in the colonial context, it was used to name a policy that exercised tolerance of Korea's local language media (Sand 2003, 214–34). But for Kanaseki and his colleagues, attempting to rescue studies and records of customs and collective memories from the discursive framework of "modernized" culture, exploring aspects of local culture supposedly untainted—although also shaped—by the forces of modernization and assimilation became an essential approach. Notably, their efforts diverged from dominant narratives on culture in the colonial metropole even as they were also inspired by such narratives.

This is not to say Kanaseki and his colleagues were the pioneers of studies in ethnography, ethnology, and local history in colonial Taiwan; on the contrary, quite a few Japanese anthropologists and ethnographers had already initiated work in Taiwan since the first year of Japanese rule. Inō Kanori (1867–1925) and Torii Ryūzō (1870–1953) were two anthropologists whose works came to be viewed as the foundational studies in the field; indeed, the tribal taxonomies they completed were used by scholars even after the end of colonial rule (Barclay 2010). The two left behind them very different legacies, however; Inō's scholarship was characterized by constant references to Chinese historical sources, whereas Torii's anthropological research into Taiwan Aborigines' physical traits earned him a lifelong career as an anthropology professor and researcher in the academy. Building on this earlier scholarship, Kanaseki and his colleagues were not only looking for new scientific approaches to the study of local histories and culture but also seeking new angles for narrating these studies. Sometimes, as I will elaborate, this meant adopting a "local's voice." And they were not alone in such endeavors in the 1940s, as the 1930s witnessed the height of the "local history movement" in Japan (Young 2013). Mainly locally oriented, local history movements were mostly taking place in the emerging cities outside of the metropole. A result of urbanization and the development of regional economies, local history movements in Japan could also be seen as part of the global trend to understand the "local" as a site of enduring value in the face of globalization.[1] Inheriting aspects of these various "movements toward the local," scholars of colonial Taiwan could have very easily joined with their predecessors in Japan to justify their purposes and approaches to studying local history.[2] And yet, as implied in Kanaseki's opening statement for *Minzoku Taiwan*, they were not interested in copying the Japanese model, instead actively proposing new interpretations and frameworks for their version of local studies. Rather than associating narratives of "culture" with the "modern" and "civilized," they tried to establish a disciplinary framework for embedding locality and a sense of nativeness in the idea of culture.[3] Their product, *Minzoku Taiwan,* thus became the only and most significant record of the groundbreaking epistemological exploration undertaken during this period when "culture" was increasingly interpreted as something ahistorical and global.

The influence generated by the publication of *Minzoku Taiwan* went far beyond the community of scholars and intellectuals involved, and the journal became the catalyst for a new wave of local and native culture studies for decades to come. To be more specific, what these scholars initiated was a complicated process of renegotiation with the nationalistic framework intrinsic to Japan's *minzokugaku*/folklore studies and, more importantly, the (re)positioning of the epistemological basis for the recognition of culture, or a (re)building of the methodology for documenting and narrating culture. After the termination of Japanese rule in Taiwan, similar projects, such as "Taiwan Fengtu" (Taiwan custom and land), a column in one of the earliest post-1945 newspapers, *Kong Lun Pao* (1947–61), continued to focus on local culture and histories. Undisrupted by the transition of political regimes, folklore and local studies writing in Taiwan remained a hub of knowledge production before and after the end of colonial rule. In negotiation with coloniality from its inception, studies of folklore and local histories offered future generations of scholars in postcolonial Taiwan a unique platform for understanding ideas related to "local culture"—as well as locality and culture itself. In this article, I demonstrate how it was not necessarily the process of othering or objectifying colonial subjects that was engendered by the scholarship of physical anthropology and folklore studies in Taiwan. Rather, what these disciplines proposed was the idea that "practices of the everyday" could be made into a subject of (scientific) documentation and study, which ultimately served as the material foundation for a new system of knowing and understanding the everyday. What I examine, then, is how these new ways of documentation, or ways of seeing, contributed to individuals' identity formations in the face of an emerging and all-encompassing nationalistic discourse. And what this reveals, I propose, is not simply coloniality but also another way of building modernity.

This article is divided into three main sections. In the first section, I survey the broader historical context of folklore studies in Taiwan by offering an overview of the introduction, reception, and translation of the concept of "folk" or "old customs." Using a case study of a major debate—which lasted for more than three issues of *Minzoku Taiwan*—on the Minnan greeting phrase "Have you eaten yet?" I point out that while the functions of folklore studies or research on "folk practices" transformed in different periods of Japan's colonial rule due to changing political circumstances, the understandings or debates surrounding these concepts were not simply a battleground for political discourse but reflections of an emerging transnational intellectual community where diverse narratives for culture, history, and nationality converged. The second section looks at the moment when this group of historians, ethnographers, and anthropologists began to identify their roles and potential subjects of study by participating in or organizing exhibitions about "local history" or the history of Taiwan. As a result of negotiations and compromises made between colonial authorities, scholars, amateur collectors, and researchers from regional organizations, these "local history exhibitions" served as laboratories for this community of first-generation folklore scholars to garner public interest and transform the meaning of "local history" to "native history." Some of their works, as subsequently published in *Minzoku Taiwan,* are the focus of the third section, which examines the struggles, successes, and failures in their attempts to establish the "authentic locals' voices."

■ THE (IM)POSSIBILITY OF TRANSLATING *MINZOKUGAKU*

While "folklore studies" was introduced as a newly imported discipline to colonial Taiwan, the building of archives for "folk practices" or "old customs" took place long before the 1940s. Indeed, the intellectual community of folklore studies was, to a large degree, indebted to the legacy of these earlier attempts. But it is also worth pointing out that the genealogy of folklore studies in Taiwan does not necessarily originate from the "old customs surveys" conducted in the early twentieth century. To begin with, the systemic survey and documentation of "old customs" *(kyūkan)* carried out by officials and researchers, including Inō Kanori, who worked for the Japanese colonial government since the beginning of colonial rule, created an enormous amount of data describing—or, more precisely, defining—the "traditional" practices of Han as well as indigenous peoples in Taiwan.[4] Since 1895, with official and civil initiatives like the Society of Taiwan Anthropology (Taiwan Jinruigak'kai) and Investigations of Taiwan Old Customs, studies of customs and "indigenous cultures" were introduced as an essential aspect of a new knowledge system validated by discourses offered by the colonial government (Chang 2006). Even so, it would take another six decades for folklore/native ethnology studies to be recognized more widely as a discipline qualified to enter the academies in Japan.[5] This separation between the construction of database and epistemology resulted largely from the difference in political contexts, but it also necessarily influenced the ways in which folklore studies was conceived by its practitioners in Taiwan.

It should be noted that *Minzoku Taiwan* was not entirely dedicated to folklore studies, according to its editors. Or, to put it differently, "folklore studies" was never really clearly defined by the folklore scholars and writers in colonial Taiwan, and like folklore studies or *minsuxue* in early Republican China, it was also very much shaped by both local and global ideas and theories (Duara 2003). In a letter addressed to the readers from the editorial board, published in 1943, the editors stated their mission thus:

> To trace the historical developments of a people, besides textual and material data provided by historical and archaeological studies, orally transmitted customs and [traditional] practices analyzed by folklore studies are also necessary. But folklore studies are different from historical and archaeological research in that...as "Volk" is people of one nation, "Volkskunde" in its single form refers to folklore studies; namely, folklore studies [is] of one nation.... On the other hand, such studies of other peoples in the world...is called "Völkerkunde," in its plural form[—studies of peoples.]...Because the utmost mission of this journal is for the popularization [of folklore studies], we do not advocate only "folklore studies of Taiwan" in its strictest sense. Articles and studies in related fields such as history, archaeology and ethnology are all welcomed, too. (Editorial Team 1943, 21)

The purpose of this statement was to "clarify the confusion between ethnology and folklore studies" experienced by one of the journal's readers.[6]

The author of this letter also cited Yanagita Kunio, while referencing the British and American definitions of *folklore* in relation to German *Volkskunde*. This was the first time the term *folklore studies* was presented in its multilingual form, yet all in Japanese transliteration (katakana). Tellingly, the actual process for translating folklore studies took place two years after the first issue of *Minzoku Taiwan* was published. Through such "belated" attention or attempts in defining while translating and transporting the concept of "folklore" and "folklore studies," the characteristics of the community for folklore studies surrounding the evolving "folklore Taiwan" journal began to show; that is, there were always multiple layers of interpretation at work for these intellectuals, who were mostly part-time "folklore scholars." Or, one could say, the translating process never stopped for folklore studies among the contributors, scholars, and students, who all had different background knowledge for understanding, and thus defining, what constitutes folklore and/or *minsu*. Like their Chinese and Japanese colleagues who came to set the foundation for the shaping of ethnology and discourses for ethnicity in the latter half of the twentieth century, this was a group of people initiating their own identitarian projects by negotiating various processes of translation (Duara 2003, 210–13).

Another reason for the hesitation among the editors of *Minzoku Taiwan* to give definitive explanations for "doing folklore studies in Taiwan" would have been the "impossibility" of transporting Japan's *minzoku* studies into the colony. The political agenda that practitioners of folklore studies in Taiwan had to confront was Japan's ideological scheme for establishing the "Greater East Asian Co-Prosperity Sphere." While the building of "Greater East Asian Folklore Studies" was occasionally brought up by the publishers of *Minzoku Taiwan*, the folklore community in 1940s Taiwan was certainly not solely driven or shaped by imperial Japan's ideological scheme. To establish *minzokugaku* in Taiwan, the researchers would have to come up with their own interpretation and approach to a discipline that had not been officially "validated" in the academic world. In Japan, *minzokugaku* defined as well as generated knowledge for Japan's *kyōdo*, or the "interiority," that is, lives and spirits of native, local Japanese (Christy 2012). Japan's native ethnology studies was thus difficult to apply to studies of the colony, as it was a knowledge system meant to function exclusively for, on behalf of, and by "native" Japanese.[7] This also implies that any assimilation movement carried out in its colonies would not create, and neither should they be creating, "authentic" or "real" Japanese, despite the fact that the Kōminka movement in Taiwan propagated the adoption of Japanese names and abandoned the usage of Minnan dialect. In reality, the Kōminka movement did not promote "Japanese culture" per se but introduced into the colony Japan's "national culture" fabricated by wartime propaganda, with the purpose of creating loyal imperial citizens rather than authentic "Japanese" citizens. It thus would be an oversimplification to claim that these "imperial Japanese" are regarded as the same as "Japanese." Tailor-made for the islanders, the cultural practices loyal Taiwan citizens should perform during the Kōminka movement, according to the colonial government, should include—among several others—installing Jingūtaima 神宮大麻 (or ōnusa, a ritual purification wand issued by the Ise Shrine, the Shintō shrine of the imperial house) in every household shrine. In no way a nationwide traditional practice in Japan, such acts served more as proof of loyalty to the emperor than as a means of cultivating Japanese "folk" customs, traditions, and authenticity among Taiwanese.

The ambiguity that existed among definitions of cultural authenticity and nativeness, together with the contradicting attitudes toward cultural assimilation shared by both colonial authorities and subjects, became an underlying issue that remained unresolved for the contributors to *Minzoku Taiwan*. While it was difficult, if not impossible, to practice "folklore studies" or native ethnology in colonial Taiwan, the methodology and scientific principles of folklore studies in the colony were being proposed, experimented with, and developed by Japanese and Taiwanese scholars. The process of these "folklorists" with different understandings and positions regarding culture and authenticity speaking with, to, or against each other made the practice of "documenting culture" through both scientific observation and the theorization of cultural traditions possible. A case study of the discussions surrounding the Minnan salutation "Are you full?" (literally, *li jia ba mei* 汝食飽未), which grew to a lengthy debate that lasted for more than three issues of *Minzoku Taiwan* (nos. 5, 8, and 9), best exemplifies this evolving methodology for documenting "local culture." It started with Higashikata Takayoshi's (1889–1957) essay analyzing the social and cultural backgrounds of this particular daily salutation (Higashikata 1941). A translator working for the colonial government, Higashikata Takayoshi was an expert in Mandarin and Minnan dialect, and in the essay, he reached his conclusion based on "years of experience observing and studying Minnan speaking." Comparing salutations in Japan, China, and Taiwan, Higashikata believed that the historical roots for the use of "Are you full?" lay in the cultural tradition of Confucian society as well as the chaotic, impoverished rural communities seen in premodern China. He first quoted from Mencius, "Appetite for food and sex is nature" (Lau 2003, 240), and argued that Confucian doctrines were the source for the everyday salutation. He then further substantiated the argument by suggesting that because Chinese people were constantly being forced out of their homes due to the unstable political and social environments of dynastic rule, it was only natural for the Chinese to share with others the concern for means of securing basic needs (Higashikata 1941). Higashikata went on to proclaim that, because under Japanese rule, Chinese in Taiwan enjoyed a peaceful and harmonious social order, such salutations from the past should be abandoned and the Japanese daily salutation "good day/evening" (kyō wa/konbanwa) should take its place in Taiwanese daily dialogue. Sharing the same cultural values originating from Confucianism, Han people in Taiwan—mostly settlers from southeast China—should find it natural to adapt themselves to everyday Japanese customs and practices. This promotion of adopting the Japanese daily salutation thus not only introduced Japanese "national" culture to the colony but also helped to lay the foundation for the discourses of the Greater East Asian Cultural Sphere.

Another Japanese scholar and sociologist, Okada Yuzuru (1906–69), also contributed to this discussion. He argued that while Higashikata's analysis mostly focused on the social and historical circumstances in China, it should be the responsibility of both authors and readers of Minzoku Taiwan to reconsider this topic by studying and observing how customs are formed within everyday lives of the island's local communities. According to Okada, the salutation was merely an extension of the cultural practice of dining with one's extended family members. Such a deduction, in Okada's words, was based on Yanagita Kunio's theory of the ritual of the family—the practice of family dining together as a ritual that binds a community. He concluded by suggesting that tracing the origins and formations of customs, and analysis of shared ideas and practices rather than historical records, should be emphasized (Okada 1941). Successfully defining and amalgamating this "Taiwanese custom" with Japanese ones, Japanese scholars' utilization of minzokugaku methods on the case study of "Are you full?" also resulted in the diminishing of the value of historical and textual analysis in Chinese. But such "minzokugaku method," in fact, did not come to dominate the methodological framework adopted by most non-Japanese authors for Minzoku Taiwan.

In response to Japanese authors' essays on this topic, Liao Han-chen (1912–80), an active writer who also specialized in Minnan proverbs, rejected the theory based on "Chinese cultural tradition" completely. In an essay titled "About 'Are You Full,'" he posed his objection to Japanese scholars' opinions based not on theories of cultural tradition but on the environmental factors that helped form common practices shared by one race (Liao 1942). Repudiating Higashikata's and Okada's explanations, Liao first quoted from works of local Taiwanese history and employed a philological approach to analyze the origins and actual usage of the salutation in local people's daily lives. Using quotes from Lian Heng (1878–1936) and Lan Ding-yuan (1680–1733), Liao pointed out that instead of "Are you full?" the more common salutation between Taiwanese people was "Have you eaten yet?" (*Jia mei?* 食未), and there is a significant distinction between these two questions. The latter, according to Liao's quote from Lian Heng, was one of the two daily salutations widely seen in the Minnan community of Taiwan; the other one would have been "Where are you going?" (*Do qi?* 佗去) (Lian 1957). Different from the question "Are you full?" which can be observed among most Chinese speaking different dialects across China during daily mealtimes, "Have you eaten yet?" was spoken by Han settler (in this case, the Minnan) communities from the seventeenth century onward in Taiwan. Liao proposed that being a settler society, early immigrants to Taiwan found this salutation a caring expression for others living in an environment constantly threatened by savages and fierce challenges posed by hostile immigrant competitors (Lian 1957). From here, Liao's analysis then began to differ from the analyses of the Han scholars he quoted.

It is undeniable that such way of greeting others originated as a social practice in mainland China, but Liao also argued that the different natural, social, and cultural environments of different regions have had a profound role in shaping how people meet and greet each other. While Taiwanese settlers and the Han Chinese communities of southern China (especially southeast China, in this case) shared this way of salutation, Liao made it quite explicit that studies of Han communities in China who were responsible for making popular this expression actually made visible a greater historical context that contradicted the narratives about cultural similarity between Han settlers in Taiwan and Japanese, as proposed by the Japanese scholars. To illustrate his point, Liao quoted extensively from the Chinese version of Ellsworth Huntington's (1927) work *The Character of Races*, selectively translated, reorganized, and renamed by Pan Guangdan (1899–1967, a sociologist) as *Natural Selection and the Character of Chinese Race (Minzuxing* 民族性) (Pan 1928). Based on Pan's translation of Huntington's theory about the interrelation between the environment and the development of racial characters, the Han migration toward southeast China that lasted for centuries had the most significant impact on the shaping of Han people's common customs and characters as a race. On one hand, the hazardous environment of the mountainous southeast regions, coupled with threats posed by the indigenous people, made the

Han people more attentive to basic daily needs. And when faced with a similar environment, a new island settlement, it seemed only natural that Han settlers would carry with them the salutation "Have you eaten yet?" to their new homes. On the other hand, however, another important factor that played a key role in shaping the character of the Han race but that the Japanese scholars failed to recognize, according to Liao, was the "mixing" of races. Just as northern Chinese developed slightly different salutations, many local communities in Taiwan also began to have different questions and sayings for daily greetings, and Liao observed these changing life customs were mainly the result of racial mixing between Han and the aborigines—similar to the situation in China, where there were intermarriages between the Han and northern non-Han tribes (Liao 1942, 28). Liao's analysis on the topic, in other words, was not a direct rejection of the Japanese authors' theories, but it nevertheless exposed the problems, if not the impossibility, of Japan's *minzokugaku* being grafted on to the propagandist discursive framework for cultural assimilation. Utilizing both Chinese and Western (albeit a Chinese translated version) sources and scholarship, Liao was clearly speaking to an audience that was not only acquainted with such methodologies but also had some knowledge of the scholarly and scientific values of the sources in his writing. Liao's challenge to Japanese authors based on his own learnings in both traditional Chinese and modern (Western) knowledge systems was, in this regard, also a call for local intellectuals to join his efforts in constructing a new knowledge system that offered different ways for interpreting and producing *minzoku* studies.

As demonstrated in this debate that took place between Japanese and Taiwanese scholars, the platform for "studying folklore" as structured by the journal *Minzoku Taiwan* necessarily entailed the establishment of not one but multiple methodologies or approaches to folklore studies. The journal became a space in which writers with different epistemological backgrounds could utilize, articulate, and exhibit their knowledge systems for understanding the concepts of culture, history, and, of course, "race." The translating of "native ethnology" or *minzokugaku* in the multilingual colony, in other words, was really a process during which competing ideas of and concepts for what constitutes cultural authenticity began to serve as major topics of intellectual discussion. For the Japanese supporting a colonial agenda, the practice of "scientific" studies of folklore in Taiwan would ultimately contribute to the reorganization of "local culture" according to principles of assimilation. But for those who shared Liao Han-chen's concern about the formers' cultural nationalistic approach toward folklore studies, the "real" scientific methods for studying folklore should have been a mixture of Chinese historical and philological study, also possibly including the latest scientific theories for analyzing ethnic origins. Therefore it might have been "impossible" to apply or translate Japan's *minzokugaku* in colonial Taiwan, but the process of translation and how such translations were negotiated were significant. One of the results of this complicated process of negotiation was the discovery of the concept of "nativeness" among the local communities, who found themselves to be no longer the immigrants to a settlement but the practitioners of cultural traditions that had already been transformed by their lived environment, or "localized."

■ FINDING LOCAL HISTORY IN "NATIVE LAND"

The kinds of epistemological experiments with old and new theories about cultural traditions and racial characters seen in Liao Han-chen's essay were already taking place decades before the 1940s. Attempts to retell—if not reinvent—narratives for customs, traditions, and a "communal past" had been undertaken by Chinese and Japanese intellectuals since the early twentieth century. Nonetheless, as mentioned before, the popularization of the grassroots local history movements that spilled over from Japan since the 1920s signaled a moment when the interest in local history might not have been purely intellectual. In 1930, the first public exhibition to propagate the theme of "Taiwan culture," the Commemoration of Taiwan Culture's Three Hundredth Year (Taiwan Bunka Sanbyakunen Kinenkai), was held in the city of Tainan. The year count of "three hundred" was mainly based on the date of the erection of Fort Provintia, seen as the symbol of the beginning of civilized rule on the island. The conception of a "cultural exhibition" was a result of collaborative efforts between local sponsors and the government-general, and in the end, it was the officials and librarians who worked within the government-general system who oversaw the curation of sections for exhibiting cultural and historical materials. With donations and assistance from local intellectuals and literati, the commemoration thus turned out to be the earliest cultural exhibition in Taiwan to feature a "historical records" section (*shiryō tenrankai* 史料展覧会) displaying manuscripts, documents, and inscriptions from the period of Qing rule.[8] The commemoration thus signaled the beginning of a series of semiofficial projects for promoting studies of Taiwan's "culture," a concept embedded in the narrative of its "three-hundred-year history." And because such recognition and commemoration entailed popular identification with key historical figures and events, the visual display of materials related to these key historical elements became crucial. This was the logic behind curating the "historical records" section:

besides being introduced to an extensive textual collection recording, praising, and portraying the achievements of Koxinga (Zheng Chenggong, 1624–62) and his Japanese relations, visitors also were made familiar with the historical connections between Japan's expeditions to the island of Taiwan. They were also invited to review some aspects of Qing officials' governance through appreciating the archaeological discoveries of Taiwan's ancient and indigenous cultures excavated and curated by researchers trained in "modern (Japanese) sciences of anthropology and archaeology."[9]

Acknowledging a historical trajectory that was shaped by both Chinese and Japanese cultural influences, Tainan's cultural exhibition went on to become a model for historical exhibitions of Taiwan, as well as the emerging narratives of "local history" that were being popularized by local history movements. In Taiwan, its culmination was the popularity of *kyōdo ten* (literally "native land/homeland exhibition") or *shiryō ten* (historical documents exhibition), which were more and more commonly seen by the late 1930s. Again, Tainan was the place where the venue for the first *shiryō ten* was located. But it was in 1934 that Taiwan's first "native museum," or *kyōdo kan*, was constructed in Jilong, and later that year, as a result of an island-wide "convention for native education" *(kyōdo kyōiku kenkyūkai)*, Jilong's first *Nativeland/Folk Reader (Kyōdo tokuhon)* was distributed, first to a Japanese primary school.[10] And in the aftermath of Taiwan's own Taiwan Expo in 1935, there have been discussions for establishing more museums of local history. On one hand, the growing attention to systemic narration of "local history" and the implicit "local memories" was one result of the amalgamation of Japan's national propaganda for "love for native land" *(kyōdo ai)* and colonial policy for the promotion of "localized" education. Also aiming to cultivate a general "love for native land," the establishment of "native/local education" and "native/local museums" in Taiwan, however, was designed to deliver a narrative of "native history" and "native culture" within the discursive framework of Japan's colonial dominance mainly among Japanese immigrants. Whereas in Japan, the *kyōdo ai* propaganda was intertwined with the formation of *minzokugaku* and partially backed by the institutionalizing knowledge of native ethnology, in Taiwan, the conception and content of the "native" still lacked an ideological basis, as there had been no intellectual discussion regarding the existence or definition of "nativeness." As I have already pointed out, Taiwan's "native land/folk readers" are found lacking in descriptions of local histories or only contain the narratives that confirm Taiwan's historical ties with Japan (Chou 1999). However, the popularity of constructing narratives and visions of native culture provided a framework for the historians and ethnographers of Taiwan to finally find a way to articulate their projects as being of popular "local history," which would then come to be associated with the concept of nativeness with the help of *Minzoku Taiwan.*

Indeed, "local," or "native" was the primary concept Ikeda Toshio (1916–81), cofounder and editor in chief of *Minzoku Taiwan,* strived to reinvent. A settler in Taiwan from Shimane prefecture, Ikeda moved to Taipei with his family when he was seven and developed a passion for Taiwan's history and culture from his youth (Ikeda 1982). After graduating from Taipei First Normal School in 1935, he worked as an elementary school teacher for five years at Longshan 龍山 public school, Maga (now Wahua) district, in Taipei. According to his memoir, he fell in love with the place (Ikeda 1982). Despite never having received any academic training in *minzoku* or folklore studies, Ikeda was an enthusiastic collector and amateur researcher of Maga's folklore and local customs. It was not until 1940, when he began to work as a commissioned researcher at the archives division *(monjo ka)* for the government-general, that his proposal for *Minzoku Taiwan* was realized with both official and academic support. The position he acquired with the government-general, preceded by ethnographers and historians like Inō Kanori, gave Ikeda opportunities to review governmental data and publications and gain access to the archive of ethnographic information built up by "investigations of local customs" as well as colonial officials' individual works—or "field reports." In Ikeda's memoir for *Minzoku Taiwan*'s initiation, he compared *Minzoku Taiwan* to *Taiwan Kanshū Kiji* (Taiwan etiquette and custom note), a periodical published between 1901 and 1907 by a semiofficial research committee consisting mainly of officials and researchers involved in the colonial "investigations of local customs" projects (Ikeda 1982). Stressing *Minzoku Taiwan*'s nonofficial status, Ikeda described *Minzoku Taiwan*'s foundation as an act of resistance by both Japanese and Taiwanese intellectuals against the cultural assimilation movement. Ikeda was a great sympathizer with the antiassimilation movement and very fluent in both Mandarin and Minnan, but it is probably also undeniable that he was a marginal, if not amateur, folklorist compared to colleagues like Kanaseki. His position on the *Minzoku Taiwan* editorial board, in other words, had more to do with his experience working with the archival sources at the government-general and his language expertise. According to Ikeda's ideal, the information offered in *Minzoku Taiwan* would be locally oriented research that reflected the popular perception of "what it was" that constituted the authentic parts of local culture. Inspired in part by China's folklore studies in the 1920s, Ikeda envisioned *Minzoku Taiwan* to be an unmediated channel for local and Japanese researchers and scholars to publish works on Taiwan's folklore as well as historical studies. Based on Ikeda's design, *Minzoku Taiwan* would challenge the colonial practice of making the locals the "objects of research." Ironically, throughout the journal's publication, Ikeda adopted quite a few Chinese pen names in trying to convince readers of the authenticity of local subjects' participation.

In other words, Ikeda not only assumed but also actively invented a "local's perspective" for ways of representing traditional practices and beliefs. The adoption of Chinese pen names—most of them female names—was, on one level, a way to enhance the impression of locals' participation in the journal when Ikeda introduced specific customs or everyday objects. For instance, with the pen name "Li Shi Xing Hua" 李氏杏花 (*xing hua* means "apricot blossoms," then a common name for girls in Taiwan), Ikeda wrote a short essay depicting the different lifestyles of a *yangnü* (adopted daughter) (Li Shi 1943). This particular way of "allowing the locals to speak for themselves" came to form a unique characteristic of the journal's style of narration; namely, it supplemented the body of folklore studies with narratives of local customs and traditions "by the locals," thus giving an authentic voice to a journal sponsored and edited mainly by Japanese authors. Although it was indeed possible that a reader familiar with the journal's publishers would notice that these "local girls" were actually Ikeda, it is also worth pointing out that "Li Shi Xing Hua" was not Ikeda's only Chinese pen name, and he used different pen names to write different kinds of articles (Ikeda 1982), so it is likely that a number of readers would have been misled. Inevitably jeopardizing the authenticity of the "locals' voices" and "local way of seeing" that the journal claimed to be documenting, Ikeda's role-playing strategy helps to reveal the struggles shared by the editorial team. Although they had to valorize the nativeness of the journal's contributors, it was also necessary that such nativeness should not challenge the value system upheld by the assimilation policy. The act of remembering and documenting supposedly performed by the "locals" as envisioned by Ikeda as well as other editors of *Minzoku Taiwan* was thus turned into a form of representation that could also be mimicked, if not "reproduced," by the expedient adoption of local names as pen names. For the true local contributors, this would also mean that they might have been involuntarily turned into collaborators by offering the documentation of their own memories, which could be juxtaposed with accounts by "fake" local writers. Yet, this was also a moment when some Taiwanese authors began to realize the possibility of reinventing or retelling native history utilizing the newfound power granted by a local identity.

■ FROM LOCAL HISTORY TO NATIVE HISTORY

The topic that best demonstrates the complications of narrating history and culture for intellectuals confronted with the issue of defining what is or should be "native" and/or "local" is the stories of Shilin 士林, to which the editorial team of *Minzoku Taiwan* dedicated a special issue. According to the editor's note, the Shilin special issue was mainly inspired by the Exhibition for Shilin's Culture *(bunka)* and Native Land *(kyōdo)* held in August 1941 by Shilin's literati association Shilin Xiezhihui (Shilin Alliance for Interculture 士林協志會) and the influential intellectuals associated with it, such as Yang Yun-ping (1906–2000). For *Minzoku Taiwan,* the special issue thus also functioned as a valuable opportunity for showing that it was both supported and recognized by the "real" local intellectuals, who, in this regard, could also be seen as the "informants" for the stories published in the journal. In other words, editorial cooperation with local authors generated a special issue that could be viewed as exemplary of native investigations into local communities, the "native land." Similarly, for intellectuals like Yang Yun-ping, the contribution to a special issue on topics with the appeal of "native culture" constituted a rare opportunity to establish, in the world of knowledge production dominated by Japanese intellectuals and theories, his own ideas for how "native land" should be theorized and defined.[11] The terminology for "native land" did not appear in the Shilin special issue, but the editorial arrangements and choice of essay topics suggest that by a particular way of documenting and narrating historical stories, sights, and memories, pieces of history could become the basis for "authentic" cultural traditions that are the defining factors for the "native land."

The Shilin special issue included essays, survey records, collections of inscriptions, temple histories, and folklore compiled by three Shilin intellectuals—Yang Yun-ping, Tsao Yung-ho (1920–2014), and Pan Nai-zhen (1918–45). Members of *Minzoku Taiwan*'s editorial team, Kanaseki and photographer Matsuyama Kenichi, also contributed. Yang Yun-ping wrote "Preliminary Collection of Biographical Data on Shilin's Forefathers" (Shilin xianzhe zhuanji ziliao chuji) and "Shilin Street" ("street," i.e., *gai* in Japanese), a short introduction to the geographic and cultural history of the Shilin district. Together with Tsao Yung-ho's "Shilin's Ancient Stelae," "Shilin's Legends" (Shirin no densetsu), "Shilin Temples Gazetteer" (written in Chinese), and "Listening to Stories in Shilin" (Shilin tingshu), the two Shilin-born intellectuals offered an account of Shilin's history that was mainly written in the traditional Chinese gazetteer style (Tsao 1941a, 1941b). Referencing pre-twentieth-century gazetteers and genealogies in the accounts of Shilin temples and forefathers *(xianzhe),* Yang's and Tsao's articles of Shilin history not only reduced the presence of colonial rule to a minimum but also seemed to disavow the theoretical framework of folklore studies. The article "Shilin Temples Gazetteer" was more like a direct copy of temples' own historical records, as readers only found information regarding the foundation and initiators of the temples and descriptions of heads of the Han clans in the Shilin community. No further interpretation or explanation was offered by Tsao. With strong passion and a sense of belonging, Yang's account of "Shilin Forefathers" essentially focused on his identification with local intellectual communities. Such writings of local histories in the traditional Chinese style bore no resemblance whatsoever to the works on local history promoted by Japanese authors and settlers, but if placed within the framework of "native history studies," the essays could then constitute another authentic "local's voice," this time much more significant because these were written by renowned local intellectuals. Moreover, Yang's and Tsao's essays on the historical past of Shilin demonstrated that they were able to acknowledge the cultural boundaries of "native history" by structuring narratives of local identity.

In fact, neither Yang nor Tsao was among the traditionally trained Chinese literati. Like their colleague Liao Han-chen, they graduated from public schools established during the colonial period. Although classically trained, they were no strangers to the Japanese/"modern" knowledge system for culture and civilization. Yet, in their writings, works by non-Chinese authors were never cited. In his short study on Shilin's toponymic history, Yang simply ignored the latest ethnological finding regarding the aboriginal origin of Shilin's old name, "Pattsiran" 八芝蘭 by Abe Akiyoshi (1942) (a linguist working for the government-general), a very obvious absence in a historical account that aims to explain the different historical names for Shilin. In Yang's and Tsao's essays, the names "Pattsiran" and "Zhishan Rock"—the cultural and geographic center of the Shilin area—simply appeared without any explanation. For those unfamiliar with Shilin, the place as depicted in Yang's and Tsao's essays would have seemed like a space constructed by historical narratives and memories rather than actual geographic research, namely, a spiritual "native land" for those who could recognize its cultural authenticity. In the essay on Shilin's legends, Tsao wrote the following foreword:

Truly, the Zhishan Rock is the [spiritual] symbol of Pattsirans, and it has been intimately connected with Pattsirans' daily life. This is where the ancestors' spirits are; this is where the ancestors spilled their blood. There is no place better suited to serve as literati's dwelling than the Zhishan Rock of Pattsiran. (Tsao 1941a, 24)

Although he also brought up the "Six Teachers Incident" in the foreword, in Tsao's essay, the cultural significance and historical relevance of the incident—the murder of six Japanese schoolteachers stationed in the first elementary school founded on Zhishan Rock—were completely ruled out in his narrative. Recounting mythical stories surrounding Zhishan Rock, Tsao's essay was made up of anecdotes that took place before the twentieth century, a style reminiscent of Yanagita Kunio's *Tōno monogatari* (Tales of Tono). Tsao's essay might have been an unwitting imitation of the *Monogatari,* but in the foreword, Tsao did compare these orally transmitted stories with *kaidan* (Japanese mystery), assuming his readers would know the similarities and differences between *kaidan* and *densetsu.*

The essay "Listening to Stories in Shilin" was also authored by Tsao. With heavy emphasis on the oral origins of these stories, "Listening to Stories in Shilin" was narrated in a more authentically "local" style: mimicking the experience of "listening to stories"—or *kóng-kó* 講古 in Minnan dialect, literally "speaking of the old"—told by local storytellers (*kóng-kó sen* 講古仙 or 講古先) in teahouses, "Listening to Stories" is composed of titleless paragraphs of local rumors and myths. The fact that local storytelling activity was also being censored in the early stages of the cultural assimilation movement would have made the essay look even more like natives' documentation of a disappearing cultural practice. In this documentation, the concept of "good fengshui" (literally, *dili* 地理)—already dismissed as a local superstition by official discourse in the 1940s—associated with the space of Zhishan Rock was evoked multiple times, and in Tsao's narrative, it was depicted as a fundamental way of understanding and describing the world shared among the locals. The fact that such a depiction of the "natives' way" for understanding the world was stressed in Tsao's essay again shows that he knew his readers' expectations: a "native's voice" was what made studies of local history authentic. Ultimately, this authenticity was to serve as the basis for resistance against the Japanese narratives of "native history."

It was not a coincidence that before Tsao's essay, Ikeda had already published essays with the title "Listening to Stories in Maga" using the female pen name Li Shi Xing Hua, thereby ascribing to the format of "listening to stories in native land" special functions for folklore studies. Although different from Tsao's approach, Ikeda did point out in these short essays that many of the stories and practices recorded were products of uncivilized beliefs and conventions. Tsao utilized Ikeda's framework for narrating local stories and beliefs to write about topics that did not necessarily fit with the assimilation agenda. Thus, in Yang's and Tsao's essays, the theoretic framework of *minzokugaku* was applied to legitimize narratives for local histories that were otherwise incompatible with the dominant colonial discourse of "(assimilated) local culture." Furthermore, by choosing different styles of documentation for topics with different cultural implications, the Shilin intellectuals Yang and Tsao were able to make their writing serve their own purposes. In their essays on Shilin, studies of local history were transformed into accounts of native history. With "ancestors' blood" and "ancestors' spirit," the community of Shilin residents began to establish their native identity with a sense of "nativeness" discovered with the help of their Japanese folklorist friends.[12]

■ **CONCLUSION**

Despite the different approaches adopted by different authors for the journal, *Minzoku Taiwan* became, for editors like Ikeda and Kanaseki as well as local intellectuals, a unique medium for developing ways to represent cultural authenticity. Of the Japanese scholars who chose to join the journal's editorial team despite it not being viewed favorably under the colonial censorship system, it could be said that they had mixed motives: on one hand, they were all emerging scholars working in the colony and needed recognition by mainstream scholars in the metropole. Coming up with theories and ideas that could potentially expand or even challenge Japan's scholarship on ethnographical and ethnological sciences thus would have been their primary mission. On the other hand, the experience living and working with Japanese settlers as well as local intellectuals gave them opportunities to rethink and review existing discursive frameworks, most notably that of "culture," which was forced into the colony with the cultural assimilation movement. What Japanese and Taiwanese intellectuals alike faced, then, became the same problem: was there any choice left besides the cosmopolitan, modern "culture" and/or Japan's nationalistic "culture" to which the Taiwanese had to "assimilate"? This was the time, after all, when public debates and discussion taking place among intellectuals in the Japanese colonial empire—Japan, Korea, Taiwan (and Manchukuo)—were supposed to echo the propagandist agenda for cultural assimilation or the promotion of a shared "Greater East Asian" cultural sphere. But this was also the time when the nationalistic framework for narrating the "culture of a people" came to serve as a globalizing force that had put pressure on the colonial governments' assimilation policies since the late 1910s. The birth of *Minzoku Taiwan* and similar publications after the end of the colonial period in Taiwan reflected the local reaction, if not resistance, to the forces of both globalization and assimilation.

When Kanaseki proposed the concept of "monument" for documenting and reporting the *minzoku* of Taiwan, he might not have anticipated the establishment of a modern scholarship "of one nation," but he and his colleagues did start a community that functioned as the active agent for creating alternative means of "memorization." The act of memorization, by definition, implies that loss is inevitable, but that which is memorized and documented is meant to be "monumental." The construction of *minzoku* studies, thus, became the pivotal process for transforming individual acts of memorization into the collective initiative for "memorialization," giving new meaning not only to the subjects documented but to the act of documentation itself. As a first collective project for memorialization that witnessed the transitional period between the end of imperial rule and the start of nationalist democratization in Taiwan, *Minzoku Taiwan* came to serve as the basis for another discursive framework, even paradigm, for the focus on local/native culture and history. The "Taiwan Fengtu" column mentioned earlier was founded and edited by students of the *Minzoku Taiwan* editors, including Chen Chi-lu (1923–2014), who later became a member of the first generation of anthropologists in post-colonial Taiwan. This legacy of native cultural studies also played an important role in the post-1950 nativist movements seen throughout East Asia, especially in Korea and Taiwan.[13] As the globalizing capitalistic economy and Western cultural paradigms were conditions met by every Asian society undergoing a struggle for decolonization in the latter half of the twentieth century, the "discovery" of nativeness and local consciousness became a shared theme for communities looking for their own place and voice on the world stage. For postwar Asian societies, including Taiwan, the search for monuments of culture is ongoing.

Anne Ma Kuo-an is a postdoctoral fellow at NYU Shanghai. She received her PhD in Chinese studies from the Chinese University of Hong Kong with her dissertation titled "Portraits from Formosa: Visual Documents and Taiwan's Colonial History (1895–1960)." Her work focuses on the visual aspects of East Asian colonial archives, with a special interest in transnational exchanges of cultural traditions. She has authored several photographers' biographies in collaboration with the National Center for Photography, Taipei. Her current research looks at the intersections of ethnographic studies and modern visual culture in East Asia.

■ NOTES

1. Prasenjit Duara has analyzed how German ideas including *Lebensraum* (geopolitics), *Gemeinschaft,* and *Gesellschaft* were developed in Japan for their rhetoric of native place as well as in China, when Fei Xiaotong discussed "localness" *(difanxing)* from the 1920s to the 1940s. The differences or distinctions between ideas for native place in Japan and Fei's role and influence on the concept of "localness" were not the focus of Duara's discussions, but these ambiguities for definitions for concepts of "local" and "native" have seldom been pointed out by historians of colonial Taiwan (Duara 2003, 214; Watsuji 1988; Fei 1992).

2. The establishment of the Taiwan Cultural Association (Taiwan bunka kyōkai/wenhua xiehui; 1921–31; TCA), according to Evan Dawley's analysis, was one of the popular movements in Taiwan led by islanders who were driven by a similar desire for the "culture life." A purely non-Japan organization, however, the more important agenda of TCA was to serve as the islanders' channel for rallying non/anti-Japanese support for locals' voices against dominant Japanese narratives, especially those of the "local history movements" initiated by Japanese settlers. Dawley also pointed out that the TCA-sponsored talks and events also helped to raise local communities' awareness toward the significance of knowing the origins of customs that were beginning to be considered as part of the communities' identity and history (Dawley 2019).

3. The concept of "nativeness" or simply the use of the term *native* has seldom appeared until the 1940s in Taiwan, and even in the articles published by *Minzoku Taiwan,* there were never clear discussions or definitions given for this term. Rather, it was always implicitly suggested, in the discussions surrounding the studies of folklore and ethnography as disciplines, that the subjects of the study would have been customs and practices native to the people of the study. Namely, it was never something comparable to the "native-place literature" promoted in Manchukuo during the 1940s, but much more subtle and nuanced (Duara 2003).

4. The Japanese government-general of Taiwan, under the supervision of chief of civil affairs Goto Shimpei (1857–1929), began to organize island-wide surveys of local customs, languages, and legal practices from 1900. This massive body of data was published as the series for "old customs of Taiwan" *(Taiwan no kanshū),* and later, fieldwork and surveys conducted among the aboriginal tribes were also published as "old customs of the savages" *(Banzoku kanshū kiji).* Compiled by groups of semiofficial writers and intellectuals who acquired their sources from the Qing records, accounts made by European missionaries, and some oral interviews made during field trips, the set of records for "old customs"

of Taiwan continued to serve as the most comprehensive and referenced material for colonial governance until the end of Japanese colonial period (see also Chang 2006).

5. Folklore studies in Japan was never officially established as an academic discipline until 1958. Yanagita Kunio turned the living room of his house into a studio for students to discuss folklore from 1927, and for the next three decades, folklore studies in Japan has remained in a particular status as an "amateur's discipline," or as adequately defined by Alan Christy (2012), a "discipline on foot."

6. The actual questions and the identity of the reader were never specified in this letter, and only the title mentioned that this was "in answer to a reader's question." It is reasonable to assume that, given the unique subject matter of folklore and ethnologic studies, both Taiwanese and Japanese readers would have been questioning the purpose and methodology adopted by authors for *Minzoku Taiwan*. In another announcement issued by the editorial board to the readers published one year after, the relevance of folklore studies to "greater East Asian folklore studies" was brought up, obviously to justify their purposes under the assimilation policy (Editorial Team 1944).

7. This characteristic of *minzokugaku*/native ethnology in Japan was made most explicit in the discussions about if, or how, *minzokugaku* could be applied to countries other than Japan. Although scholars who participated in the discussions held ambivalent views as to whether Japan's *minzokugaku* should have been a "one-nation science," most of them agreed that the development of *minzokugaku* in Japan could help elevate the nation from its originally "marginal" position to the position of a "leader" in Western-centric discourses about advancement of cultures and civilizations (Christy 2012, 135–55).

8. Part of the content of the exhibition—including the items and documents exhibited—was recorded in an exhibition catalog titled *Taiwan shiryō shūsei* (Collection of Taiwan's historical materials) (Taiwan Bunka Sanbyakunen Kinenkai 1931) compiled by the curators of the exhibition, who were members of the network of either amateur collectors or official/academic researchers in the emerging field of archaeology and anthropology.

9. The "historical records" section of the exhibition was basically cataloged in full in *Taiwan shiryō shūsei*.

10. As Evan Dawley (2019) pointed out, the characteristics of Japan's settler community in Jilong contributed significantly to the formation of local identity. Part of his analysis elaborated on how the narratives for "local culture" and "local history" constructed by Japanese settlers

in Jilong became the object of collective discontent among Taiwanese communities, who began to recognize the existence of "Taiwanese local identity."

11. A famous cultural figure from one of Shilin's most prestigious and ancient families, Mr. Yang has been involved with the publication of *Minzoku Taiwan* since the first issue by sending to the editors his comments on the founding principle of the journal. After seeing "notes from the editors" in the first issue, Yang wrote to *Taiwan Nichinichi Shinpō* expressing his doubts regarding the sincerity of the editors' attitude and questioned if Kanaseki's editorial statement—an open admittance of the "inevitable" disappearance of local customs—was a sign of disbelief and lack of understanding of the cultural significance of local customs. However, satisfied with Kanaseki's response published in the follow-up issue, Yang was convinced the editors—including Kanaseki—shared with him a kindred spirit with a "love" of customs and traditions and promised to offer his support for the journal. Thus, two months later, when attending the Shilin cultural exhibition, the editors of *Minzoku Taiwan* asked for Yang's help to compile a special issue dedicated to studies of Shilin. The Shilin special issue, coedited by Yang, was to become the first of the "special issue" series that featured cultural and historical studies surrounding a special theme proposed by either the editors or corresponding writers.

12. After the end of colonial rule, the two continued to play active roles in the intellectual communities of studies of Taiwan history and joined the Department of History at National Taiwan University.

13. Korea and Taiwan both witnessed two waves of native-place or nativist literature movements in the twentieth century, one around the 1930s, the other roughly during the 1960s to 1970s. The movements in both colonies shared another similarity in that the nativist literature movements initiated by local (Taiwanese and Korean) writers in their colonies were both aiming to be experimental projects for literary realism, as works depicting the everyday, real-life experiences of local people living under colonial rule necessarily involved descriptions of oppression and exploitation enforced by the colonial government. Resistant by nature, the nativist movements in colonial Korea and Taiwan were both inherited by postcolonial writers as well. The postwar nativist movements in Korea and Taiwan within the context of the Cold War, however, diverged in their central agenda—for Koreans, the postwar cultural productions that revisited the theme of nativism were part of a larger project for the review and reexamination of colonial history, whereas for activists in Taiwan, the postwar nativist movement dealt mainly with the issue

of Chinese (vs. Taiwanese) identity. For analysis of Korea's postcolonial nativist movement, see An (2018).

■ WORKS CITED

Abe, Akiyoshi. 1942. "Shirin No Chimei" [Shilin's old names]. *Minzoku Taiwan* 2, no. 2: 13.

An, Jinsoo. 2018. *Parameters of Disavowal: Colonial Representation in South Korean Cinema* (1st ed.). Berkeley: University of California Press.

Barclay, Paul D. 2010. "An Historian among the Anthropologists: The Inō Kanori Revival and the Legacy of Japanese Colonial Ethnography in Taiwan." *Japanese Studies* 21, no. 2: 117–36.

Chang, Lung-chih. 2006. "From 'Old Customs' to 'Folklore': Modern Japanese Knowledge Production and Cultural Politics in Colonial Taiwan." *NTU Studies in Taiwan Literature* 2: 33–58.

Chou, Wan-yao. 1999. "Education and National Identity in Colonial Taiwan: The Case of 'National Language' Books, 1923–1937." *Taiwan Historical Research* 4, no. 2: 37–38.

Christy, Alan. 2012. *A Discipline on Foot: Inventing Japanese Native Ethnography, 1910–1945*. Lanham, Md.: Rowman and Littlefield.

Dawley, Evan N. 2019. *Becoming Taiwanese: Ethnogenesis in a Colonial City, 1880s–1950s*. Cambridge, Mass.: Harvard University Asia Center.

Duara, Prasenjit. 2003. *Sovereignty and Authenticity: Manchukuo and the East Asian Modern*. Lanham, Md.: Rowman and Littlefield.

Editorial Team. 1943. "Tenshin." *Minzoku Taiwan* 3, no. 5: 21.

Editorial Team. 1944. [Announcement]. *Minzoku Taiwan* 4, no. 5: 1.

Fei, Xiaotong. 1992. "Special Characteristics of Rural Society." In *From the Soil: The Foundations of Chinese Society—A Translation of Xiangtu Zhongguo*, translated by Gary G. Hamilton and Zheng Wang, 37–44. Berkeley: University of California Press.

Harootunian, H. D. 1990. "Disciplining Native Knowledge and Producing Place: Yanagita Kunio, Origuchi Shinobu, Takata Yasuma." In *Culture and Identity: Japanese Intellectuals during the Interwar Years*, edited by Thomas Rimer, 99–127. Princeton, N.J.: Princeton University Press.

Higashikata, Takayoshi. 1941. "'Jia ba mei' to 'Kyō wa'" ["Are you full?" and "Good day"]. *Minzoku Taiwan* 1, no. 5: 19–20.

Huntington, Ellsworth. 1927. *The Character of Races as Influenced by Physical Environment, Natural Selection and Historical Development*. New York: Scribner's.

Ikeda, Toshio. 1982. "Shokuminchika Taiwan no Minzoku Zas'shi" [Taiwan's folklore journals under colonial rule]. *Taiwan Kin-Gendaishi Kenkyū* 4: 169–77.

Kanaseki, Takeo. 1941. "Foreword." *Minzoku Taiwan* 1, no. 1: 1.

Lau, D. C., trans. 2003. *Mencius*. Hong Kong: Chinese University Press.

Lian, Heng. 1957. *Taiwan yu dian II* [Dictionary of Taiwanese dialect II]. Taibei: Zhonghua Congshu Weiyuanhui.

Liao, Han-chen. 1942. "'Li Jia Ba Mei' Ni Tsuite" [Discussions regarding "Are you full?"]. *Minzoku Taiwan* 2, no. 2: 26–28.

Li Shi Xing Hua. 1943. "Yangnu Jueshu"/"Yōjo Kakusho" [Confessions from an awakened adopted girl]. *Minzoku Taiwan* 3, no. 11: 32–33.

Okada, Yuzuru. 1941. "Li Jia Ba Mei" [Are you full?]. *Minzoku Taiwan* 1, no. 6: 17.

Pan, Guangdan. 1928. "Ziran Taotai yu Zhongguo Minzuxing" [Natural selection and the character of Chinese race]. *Xin Yue* 1, no. 6.

Sand, Jordan. 2003. *House and Home in Modern Japan: Architecture, Domestic Space, and Bourgeois Culture, 1880–1930*. Cambridge, Mass.: Harvard University Asia Center.

Taiwan Bunka Sanbyakunen Kinenkai. 1931. *Taiwan Shiryō Shūsei*. Tainan: Taiwan Bunka Sanbyakunen Kinenkai.

Tsao, Yung-ho. 1941a. Foreword to "Shirin no Densetsu" [Shilin's legends]. *Minzoku Taiwan* 1, no. 6: 24.

Tsao, Yung-ho. 1941b. "Shilin tingshu" [Listening to Stories in Shilin]. *Minzoku Taiwan* 1, no. 6: 44–45.

Watsuji, Tetsuro. 1988. *Climate and Culture: A Philosophical Study*. Translated by Geoffrey Bownas. New York: Greenwood Press.

Young, Louise. 2013. *Beyond the Metropolis: Second Cities and Modern Life in Interwar Japan*. Berkeley: University of California Press.

LILY W. LUO

Intimacies of the Future: Techno-Orientalism, All-under-Heaven (Tian-Xia 天下), and Afrofuturism

ON JUNE 23, 1982, Vincent Chin, a Chinese American man, was beaten to death in Michigan by two white men who mistook him for being Japanese and blamed him for the decline of U.S. automobile factories.[1] The militaristic fear of a Japanese takeover during World War II had turned into economic anxiety about Japanese cars taking over the U.S. automobile industry (Choy 1987). Three days later, on June 25, 1982, *Blade Runner* was in theaters across the United States. Set in an imagined 2019 Los Angeles that is clearly Orientalized, the set of *Blade Runner* was filled with looming images of Japanese corporations. The world of *Blade Runner* betrayed that fear on the screens, but the brutal murder of Vincent Chin was that fear made alive.

The film's production executive, Katherine Haber, remarked that they tried to create a "multi-national, multi-racial society" where they had tons of "punks, Blacks, and Mexicans . . . a mélange of every part of society you can imagine" (Yu 2008, 55). The actual makeup of background actors on the streets challenges this assertion. As many Asian American theorists have noted, the Orientalized dystopia of productions like *Blade Runner* (1982), *The Matrix* (1999), *Cloud Atlas* (2012), and *Altered Carbon* (2018) betray a techno-Orientalist imagination of the future while at the same time cutting Black or Mexican characters out of that future altogether (Locke 2009). Despite the production's stated intentions, the imagined world of *Blade Runner* reveals a much deeper and perhaps subconscious fear of Asia and Asians while simultaneously contributing to the erasure of Black people from science fiction. If techno-Orientalism reveals white anxieties about Asia's technological and economic rise, Afrofuturists argue that the invisibility of Black actors in science fiction reveals the inability of the white imagination to conceive of the survival of Blackness into the future.

So, what will the future actually look like? Or better yet, what *could* it look like? At a time when the future of the globe seems uncertain, securing capital, borders, and power seems to be the main focus of speculation, especially within the field of international relations (IR). In this article, I bring together the study of speculative fiction and the field of IR to highlight how our imaginations of the future contain both the blueprint of global systems of oppression and the keys to destroying them. Techno-Orientalism and Afrofuturism, alongside All-under-Heaven (Tian-Xia 天下), a reemergent Chinese geopolitical philosophy, are speculative theories of the future that can help us understand historically who has claimed a monopoly over modernity, who has been shut out, and who are trying to theorize their way into it today.[2] I use Lisa Lowe's framework of intimacies to link these seemingly unconnected topics and transgress geographical and academic borders with colonial valances. Lowe's exploration of the linear progress narrative which Western liberal philosophy has long relied on to justify its attempts at global domination plays a central role in my reading of speculative fiction productions and IR theory. As I move though an introduction to and close reading of techno-Orientalism, Tian-Xia, and Afrofuturism, I assess the extent to which techno-Orientalism, Tian-Xia, and Afrofuturism offer visions for the future that either reinscribe or try truly to depart from the speculations of Western modernity.

■ INTIMACIES OF THE FUTURE

A crucial theme of Lisa Lowe's 2015 book *Intimacies of Four Continents* is the importance of paying attention to understudied connections between disciplines and geographic areas of study. For those who are interested in the changing scope of the multidisciplinary study of "Asia" and "Asian America," *Intimacies* significantly expanded the study of Global Asias and broke down all kinds of disciplinary boundaries in the study of geography, literature, history, and political science. Joanna Tidy and Joe Turner's (2020, 132) article "Intimate International Relations of Museums: A Method" turns to Lowe's framework of intimacies to note that "intimacy helps question the division of the world into domestic/international, local/global and complicates common sense understandings of the 'far' and 'near' and 'past' and 'present.'" Lowe complicates and transgresses these divisions as she delves into the British colonial archives to expose the intentional divisions imposed on differently racialized groups throughout the colonized world. She proposes an emphasis on "a constellation of asymmetrical and unevenly legible 'intimacies'" which serve to "unsettle the dominant notion of intimacy" and "involves considering scenes of close connection and relation to a global geography that one more often conceived [of] in terms of vast spatial distances" (Lowe 2015, 18). Inspired by this approach, I attempt to knit together the vast spatial distances between the fields of IR, Asian American studies, contemporary Chinese political philosophy, speculative fiction, and critical Black futures to break open imaginations of the future that resist linear logics of progress and conventional ideas of modernity. This not only allows for dialogue between these disciplines but also emphasizes the liberatory significance of doing so. By linking IR theory and speculative fiction, we can begin to observe the ways pop culture both expresses and influences how citizens anticipate their own nation's future.

In this article, I build on the work of critical and global IR theory scholars whose writings speak to questions of modernity, racism within IR, and the broader movements to challenge the Eurocentric foundations of the field itself.[3] I hope to cut through the "great powers" debate that often dominates discussions of the relationship between China and the United States to get at underlying visions of the future that exist both within and outside a binary understanding of "East" and "West."[4] I also seek to contribute to the growing literature about "everyday IR" that is moving the field away from the study of state behavior to pay more attention to how regular citizens imagine—through everyday interactions, mass media, art—the future of global relations.[5]

In trying to explore the connection between politics and speculative fiction, starting from the study of techno-Orientalism makes sense because many Asian American theorists have already made the link between speculative fiction, racial politics, and global affairs. The study of techno-Orientalism claims that, historically, the genre of speculative fiction has largely portrayed a future that can only legitimately belong to the "West," with the United States being the current heir to that imagined geography. They argue that the often-Orientalized aesthetic of the future found within seminal speculative fiction productions betrays a much deeper Western fear of losing its supposed monopoly on the future. David Roh, Betsy Huang, and Greta Niu (2015, 2) describe techno-Orientalism as the "phenomenon of imagining Asia and Asians in hypo- or hyper-technological terms in cultural productions and political discourse," which they argue is an "expressive vehicle for [white] aspirations and fears" about the imagined "East" taking over. Given that this analysis comes primarily out of literary studies, I make the link between their questions about Asian representation in speculative fiction to the foundational questions of political science, specifically IR. By bringing in Lowe's work on liberalism, I seek to make explicit the link between studies of techno-Orientalism and the linear liberal progress narrative. This is especially important as it relates to Afrofuturists' critique of the invisibility of Black characters in speculative fiction.

While older techno-Orientalist films betrayed an underlying anxiety about 1980s Eastern capitalism exemplified by Japan's economic growth, China's rise in the twenty-first century poses an even deeper threat to the idea that legitimate progress can happen only within the constructs of Western liberalism and free market capitalism. Although this essay analyzes the specific geopolitical theory of Tian-Xia, as a way to link IR theory to the study of speculative fiction, the recent rise in literature on "Sino-futurism" is definitely related to the topics addressed in this article and warrants deeper analysis.

Tian-Xia (天下), commonly translated to "All-under-Heaven," tries to wrest the future away from the U.S. Empire and ostensibly imagines a future that could actually belong to the entire world collectively. I mainly draw on Zhao Tingyang's work on Tian-Xia, which argues that a turn to Chinese philosophy does not only benefit China (Zhao 2006, 2009, 2012, 2021). Zhao takes a concept that gained prominence in the Zhou dynasty more than three thousand years ago and argues for its increasing relevance in modern global politics. Literally translated, Tian-Xia refers to the entire earth, meaning the universe or the whole world. It can also mean the "hearts of the people" or the "general will of the people" (Zhao 2006, 30). Historically, it also referred to all the lands, spaces, and peoples that were under the rule of the emperor of China, who had received the Mandate of Heaven. Zhao's contemporary vision for this concept, however, is not dependent on a Chinese emperor ruling the world:

> The conceptually defined Empire of All-under-Heaven does not mean a country at all but an institutional world instead. And it expects a world/society instead of nation/states. All-under-Heaven is a deep concept of the world, defined by the trinity of the geographical, psychological, and political worlds. (30)

This is the updated Tian-Xia that Zhao champions: an ethical and/or political vision of a world institution or a universal system for the world. My inclusion of Tian-Xia in this article is meant to contribute to the larger turn within Asian American studies toward the study of Global Asias and to point out that the "Western" gaze is not the only gaze relevant to the study of IR today. Despite the various articles that have been written about China's rise, many critical scholars note that Western IR frameworks have been slow to catch up to prominent IR theories coming out of China itself. I argue that Tian-Xia, like other political theories of global order, engages in a quintessential element of speculative fiction: world building. What sets speculative fiction apart from other kinds of fiction is that the world in which it is set has some core element that differs from the one in which we are currently living. I argue that reading IR theory as speculative fiction allows us to see how it creates an image of the world as much as it proposes to describe it. Through this lens, the question then becomes, what kind of different world does Tian-Xia imagine, and does it actually radically differ from the one in which we live today?

Reading Tian-Xia, and IR theory more generally, as speculative fiction brings up useful questions about the fundamental purpose of theory itself. Is it to create a "realistic" model of human affairs, or is it to articulate a "normative" vision for an ideal world? Whose "normative" vision has been deemed universal, and whose visions relegated to the realm of the particular? To answer these questions, I propose turning to Afrofuturism as a prime example of a speculative arts genre that should be seen as IR theory. Zhao argues that Western liberal IR theories have often made the mistake of conflating universal interest with the narrow interests of the few, and Afrofuturism certainly has much to contribute to that conversation. Afrofuturist art and the study of critical Black futures offers meaningful resistance to the dominant narratives regarding modernity and liberalism that have long sought hegemonic power over our imaginations of global futures. Whereas both Western liberalism and Tian-Xia claim to be theories of the future that do not privilege a particular social or political location, Afrofuturism is an artistic and philosophical movement that chooses to center Blackness specifically. A deeper dive into the theories and recurring questions of this speculative arts movement can reveal unique insights if our goal is to imagine our way past a hierarchical global order. Reynaldo Anderson (2016, 230) writes in "Afrofuturism 2.0 and the Black Speculative Arts Movement,"

> Afrofuturism is the current name for a body of systematic Black speculative thought originating in the 1990s as a response to postmodernity that has blossomed into a global movement the last five years. Although contemporary Black speculative thought has roots at the nexus of 19th century scientific racism, technology, and the struggle for African self-determination and creative expression, it has now matured into an emerging global phenomenon.

Given that Western imaginations of Africa and the Black diaspora have long linked Blackness to the very antithesis of modernity, Afrofuturism comes at the question of futurity from the positional standpoint of those who have been shut out of the future altogether. As Phillip Butler (2021, 3) points out in the recently published anthology titled *Critical Black Futures: Speculative Theories and Explorations,* "mainstream futuristic depictions are fraught with extravagant designer technologies, ecological possibilities, and scientific explorations that often exclude, relegate, or invisibilize Blackness into irrelevance/obscurity or extinction." Because of this, Afrofuturism offers a radical departure from the "great powers" debate ever present in IR and the linear progress narrative within Western liberalism that is constantly adjudicating who can or cannot be the next protagonist on the stage of world history. By looking at Afrofuturism in the context of IR, we open up a whole new set of questions. Instead of the ever-looming IR question "who will be the world's next hegemon?" seeing Afrofuturism as IR invites us to ask different questions. What will the future look like for Black people? What must it look like if Black people are to thrive? Why is it important to attend to the future of Black people if we want to build a future without domination for everyone? If mainstream techno-Orientalist speculative fictions reflect the dominant anxieties of the U.S. Empire, Afrofuturist creations try to imagine a future that is not foreclosed but rather radically open.

The main argument of this article is that these three seemingly unrelated examples are all, at their core, attempts to imagine the future.[6] Lowe (2015) points out that one of the core tenets of liberal philosophy is a linear narrative of human progress. In that story of human history, certain cultures and peoples are categorized not only as less than human but also as less developed or belonging to a different time. Terms like *backward* and *barbaric* evoke not only a sense of inferiority but also a sense of not quite belonging to the present or the future. Lowe's book delves into the political consequence of categorizing the histories of multiple continents into neat and separate categories. She notes that the connections between the four continents and the differently racialized groups throughout the colonized world are underrepresented in history because those different groups served "specific Imperial functions and purposes" (173). Thus she sees the project of uncovering intimacies as crucial to breaking down those intellectual barriers set up by imperial necessity. Where Lowe finds this separation physically represented in documents filed separately in the British colonial archives, today we can see similar distinctions operating within the departments of the U.S. Empire's State Department bureaus or Central Intelligence Agency mission centers (Barnes 2021). By putting the studies of techno-Orientalism, Tian-Xia, and Afrofuturism into conversation with one another, I am hoping to continue Lowe's work by uncovering the intimacies not only of the past but also of the future.[7]

■ TECHNO-ORIENTALISM AND THE LINEAR PROGRESS NARRATIVE

The future that *Blade Runner* imagined did not come true literally, but the fear of the "East" and its potential to surpass the "West" as a new center of power has stayed relevant well into the twenty-first century.[8] China has replaced Japan as the main focal point of Western anxiety, especially from the perspective of the United States. In 2020, Donald Trump's rhetoric about the global Covid-19 pandemic brought the fear of the Orient into new forms with phrases like "Kung Flu" and "Wuhan Virus" specifically racializing its origins in China (*Guardian* 2020). Building on insights from scholars of techno-Orientalism, I argue that art, especially speculative fiction, is not only expressive of existing political dynamics but also a creator of it. If IR theory is fundamentally about trying to make sense of the global relations to come, then what is speculative fiction if not that for the general public? The pervasive use of techno-Orientalist imagery in popular speculative fiction films and television captures, through specifically East Asian aesthetics, both the obsession with and fear of the rise of Japan in the twentieth century and China in the twenty-first. This fear relates to the linear narratives of progress that had dominated the liberal political theory of the British Empire from the eighteenth century onward and more recently the liberalism espoused by the U.S. Empire. These definitions of human progress paint a picture of a universal linear path toward higher levels of morality, reason, and, ultimately, liberal democracy (Fukuyama 1992; Kant et al. 2006).

One of the points that Lowe's *Intimacies* highlights is that for all its universalizing statements regarding human progress, this "narrative of freedom overcoming enslavement . . . at once denies colonial slavery, erases the seizure of lands from Native peoples, displaces migrations and connections across continents" (Lowe 2015, 3). For Lowe, these erasures are no simple oversight. She argues that the division of subjects and societies between rational human beings capable of progress and those who were, in the words of John Stuart Mills, "unfit for liberty" was in fact a signature feature of "liberal modes of distinction" (16). These linear narratives reveal a future that is ostensibly for everyone but, at its core, actually only for those who follow in the exact footsteps of highly industrialized and majority-white Western European and North American democratic nation-states.[9]

This contradiction is one that consistently shows up in Western speculative fiction productions. Though some IR theorists value the genre of speculative fiction precisely for the radical conditions of possibility that exist in its imagination, those same possibilities are often denied to those deemed outside of modernity. It is telling that in a genre where anything is possible, where people can be cloned and cars can fly, it had often been hard to find a single Black lead. In a genre where the future could look like anything, it had consistently looked like a bad copy of downtown Tokyo or Shanghai. Whereas Edward Said's (1978) seminal book *Orientalism* noted that, historically, the study of the Orient situated the East in the past as a backward, antiprogressive, and primitive place, techno-Orientalism suggests the opposite: that the East is too forward, too technological, too robotic. In techno-Orientalist fantasies, it is common for the viewer to discover some kind of moral decay hidden under the shiny technological advances. The underlying message: these advances have come at a cost. Japan's or China's uniquely Asian brand of progress is not the correct kind of human or moral progress. There is something uniquely dangerous about Eastern progress, something that threatens to infect the United States if left unchecked. The past fears of "Chinamen" dwelling in opium dens spreading moral decay passed through the model minority filter and turned into Chinese spies slithering their way into U.S. labs (Ruwitch 2022; Prasso 2021)—yellow peril turned yellow technological peril.

The hypervisibility of East Asians and the invisibility of Black actors in Western speculative fiction at their core betray an underlying assumption about a linear model of human progress that touts Western liberalism as advancement. Despite the significant economic and technological rise of certain East Asian nation-states, such as China, Japan, Korea, and Singapore, the future cannot belong to them. Their progress cannot be considered legitimate human progress because they are not "real" humans. By setting up metrics to determine humanity and progress that propose universal relevance but ultimately monopolize it for white supremacy, the linear progress narrative also claims a monopoly on the future. The implication is clear. If we allow the "East" to continue advancing, there will be no future at all. Earth itself will become uninhabitable, not because of Western capitalism, but because of Eastern capitalism. As the United States' role of sole superpower and rightful inheritor of Euro-modernity becomes threatened in the twenty-first century, techno-Orientalist language can be found most intensely directed at what it perceives to be its main rival on the world stage: China.

If the United States was the inheritor of Britain's, and more broadly Western Europe's, hegemonic power in the twentieth century, the specter of China's imagined future haunts the discourse of twenty-first-century global order. China's rise poses an existential threat to the United States, in particular the tenuous hegemony that it built in the aftermath of World War II and the dissolution of the Soviet Union. Chengxin Pan and Emilian Kavalski (2018, 290) note that "China's emergence into an increasingly powerful and consequential global actor in international relations" is studied "primarily [through] applying existing theories to it in order to explain its policy and practical implications" rather than as a theory-*generating* event. In speculative fiction terms, China's rise can only be assimilated into preexisting narratives about the future rather than an event that could potentially generate whole new plotlines altogether. The protagonist of human history has already been cast; the only other role left is the role of the antagonist. Pan and Kavalski note that this is due to Western IR's tendency to try to assimilate "raw data" from other parts of the world into preexisting Western IR frameworks, which are deemed universal:

> That is, when it encounters "other" concepts, practices, and experience of the "international," IR more often than not reverts to the prism of its Columbus syndrome: either it recognizes them as narratives about world politics but does not acknowledge that they are different; or acknowledges that they are different, but refuses to admit that they are part of IR (thereby relegating them to fields such as cultural studies, area studies, and anthropology). (296)

The dominance of U.S. and Eurocentric IR frameworks mirrors the narrow definitions of progress that scholars of techno-Orientalism critique. Pan and Kavalski see China's rise on the global stage as one that should be studied as a "paradigm-shattering phenomenon in global life that, on the one hand, requires fresh and innovative theorizing in and beyond IR and, on the other hand, potentially offers new insights for us to rethink world politics more broadly" (289). This rethinking of world politics at once provides new dimensions to the field of IR and has the potential to deconstruct it altogether. If techno-Orientalist imagery betrays an underlying assumption that the future can only legitimately belong to the United States and its vision of a liberal world order, how are Chinese politicians and philosophers making sense of their place in world politics? If mainstream Western speculative fiction productions are a form of IR theory, then can we view Chinese IR theory as a form of speculative fiction? If techno-Orientalism represents the "Western" gaze toward the "East," then how is the "East" gazing back?

■ BACK TO THE FUTURE: ALL-UNDER-HEAVEN (TIAN-XIA 天下) FOR THE TWENTY-FIRST CENTURY

In the discussion of China's twenty-first-century rise in global power, it is important to understand that much of the political elite's rhetoric around China's global role references China's past as a regional hegemon that had been weakened by the previous "百年国耻," translated as "A Century of Humiliation." Xi Jinping (2021) references this at the ceremony marking the centenary of the Chinese Communist Party and proclaims that a "national rejuvenation" is "the greatest dream of the Chinese people and the Chinese nation." In his article "The Rise of Chinese Exceptionalism," Zhang Feng (2013) identifies several major themes that had emerged between 2005 and 2010 within Chinese foreign relations ideology, all of which play a role in the vision Xi articulated in 2021. Among these ideological themes is the idea of "Great Power Reformism," whereby

> a rising China cannot just be a great power of material strength, which would make it no different from other great powers in history; instead, it must also become a "knowledge producer," by digging deep into China's traditional historical and cultural resources, so as to be able to develop unique qualities for playing its role in the new era. (311)

Many believe that the way forward for China as an emerging great power is to look to ancient concepts like Tian-Xia for philosophical guidance.

Core to Zhao Tingyang's argument that a contemporary articulation of Tian-Xia is the best way forward for the global community is his criticism of the current Western conception of the international. Zhao (2006) argues that unlike Western political theory, which ultimately takes the nation-state as the biggest unit of analysis, in the framework of Tian-Xia, the world in its entirety takes precedence. Indeed, he claims, "Western imaginations of the world are nothing higher and greater than international alliances or unions of nations/states, not going beyond the framework of nations/states" (30). If national sovereignty is the highest goal of a peaceful world order, then it would make sense that a dystopic future would include the Orientalization of spaces like Los Angeles or San Francisco because that would mean that the "sovereignty" of the United States had been threatened. It is ironic that the vision displayed in techno-Orientalist productions is precisely the one that has already happened the world over, though it is the rest of the world that has been overtaken by U.S. American corporations like McDonalds and advertisements featuring Eurocentric beauty standards. From Zhao's revived Tian-Xia perspective,

> our supposed world is now still a non-world, for the world has not yet been completed in its full sense. World institution and full popular support are still missing. We are talking nonsense about the world, for the world has not yet been fulfilled with its world-ness. (30)

Tian-Xia as a philosophy is supposed to provide a path to true world-ness by being a unique alternative to the Westphalian nation-state system. Interestingly, "world building" is actually one of the central tenets of the genre of speculative fiction itself. Audiences often comment on the skill or lack of world building as a key element of determining the quality of a work of speculative fiction. The same could be said for IR theories of the future. How well thought out is this particular system of global governance? Even if it marks a radical departure from the way things currently are, does it follow its own internal system of logic? What are the core differences that make the world of the story/theory different from our own?

Zhao identifies two key elements of Chinese philosophy that he believes positions it as a compelling counternarrative to the competitive, nation-state-centered model on which Western IR is founded. First, relationships are foregrounded in politics rather than the individual. Second, the ultimate goal of politics is not "freedom" or even "peace" but "harmony." In this, relationships matter more in the work of politics than abstract ideals of "liberty" or "freedom." This stands in direct contrast with the narrative of liberal progress that dominates Western understandings of the future as a linear progression toward goals like increased freedom for individual people or nation-states. Harmony, on the other hand, is not an end goal to be pursued but rather a balance to be constantly attended to. Zhao notes that concepts like "freedom," while ostensibly framed as universal, really work to universalize the entire world into a narrow vision of Western modernity. World organizations like the United Nations, which are supposed to be the kind of world institutions that Tian-Xia calls for, in reality "[have] taken Oneness as a mission of western modernity to be accomplished" (Zhao 2006, 37). He points out that universalism is really a theory meant to "universalize the self instead of others, thus a sort of fundamentalism that insists on the ideology of making others the pagan" (37).

By contrast, Zhao's (2009) vision of Tian-Xia gestures toward a future that can belong collectively to the entire world by respecting all cultures and promoting cooperation for the common good. In setting up Tian-Xia as a meaningful alternative to Western liberal world order, Zhao's analysis of the unsustainability of prioritizing individual nation-state freedom over global harmony cuts to the core of some of the biggest questions in IR. Like Lowe, Zhao points out that the "universal" ideals of freedom supposedly espoused by Western nations like the United States actually closely resemble the imperialist systems of the past when put in practice. Zhao contends that "imperialism has definitely proven not to be a solution to the problems of world politics, since it is imposed on the world, rather than being of and for the world, or by the world" (6). For Zhao, a world theory is possible only when "universal wellbeing takes priority over that of the nation-state," a world theory that he believes Tian-Xia can provide (6).

■ GLOBAL HARMONY OR CHINESE EXCEPTIONALISM?

The image Zhao paints of a future world governed by the logic of Tian-Xia is clearly utopian. Yet, if we were to dig a little deeper into this utopian vision, it seems not to adequately address China's own historical and contemporary power. Korean scholar Jun-Hyeok Kwak (2021, 292) points out that Zhao's telling of history conspicuously leaves out the largely uneven power relations between China and its neighboring countries:

> At first sight, such advocacy of Chinese-style cosmopolitanism appears to be "egalitarian" in the sense that it is concerned with "diverse" or "plural" voices in international relations. However, it can hardly be denied that the advocates of Chinese-style cosmopolitanism do not pay appropriate attention to the problem of domination in the historical practices of tianxia in which China was placed at the center of a hierarchical world while neighboring countries were nothing but tributary states.

This unanswered question of domination leaves gaps in the world-building logics of Zhao's theory. Zhao *is* explicit that the historical conception of China being the center of the world does not have a place in this updated version of Tian-Xia. Kwak himself notes that there is nothing inherently parochial about the fact that Tian-Xia emerged in a Chinese context. However, he points out that Zhao also does not address the issue of domination directly:

> It is not because the world institution espoused through the notion of tianxia implicitly represents China as a new hegemon in world politics. It is because Chinese-style cosmopolitans do not provide us with a regulative

principle with which we can guard ourselves against the cultural as well as political domination of one state over other states. (Kwak 2021, 292)

Kwak's critique of Tian-Xia, taken alongside Xi Jinping's vision of a rejuvenation, raises some questions about Zhao's claims of the universal well-being that this theory could provide. His critique of the colonialist logic behind Western narratives of progress and modernity, while compelling, also serves narratively to create a contrast to a better, Chinese way of thinking about global relations. Though he is careful to note that China does not need to be the protagonist in this new story, it is clear that the United States, and the rest of the Western world, is the antagonist.

On its face, Tian-Xia represents a reimagination of the future that strongly opposes the universalizing rhetoric of Western liberalism. Tian-Xia positions itself as an "institutionalized system [that can] promote universal wellbeing, and not just the interests of some dominating nations" (Zhao 2009, 6). However, Zhao is conspicuously silent on who may be the authority in this new institutionalized world system. Kwak's (2021) work, similar to Lowe's, exposes the contradictions between the philosophical ideas of certain schools of thought and the ways they have been implemented in practice throughout history. These contradictions in Western liberalism and Tian-Xia center around questions of domination in the global sphere. As Kwak points out, "without an equal discursive stance, a cooperative relationship or normative Confucian justification can easily degenerate into domination" (294). In such cases, "the notion of tianxia would be just another normatively parochial value" (293), not at all the radical alternative to global order that Zhao imagines. Although Zhao's critique of Western liberalism and its narrow understanding of global order has merit, without addressing the problem of domination head-on, his renewed version of Tian-Xia is in danger of replicating the same trap that he accuses Western liberalism of creating: mistaking one's own interests with the interests of the whole world.

■ **AFROFUTURISM AND THE BLACK SPECULATIVE ARTS MOVEMENT**

Whereas East Asian aesthetics have become a stylistic trope for the future, African aesthetics have been persistently linked to the past or relegated to somewhere outside history altogether. For this very reason, many Black creators have been drawn to the genre of speculative fiction as a way of reclaiming modernity and futurity. Inspired by "afro-futurist artists and writers who highlight the need for Black people to claim their place," in 2017, Alisha Wormsley created a billboard installation that displayed the words "THERE ARE BLACK PEOPLE IN THE FUTURE" in white text against a black background in East Liberty, Pittsburgh, a neighborhood that was being gentrified (Wormsley 2018). When the billboard was removed by the city because of landlord complaints, community members rallied around both the billboard and the sentiment, replicating its words in Pittsburgh and multiple other cities. Much like the statement "Black Lives Matter," the assertion that there are indeed Black people in the future is only radical because we live in a world that consistently separates Blackness from narratives of progress, projects of modernity, and imaginations of futurity. To open up the future, we must start from those who have been relegated to the past. If we want to rethink our imagination of the future, then we must shatter the constructs that reduce Blackness to a past stage of human development.

First written down in a 1994 interview Mark Dery conducted with Samuel R. Delany, Greg Tate, and Tricia Rose, the term *Afrofuturism* itself is one that has been retroactively placed upon writers like Octavia Butler or the famous experimental musician Sun Ra. Dery noted that while few Black authors were prominent in mainstream science fiction at the time, the genre itself seemed perfectly suited to explore the themes of alienation, abduction, and estrangement that were commonplace tropes in both the genre and the Black diasporic experience. He grapples with the contradictions that come with the very notion of Afrofuturism:

> Can a community whose past has been deliberately rubbed out, and whose energies have subsequently been consumed by the search for legible traces of its history, imagine possible futures? Furthermore, isn't the unreal estate of the future already owned by the technocrats, futurologists, streamliners, and set designers-white to a man-who have engineered our collective fantasies? (Dery 1994, 180)

Dery's observation that the unreal estate of the future seemed dominated by white imaginations echoes the same concerns that scholars of techno-Orientalism identify in mainstream speculative fiction. The question of whether Black people can imagine the future given the erasure of their history has long since been answered. Many have also pointed out that the act of speculative imagination has always been part of Black survival and critical discourse.[10] In a conversation commemorating twenty-five years of Afrofuturism and Black speculative thought, Anderson notes,

> To be unfree and write about freedom—to imagine a utopia where black folks are free from bondage—was science fiction, it was speculative thought, even

though it wasn't necessarily canonized or characterized as such. (quoted in Barber 2018, 138)

While the term *Afrofuturism* originally appeared in an interview with African American artists and scholars, Afrofuturism has always been about transnational connections. Anderson asserts later in that same conversation, "If there's no Africa in your Afrofuturism, then you're doing somebody else's futurism" (quoted in Barber 2018, 140). After all, the linkage of Africa and Blackness with both an absence of history and the antithesis of futurity are global phenomenona.

Blackness as we understand it today originated with the rise of European colonialism and the transatlantic slave trade. Like the relations between different Indigenous nations that do not fit within liberal definitions of "nation" or "state," the Black diasporic experience is rarely included in the mainstream theories of IR. If, following Zhao's rearticulation of Tian-Xia, we were to rethink the "international" in "international relations," it would only be natural that we should pay attention to the past and present of the Black diaspora. After all, what could be more relevant to a reimagined "international relations" than the history of Blackness, which has been defined by the breaking of relations, the creation of new ones, and the formation of new nations within a nation? The project of expanding the study of IR must include a recognition of spaces where relations are happening outside of various nation-states' competition to be the next hegemonic world power. Zhao's utopian imagination of a world governed by the logics of Tian-Xia seems to gesture toward a different way of doing IR theory. Given China's historical role as a regional hegemon and the Chinese Communist Party's current ambitions to be perceived as a "better" world leader, Kwak's point about the lack of discussion of domination within Zhao's theories is not something we can gloss over.

The problem of domination is one that Afrofuturists face head-on. Liberation from domination is a particularly important theme within Afrofuturism. Ytasha Womack (2013, 9) sees it as "a way of imagining possible futures through a black cultural lens . . . as a way to encourage experimentation, reimagine identities, and activate liberation." In some cases, "it is a total re-envisioning of the past and speculation about the future rife with cultural critiques" that carries with it incredible hope and "expectation for transformative change" (42). Afrofuturism is not simply about increasing the representation of Black characters in speculative fiction. It is about challenging the way Black people's history has been portrayed and the deeper systems that have contributed to the erasure of Black characters from the future. As Anderson (2016, 230) proclaims, future-looking Black scholars, artists, and activists are not only reclaiming their right to tell their own stories, but also to critique the European/American digerati class of their narratives about cultural others, past, present and future and, challenging their presumed authority to be the sole interpreters of Black lives and Black futures.

This drive to expose the constructedness of the past and reshape our understanding of history is also reflected in Lowe's (2015) work. Lowe urges us to "defamiliariz[e] both the objects of the past and the established methods for apprehending that object" in order to make "possible alternative forms of knowing, thinking, and being" (137). Womack (2013, 153) believes that the path to undoing past harmful ways of relating to one another must come through "the power of thought, word, and the imagination" because they "can somehow transcend time." What connects the theory of Afrofuturists and scholars like Lowe is a shared project to reclaim the narratives of the past in order to reopen our imaginations of the future.

■ TOWARD AN AFROFUTURIST FEMINIST MANIFESTO

The political project and creativity found within Afrofuturism represents a powerful tool against the Western liberal vision of futurity. In such imaginations, whether in IR theory or speculative fiction, the protagonist of human history remains white. Like Alisha Wormsley's billboard art, Renina Jarmon's (n.d.) #Blackgirlsarefromthefuture seeks to recast who exactly belongs in the future. Jarmon's hashtag is not simply a fantastical statement but also a "brand, narrative, and oppositional standpoint for black girls." It emphasizes how Black women, by interacting with technology in innovative and unexpected ways that would later be adopted by the broader culture, have been pioneers in the digital space. On her website, she writes, "#Blackgirlsarefromthefuture because they were hashtagging *before* corporations knew what a hashtag was." According to Jarmon, Black girls are from the future because they are the creators of the world they want to see, and in those acts of creation, they "redefine culture and notions of Blackness for today and the future." The claims that Black people are in the future or that Black girls are from the future play two roles: it challenges the standard logics of Western philosophy and Western IR theory, which relegates Black people to the past while at the same time building up an alternative vision of the future.

In trying to grasp the importance of Jarmon's hashtag, it is important to understand it not only from an Afrofuturist lens but also a Black feminist one. After all, as Jarmon (n.d.) puts it, "Black Girls are from the

Future is a theory premised on the day to day lived experience of Black girls." In her chapter from *Critical Black Futures*, Caitlin O'Neill (2021) uses Jarmon's hashtag as an example to lay out the beginnings of an Afrofuturist Feminist Manifesto. In it, she calls back to the influential Combahee River Collective Statement to argue for the importance of Black women's speculative fiction:

> If, as the Combahee River Collective Statement asserts, freeing black women "would necessitate the destruction of all the systems of oppression" thus resulting in planet-wide liberation, then there is an urgent and present need for Black women's speculative fiction and thought that explores possible paths to liberation. (66)

The point articulated by the Combahee River Collective and other Black feminists is that because of Black women's position at the bottom of existing hierarchies, their struggle for freedom would necessarily destroy the whole system from the bottom up. Speculative fiction serves as an important tool for Black women's imagination: if the rules of *this* world have cast aside Black women's creativity and survival, then Afrofuturist feminists can use their imagination to build a *different* world altogether. It follows that Black women's speculative fiction has something to say not only about their own liberation but also about the collective well-being of the planet—a concern shared by Tian-Xia and other normative IR theories. O'Neill's Afrofuturist Feminist Manifesto links Black women's speculative fiction to both their own liberation and planet-wide liberation. Her point is that Black women's speculative fiction is integral to the creation of a world without the current oppressive hierarchies that dominate domestic and global politics. As she notes,

> in this way, #blackgirlsarefromthefuture takes on new meaning as black women and girls the world over imagine themselves as thriving, creating spaces where they are celebrated, engaging in an act of time travel and making present a world that does not yet exist. A world in which black women and femmes are safe and valued. A world yet to come. #Blackgirlsarefromthefuture because they have to be. (63)

What would such a world look like? A recent example of one such imagination comes from an episode of the TV show *Lovecraft Country*, developed by Misha Green. The episode "I Am" centers on Hippolyta, a recently widowed woman who is unexpectedly transported to another dimension while investigating the suspicious circumstances of her husband's death. Though Hippolyta had previously only been a supporting character on the show, this episode sinks into her inner life after she falls into a portal to another dimension. What follows is an extraordinary exploration of the limitations and radical possibilities of Black womanhood and motherhood.

At first, she finds herself trapped in a sterile white room, greeted by a tall Black being in a white spacesuit with a large Afro. The figure (named Beyond C'est) keeps repeating the same phrases: "You are not in a prison." "Where do you want to be?" "Name yourself." At first, Hippolyta is terrified and confused by this new place of possibility. But as she acclimates, she hastily utters the first idea of freedom she can think of: "I want to be dancing on the stage in Paris with Josephine Baker." Immediately, she is in that very place, surrounded by the hazy joy of the burlesque scene. The taste of this freedom prompts her to reflect on the life she had been living back in Chicago:

> All those years I thought I had everything I ever wanted, only to come here and discover that all I ever was, was the exact kind of Negro woman white folks wanted me to be. I feel like they just found a smart way to lynch me without me noticing a noose. . . . Sometimes I just, I wanna kill white folks. And it's not just them . . . I hate me, for letting them make me feel small. (Green 2020)

After her time with Josephine Baker, Hippolyta then transports to a female warrior camp, her old bedroom with her dead husband, and to new planets where she is allowed to freely roam as a scientist. Hippolyta's journeys through space, time, and reality represent the exploration of the confined pieces of her being that previously had been stifled by a white supremacist world. Her story, as a whole, explores the incredible possibilities of a reality where Black people may be free while simultaneously being a mirror to the ways our society has failed to imagine Black futures.

In the midst of white supremacy gone amok, the show takes us to outer galaxies and an alternate universe to center the spiritual, emotional, and spatial journey of a middle-aged Black woman who, up until this point, is defined mostly by her relationship to her husband and her daughter. O'Neill (2021, 63) delves into precisely why this kind of narrative choice matters:

> For if, as Walidah Imarisha claims, "Whenever we try to envision a world without war, without violence, without prisons, without capitalism, we are engaging in speculative fiction," then the act of a black woman choosing to enact self-care and advocacy, however briefly, is an act of speculative and science fiction.

This is true precisely because the world Hippolyta lived in actively sought to dictate the limits of her imagination and her future possibilities. That makes her act of cosmic and psychological exploration all the more powerful. Therein lies the valuable orientation of Afrofuturism. O'Neill challenges us to see that Black feminist Afrofuturism is linked not only to Black women's liberation but also to our imaginative capacity to envision a world without war, without violence, without prisons, and without capitalism. "I Am" challenges us to reexamine our relationship to Black women as well as Black women's relationships to themselves, and O'Neill posits that this holds a key to imagining a world without oppression or domination. After all, if we cannot imagine such a world, how can we really strive to fight for it?

The linkage of Black women's liberation with collective liberation is one that has thoroughly been explored in decades of Black feminist thought.[11] Afrofuturist feminist art utilizes a long history of speculative imagination to pose critical interventions into how we think about the future. Afrofuturist feminist art and theory allow us to come at questions of global futurity firmly rooted in the specific experiences of Black women while also gesturing toward a broader claim about planet-wide liberation. Afrofuturism offers a radically different orientation to the question of both futurity and belonging, one that uses time travel and interdimensional exploration to break open our imaginations—not only about advanced technologies but also, more importantly, about transformed relationships. Like the most powerful speculative fictions and philosophical theories, its most innovative works focus not on new technologies that will drastically reshape society but rather on the disruptive potential of reimagining our relationships with each other and ourselves.

■ TO INFINITY AND BEYOND

Using techno-Orientalism, Tian-Xia, and Afrofuturism as objects of analysis in this article serves two purposes. The first is to build on Lowe's intimacies framework and use it to draw out the intimacies of these differently located imaginations of the future. The second is to bring together the fields of IR theory and speculative fiction. It is meant to contribute to the growing IR literature that seeks to reimagine the "international" altogether and foreground the kinds of relationships that might be possible in such a reimagination. Techno-Orientalism betrays the underlying racism that continues to dominate imaginations of the future. In a time when the role of both U.S. American and Chinese global leadership is in flux, the introduction of Tian-Xia demonstrates that IR cannot conceptualize "China's rise" by recycling the same frameworks for thinking about "great power struggle." Its claim that the Western liberal order is not even a world yet, just a chaotic globe filled with individual nation-states all vying for dominance, with no regard for actual global order/harmony, is certainly compelling. At the same time, the problem of domination in the global sphere remains unaddressed in its utopian vision for the future. This is where Afrofuturism's orientation toward the future could greatly enhance IR's imagination of modernity/futurity, not as a space to be conquered or owned, but rather as a place of radical possibility[12]— possibility that depends less on a shiny new technological advancement and more on the transformation of human relations that will be needed for a less oppressive world. Afrofuturism represents a radical opening of imagination while at the same time not ignoring the oppression that Black people face. This boundary-less yet still centered aesthetic and orientation toward the future represents a way we, too, could approach the future of IR. If traditional IR theories are born out of the need to imagine victory for the state and the Empire, then perhaps Afrofuturism and other radical speculative fictions can provide the blueprint for imagining a future in which relation rather than victory is the ultimate goal. This future will not be easy to attain, nor is it guaranteed. But, to quote Baby Suggs from *Beloved*, with a little twist, the only future we can have is the future we can imagine; if we cannot see it, we will not have it.[13]

Lily Luo is a scholar, poet, and visual artist who is a PhD candidate at the University of Connecticut's Political Science department. She is currently working on a dissertation about the revolutionary legacy of Grace Lee Boggs and the power of embracing contradiction in political struggle.

■ NOTES

This article would not have been possible without help and encouragement from all my friends, colleagues, and mentors, in particular, Professor Terry Park, in whose class I first developed these ideas, and Professor Fred Lee, who has edited countless drafts of this article. A special thanks to all those who gave me thought-provoking and much-needed feedback at various Asian American and Africana studies conferences over the years.

1. In this article, I use the term *American* specifically to refer to the "United States of America" and not to the entire continents of North and South America. This is for purposes of legibility within the preestablished academic fields to which I refer, such as Asian American studies. However, I do want to acknowledge that this linguistic choice is made possible because of the United States' continued hegemonic power in the Americas, which warrants further reflection.

2. Taking Aimee Bahng's lead in *Migrant Futures*, I choose to use the term *speculative fiction* rather than *science fiction*, not to identify a genre wholly distinct from science fiction, but to use a more expansive term that might include related genres, such as fantasy, horror, and historical fiction, and that highlights the speculative mode of the "what if?" (Bahng 2018, 13).

3. Many authors have already addressed the issue of Western dominance in the study of IR and the realm of the "global" as a whole (Alejandro 2020; Anievas, Manchanda, and Shilliam 2015; Dussel and Mendieta 1996; Fonseca 2019; Kelley 2002; Linklater 1992; Mignolo 2011; Ní Mhurchú 2016; Shilliam 2011).

4. My work is inspired by many other thoughtful IR texts about China's growing global power (Ling et al. 2017; Pan and Kavalski 2018; Wang and Huters 2011).

5. There has been an expanding literature on the varied, unexpected places we might find IR theory (Sylvester 2009; Tétreault and Lipschutz 2009; Guillaume 2011).

6. Some notable articles and workshops do address the connections between these topics (McLeod 2013; Kaya Press 2021). A recent call for chapters for an upcoming second volume of *Techno-Orientalism* edited by David S. Roh, Betsy Huang, Greta Niu, and Christopher T. Fan is even specifically looking for works that are in dialogue with "Afrofuturism and indigenous futurisms," so clearly this intersection is gaining interest (Roh 2022).

7. Although it lies beyond the scope of this essay, I also have to note that we cannot talk of Afro-Asian solidarity without acknowledging the realities of China's unequal economic and political relations with various African states, most prominently with nations such as Kenya.

8. *East* and *West* here are in quotation marks as a nod toward the constructed nature of these geopolitical realms. It should be noted that Said's (1978) seminal work *Orientalism* primarily focused on British, French, and later American studies of what is now termed the "Middle East." Techno-Orientalism, on the other hand, while continuing the theoretical claims of Said, is focused on what had historically been deemed the "Far East," most predominantly China, Japan, and Korea.

9. Lowe's point here builds on the work of scholars like Cedric Robinson, Saidiya Hartman, Uday Singh Mehta, Paul Gilroy, Dipesh Chakrabarty, Saree Makdisi, Walter Mignolo, Susan Buck-Morss, Jodi A. Byrd, and others.

10. Butler (2021, 2) writes in the introduction to *Critical Black Futures*, "One of the underlying notions of this volume is that Black critical

discourse is steeped in the speculative. . . . Black critical discourse relies heavily on Black speculative imagination(s)."

11. Several compilations have been published that provide a thorough overview of the political stance of Black feminist thought, of which these are only a few (Hill Collins 1990; Taylor 2017; Smith 2000).

12. In fact, some IR theorists are already starting to think about the aesthetics and design of futurity and are pushing the field to critically engage with a diverse array of subjects (Austin and Leander 2021).

13. This is a play on a quotation from Toni Morrison's (2004, 103) book *Beloved* that goes as follows: "She told them that the only grace they could have was the grace they could imagine. That if they could not see it, they would not have it."

■ WORKS CITED

Alejandro, Audrey. 2020. *Western Dominance in International Relations? The Internationalisation of IR in Brazil and India.* London: Routledge, Taylor and Francis.

Anderson, Reynaldo. 2016. "Afrofuturism 2.0 and the Black Speculative Arts Movement: Notes on a Manifesto." Obsidian 42, no. 1/2: 228–36.

Anievas, Alexander, Nivi Manchanda, and Robbie Shilliam, eds. 2015. *Race and Racism in International Relations: Confronting the Global Colour Line.* Interventions. London: Routledge, Taylor and Francis.

Austin, Jonathan Luke, and Anna Leander. 2021. "Designing-With/In World Politics: Manifestos for an International Political Design." *Political Anthropological Research on International Social Sciences* 2, no. 1: 83–154.

Bahng, Aimee. 2018. *Migrant Futures: Decolonizing Speculation in Financial Times.* Durham, N.C.: Duke University Press.

Barber, Tiffany E. 2018. "25 Years of Afrofuturism and Black Speculative Thought: Roundtable with Tiffany E. Barber, Reynaldo Anderson, Mark Dery, and Sheree Renée Thomas." *TOPIA: Canadian Journal of Cultural Studies* 39 (April): 136–44.

Barnes, Julian E. 2021. "CIA Reorganization to Place New Focus on China." *New York Times,* October 7, sec. U.S. https://www.nytimes .com/2021/10/07/us/politics/cia-reorganization-china.html.

Butler, Philip, ed. 2021. *Critical Black Futures: Speculative Theories and Explorations.* London: Palgrave Macmillan.

Choy, Christine, dir. 1987. *Who Killed Vincent Chin?* Filmmakers Library.

Dery, Mark, ed. 1994. "Black to the Future: Interviews with Samuel R. Delany, Greg Tate, and Tricia Rose." In *Flame Wars: The Discourse of Cyberculture,* 179–222. Durham, N.C.: Duke University Press.

Dussel, Enrique D., and Eduardo Mendieta. 1996. *The Underside of Modernity: Apel, Ricoeur, Rorty, Taylor, and the Philosophy of Liberation.* Atlantic Highlands, N.J.: Humanities Press.

Fonseca, Melody. 2019. "Global IR and Western Dominance: Moving Forward or Eurocentric Entrapment?" *Millennium: Journal of International Studies* 48, no. 1: 45–59.

Fukuyama, Francis. 1992. *The End of History and the Last Man.* New York: Free Press.

Green, Misa, dir. 2020. "I Am." *Lovecraft Country,* season 1, episode 7, aired September 27.

Guardian. 2020. "Donald Trump Calls Covid-19 'Kung Flu' at Tulsa Rally." June 20. https://www.theguardian.com/us-news/2020/jun/20/trump -covid-19-kung-flu-racist-language.

Guillaume, Xavier. 2011. "The International as an Everyday Practice." *International Political Sociology* 5, no. 4: 446–62.

Hill Collins, Patricia. 1990. *Black Feminist Thought: Knowledge, Consciousness, and the Politics of Empowerment.* Perspectives on Gender 2. Boston: Unwin Hyman.

Jarmon, Renina. n.d. "Black Girls Are from the Future." http://blackgirls arefromthefuture.com/.

Kant, Immanuel, David L. Colclasure, Jeremy Waldron, Michael W. Doyle, and Allen W. Wood. 2006. *"Toward Perpetual Peace" and Other Writings on Politics, Peace, and History.* New Haven, Conn.: Yale University Press.

Kaya Press. 2021. "A Transnational Dialogue on Science Fiction: Nalo Hopkinson & Kim Bo-Young." September 14. https://kaya.com/2021/09/a -transnational-dialogue-on-science-fiction-nalo-hopkinson-kim-bo -young/.

Kelley, Robin D. G. 2002. "How the West Was One." In *Rethinking American History in a Global Age,* edited by Thomas Bender, 123–47. Berkeley: University of California Press.

Kwak, Jun-Hyeok. 2021. "Global Justice without Self-Centrism: Tianxia in Dialogue on Mount Uisan." *Dao* 20, no. 2: 289–307.

Ling, L. H. M., Xiao Ren, Yiwei Wang, Xueqing Han, Weixing Hu, Teng-chi Chang, Nele Noesselt et al. 2017. *Constructing a Chinese School of International Relations: Ongoing Debates and Sociological Realities.* Edited by Yongjin Zhang and Denggi Zhang. London: Routledge.

Linklater, Andrew. 1992. "The Question of the Next Stage in International Relations Theory: A Critical-Theoretical Point of View." *Millennium: Journal of International Studies* 21, no. 1: 77–98.

Locke, Brian. 2009. "White and 'Black' versus Yellow: Metaphor and *Blade*

Runner's Racial Politics." *Arizona Quarterly: A Journal of American Literature, Culture, and Theory* 65, no. 4: 113–38.

Lowe, Lisa. 2015. *The Intimacies of Four Continents.* Durham, N.C.: Duke University Press.

McLeod, Ken. 2013. "Afro-Samurai: Techno-Orientalism and Contemporary Hip Hop." *Popular Music* 32, no. 2: 259–75.

Mignolo, Walter. 2011. *The Darker Side of Western Modernity: Global Futures, Decolonial Options.* Latin America Otherwise: Languages, Empires, Nations. Durham, N.C.: Duke University Press.

Morrison, Toni. 2004. *Beloved.* 1st Vintage International ed. New York: Vintage International.

Ní Mhurchú, Aoileann, ed. 2016. *Critical Imaginations in International Relations.* Interventions. London: Routledge, Taylor and Francis.

O'Neill, Caitlin. 2021. "Towards an Afrofuturist Feminist Manifesto." In *Critical Black Futures: Speculative Theories and Explorations,* edited by Philip Butler, 61–91. London: Palgrave Macmillan.

Pan, Chengxin, and Emilian Kavalski. 2018. "Theorizing China's Rise in and beyond International Relations." *International Relations of the Asia-Pacific* 18, no. 3: 289–311.

Prasso, Sheridan. 2021. "China Initiative Set Out to Catch Spies. It Didn't Find Many." December 14. https://www.bloomberg.com/news/features/2021-12-14/doj-china-initiative-to-catch-spies-prompts-fbi-misconduct-racism-claims.

Roh, David. 2022. "Edited Collection: Techno-Orientalism, Vol. II." June 14. https://networks.h-net.org/node/73374/announcements/10378990/edited-collection-techno-orientalism-vol-ii.

Roh, David S., Betsy Huang, and Greta A. Niu, eds. 2015. *Techno-Orientalism: Imagining Asia in Speculative Fiction, History, and Media.* Asian American Studies Today. New Brunswick, N.J.: Rutgers University Press.

Ruwitch, John. 2022. "A Jury Finds a Kansas Scholar Guilty of Fraud and Hiding Ties to China." April 7. https://www.npr.org/2022/04/07/1091090565/feng-franklin-tao-china-initiative-university-of-kansas.

Said, Edward W. 1978. *Orientalism.* 1st ed. New York: Pantheon Books.

Shilliam, Robbie, ed. 2011. *International Relations and Non-Western Thought: Imperialism, Colonialism and Investigations of Global Modernity.* Interventions 1. London: Routledge.

Smith, Barbara, ed. 2000. *Home Girls: A Black Feminist Anthology.* New Brunswick, N.J.: Rutgers University Press.

Sylvester, Christine. 2009. *Art/Museums: International Relations Where We Least Expect It.* Media and Power. Boulder, Colo.: Paradigm.

Taylor, Keeanga-Yamahtta, ed. 2017. *How We Get Free: Black Feminism and the Combahee River Collective*. Chicago: Haymarket Books.

Tétreault, Mary Ann, and Ronnie D. Lipschutz. 2009. *Global Politics as If People Mattered*. 2nd ed. Lanham, Md.: Rowman and Littlefield.

Tidy, Joanna, and Joe Turner. 2020. "The Intimate International Relations of Museums: A Method." *Millennium: Journal of International Studies* 48, no. 2: 117–42.

Wang, Hui, and Theodore Huters. 2011. *The Politics of Imagining Asia*. Cambridge, Mass.: Harvard University Press.

Womack, Ytasha. 2013. *Afrofuturism: The World of Black Sci-Fi and Fantasy Culture*. Chicago: Chicago Review Press.

Wormsley, Alisha. 2018. "There Are Black People in the Future on the Last Billboard." April 6. https://www.alishabwormsley.com/tabpitf.

Xi, Jingping. 2021. "Speech at a Ceremony Marking the Centenary of the Communist Party of China." http://www.xinhuanet.com/english /special/2021-07/01/c_1310038244.htm.

Yu, Timothy. 2008. "Oriental Cities, Postmodern Futures: 'Naked Lunch,' Blade Runner,' and 'Neuromancer.'" *MELUS* 33, no. 4: 45–71.

Zhang, Feng. 2013. "The Rise of Chinese Exceptionalism in International Relations." *European Journal of International Relations* 19 (June): 305–28.

Zhao, Tingyang. 2006. "Rethinking Empire from a Chinese Concept 'All-under-Heaven' (Tian-Xia)." *Social Identities* 12, no. 1: 29–41.

Zhao, Tingyang. 2009. "A Political World Philosophy in Terms of All-under-Heaven (Tian-Xia)." *Diogenes* 56, no. 1: 5–18.

Zhao, Tingyang. 2012. "All-under-Heaven and Methodological Relationism." In *Contemporary Chinese Political Thought*, edited by Fred Dallmayr and Zhao Tingyang, 46–66. Debates and Perspectives. Lexington: University Press of Kentucky.

Zhao, Tingyang. 2021. *All under Heaven: The Tianxia System for a Possible World Order*. Translated by Joseph E. Harroff. Great Transformations 3. Oakland: University of California Press.

ELIZABETH WIJAYA

Insomniac Nights and an Aesthetics of Passivity: On Tsai Ming-liang's Walker Series

■ THE VANISHING SCREEN

Tsai Ming-liang's *No No Sleep* exhibition at the Museum of National Taipei University of Education (MoNTUE) ran from March 26 to April 24, 2016. During the exhibition, the museum opened from 6:00 P.M. to midnight on weekdays, and hours were extended until daybreak on weekends. On the first floor, the titular film, *No No Sleep* (2015), was projected concurrently on two adjacent screens. On the second floor, the films *Autumn Days* (2015) and *Journey to the West* (2014) alternated. The third floor was dedicated to screenings of *Journey to the West*. As seen in Figure 1, at daybreak, the nightscape of the film *No No Sleep* shone against the breaking light of day entering through the museum's lattice glass windows. The sleeping and somnambulating bodies appeared no less cinematic than the flickers within the looping screens.

This article reads the Walker series and the exhibition of two of the films from the series in the MoNTUE for the polyphonic rhythms of what I am calling an "aesthetics of passivity." Returning to the root of aesthetics as sensory perception, the term *aesthetics of passivity* highlights the way Tsai's cinema foregrounds the sensuality of perception through the radical slowing down of character movements, the reduction of plot-based action, and the lengthening of shot duration to emphasize rather than cut away from quotidian acts like walking or sleeping. The concept behind the series is simple: dressed as a monk, the actor Lee Kang-sheng walks or rests at an astoundingly slow pace across global locations. The films do not abandon the cinematic devices of narrative and character. Through a slow rhythm of cuts and on-screen action by the focal character even as

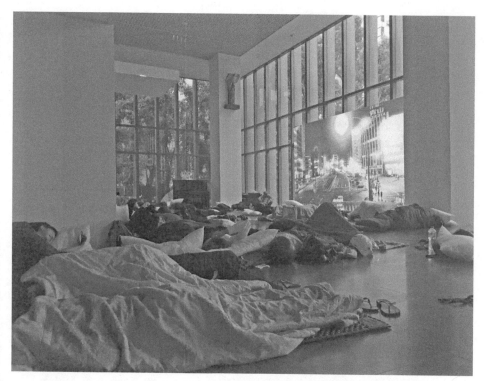

Figure 1. Daylight at the *No No Sleep* exhibition. Photograph by Elizabeth Wijaya.

the passersby in the scene maintain a conventional pace, relational and cinematic tensions remain discernible. With this minimal approach to narrative, which draws attention to the rhythms of fleshly and vulnerable bodies in distant social existence, Tsai's cinema of passivity reclaims time itself and the interrelational possibilities within it as the focus of the cinematic experience. In so doing, the Walker series shows the tensions between action and nonaction, movement and nonmovement, at work in the cinematic medium and suggests that the potential of cinema lies not in where a work is screened but in its ability to create experiential moments for alternative rhythms and shapes of collective existence. Reading Tsai's form of slow cinema through the aesthetics of passivity, I stress the ethical dimension of slow cinema and its minimal power to disrupt conventional rhythms and ways of thinking collective actions and being. Though the films are stripped of outwardly dramatic actions, on the level of desire and also as the exhibition conditions of *No No Sleep* show, the cinema of passivity is not an ascetic cinema of renunciation. The spectator is invited to experience the interrelation of time, existence, and queer attachments within a multifarious cinematic world that lingers on as a counterforce to rhythms of rapid progress and productivity. Even when figures on-screen and the spectators off-screen seem to be separated by differences marked by silence or arrythmias, and very little seems to be happening, the Walker series reveals the bodily entwinement between ethical and social existence.

On-screen passivity welcomes a spectatorial passivity. With the minimal and slow-paced action on-screen, the spectator is free to luxuriate in the rhythmic interplay within and between the filmic world and the world in which the spectator is embedded. With the slowness on-screen freeing the audience to look away, to sleep, and even to dream, there is a chance for attunement toward the passive nature of cobelonging underpinned by an interrelationality that is always already there, even before the formation or action of an individual. Tsai's aesthetics of passivity and the soporific screening conditions of the *No No Sleep* exhibition not only invite an intellectual consideration of the ethics of social existence but create the conditions in which the audience can have a corporeal experience of distant intimacy, shared vulnerability, and lying horizontally together while sheltered by the light of the screen. The disorienting tendencies of the Walker series and its horizontal inclinations have the potential to disrupt hierarchical modes of orientation, such as the mythemes of East and West. The aesthetics of passivity thus draws attention to the ethical significance of passive gestures like retiring, withdrawing, lying down, sleeping, moving slowly, and waiting.

In and through these films, queer desire radiates. With the horizontal bent of the bodies on-screen and in the exhibition, the rhythm and direction of the films disrupt the notion of time conceived as forward momentum. By challenging cinematic conventions of narrative development with the downward force of the soporific, the film offers an alternative to the visual language and ideology of progress and development. In the spaces for cinema and spaces within cinema, there is the possibility of dwelling for longer in the spacing between action and a return to the vibrations of the body in its minimal movements. For example, in the coda of the film *No No Sleep*, we watch the vibrational intensities of flesh on-screen in the moment between sleep and wakefulness doubled by another body in a similar but separate space. Through the camera and editing, the mundane act of getting to sleep becomes a corporeal drama of social existence even when it seems that the body is alone in an enclosed space. Beyond the scenes of suggestive same-sex desire, in its languorous pace, the Walker series embraces the bodily vulnerability and intimacies of everyday acts. The undercurrents of queer desire in the series create divergent rhythms of collective existence that challenge the normalization of heteronormative and capitalist modes of existence. The celebratory mode of the *No No Sleep* exhibition shows that even with the portrayal of fatigued and languid bodies, the aesthetics of passivity harbors space for queer attachments and does not necessitate the relinquishing of worldly pleasures.

There are ethical and political stakes to a reconsideration of passivity and its minimal, productive potential. Attunement to ethical responsibility can arise from doing very little, almost nothing, particularly while collectively apart. During the isolation of this interminable pandemic, my thoughts returned to the experience of being insomniac and attempting to fall asleep among strangers. In a time of curfews or quarantine orders with increased border control measures on the local, state, and international levels and magnified protectionist measures on the national scale, the question of what we have in common while physically distanced from one another has taken on increased urgency. With ethical, and sometimes legal, imperatives to isolate from others in the concerted effort to mitigate the spread of a contagious virus, in recent years, the term *social distancing* has entered everyday speech. The collective responsibility of practicing the art of staying apart brings to attention how the withdrawal of action can arise from a recognition of a fundamental, entangled cobelonging. In these isolating times, it becomes even more important to trace out what underpins responsibility for unseen and untouched others. Other than isolation, this pandemic has also intensified a rhythmic disjunction. Life for some has slowed down, while for others it has accelerated with little respite. It is precisely when social and transnational interactions have decreased that it becomes even more critical to dream of radical possibilities for an alternative body politic and collective life.

Tsai Ming-liang's ongoing Slow Walk, Long March series, also known as the Walker series, currently comprises the following films: *No Form* (2012), *Walker* (2012), *Sleepwalk* (2012), *Diamond Sutra* (2012), *Walking on Water* (2013), *No No Sleep,* and the feature-length films *Journey to the West* and *Sand* (2018). I will first contextualize the films within Tsai's declared retirement from filmmaking. I will then address the asynchronous rhythms and the significance of slow-motion steps in the earlier films, *Walker* and *Walking on Water*. I situate the polyphonic rhythms in the Walker series within the discourse on slow cinema as well as Emmanuel Levinas's meditation on time. Next, I will show how *Journey to the West* performs a minimal dislocation of the mytheme of the "West." Arguing that *Journey to the West* gestures toward a horizon of shared, rhythmic sociality, I turn to the film *No No Sleep* before returning to the *No No Sleep* exhibition. Finally, I discuss the rhythmic tensions between withdrawal and proliferation and the stakes of recognizing the potential of an aesthetics and ethics of passivity.

To illuminate the interrelational roots of passivity, this article draws on and responds to formulations of ethical passivity in Levinas's thought. In both Levinas's inspiration from Jewish thought and Tsai's engagement with Buddhist thought, there is a potential of interreligious discourse.[1] The Walker series forms Tsai's most explicit engagement with Buddhist scripture, mythology, and motifs. Ng Teng Kuan (2018, 200) reads Lee Kang-sheng's steps in *Walker* as the performance of Zen walking meditation that cultivates attentiveness against the speed of metropolitan life. *Journey to the West* concludes with a quotation from the Diamond Sutra:

> All conditioned phenomena / Are like a dream, an illusion, a bubble, a shadow / Like the dew, or like lightning / You should discern them like this

My emphasis is less on the religiosity of the works than on how the minimality of the narrative, cinematography, and editing in the films reveals the vanishing nature of cinema and its potential for queering worlds. In positing these films as rhythmically and thematically queer, I'm following the work of Karl Schoonover and Rosalind Galt (2016, 5), who propose that "queer cinema elaborates new accounts of the world, offering alternatives to embedded capitalist, national, hetero- and homonormative maps; revising the flows and politics of world cinema; and forging dissident scales of affiliation, affection, affect, and form." I am also inspired by Arnika Fuhrmann's (2016) suggestive reading of how queer desire and attachments in Apichatpong Weerasethakul's films draw on and challenge Buddhist notions of impermanence and the disavowal of worldly desires.

Writing on Levinas and cinema has frequently focused on French (Cooper 2006), American Hollywood (Girgus 2010), or European cinema (Cooper 2007). Considering Levinas's (1997, 160) fear of the "arrival on the historical scene of those under-developed Asiatic masses," this article enacts a disjunctive, reparative encounter between the two to draw out the potential in both bodies of thought to transgress prefigured regionalization of East/West. By putting what appears to be cross-cultural, cross-media embodiments of thought in dialogue, this article enacts what Tina Chen (2021) has termed an "ageographical" encounter. I examine these bodies of work for disruptions of formations of the self that dislocate and disorient us from inherited notions of origins and mapping of where the self and the other, and the East and the West, begin or end.

Shaped by the dark times of the twentieth century, Levinasian philosophy adopts a vocabulary of trauma: shadow, escape, obsession, horror, pain, persecution, insomnia, fatigue, captivity.[2] In Levinasian (1998, 44) thought, responsible action stems not from conscious, individual choices but from an embodied and sensuous passivity in the intersubjective relation to the other that disrupts the experience of time as continuous. The interplay between action and nonaction in the movements of cinema has been extensively debated via Bergson and Deleuze as a general condition of the moving image.[3] Levinas and Bergson distinguish between the synchronized presentation of clock and calendar time and the experience of time as continuous duration. Unlike Bergson, Levinas's (1979, 284) understanding of time is tied not to intention but to the dispossession of the self in the encounter with alterity, where "time is discontinuous; one instant does not come out of another without interruption, by an ecstasy."

In the Levinasian model of time, the hope for futurity lies in the encounter with the radically other, which rescues the self from impersonal, anonymous existence. Guided by the Levinasian understanding of the trace presence of the other that causes a rupture in time (which makes time possible), I see the Walker series' recuperation of the moods and modes of passivity, including fatigue and insomnia, as the holding open of a space of encounter for the possibility of rhythmic sociality, even if physically and metaphorically the characters are not in the same frame. Through the Walker series, I see in Levinas a queer potential to embody erotic relation beyond the phallocentric, limited humanism that has been critiqued by philosophers ranging from Luce Irigary (1991) to Judith Butler (2012a) and Howard Caygill (2002).

■ A RETIRING CINEMA

In this section, I consider Tsai's postretirement works to suggest that "retiring" is a passive action that enables a proliferation of possibilities. By further renouncing the conventions of cinematic rhythms, Tsai finds more space to do less. Tsai Ming-liang bid farewell to celluloid cinema with the release of *Visage* (2009), commissioned and coproduced by the Louvre Museum. When he visited National Central University (NCU) in Taiwan on May 26, 2010, to promote *Visage,* Tsai expressed the fatigue of consumption and the desire for everything to be stopped. It might thus seem contradictory that Tsai's talk at NCU ended with the promotion of his coffee on sale as part of his installation *Moonlight on the River* at the Taipei Fine Arts Museum:

> The coffee I sell is also food for thought, and I guarantee you, it's delicious homemade coffee. If you visit the exhibition, you will understand why I have

integrated the process of brewing coffee. It is part of the recycling concept: nothing in our life should be tossed away easily. (Tsai 2011)

This oscillation between exhausted anticonsumerism and the self-promotion of his auteurist coffee is indicative of the tensions within Tsai's career of contradictions—of desire and withdrawal, of quietude and hints of inner drama, of passivity and relational possibilities.

In 2013, during the release of his first full-length digital film, *Stray Dogs,* Tsai cited fatigue as he announced his retirement at the Venice Film Festival.[4] *Stray Dogs* later formed Tsai's first solo museum exhibition, *Stray Dogs at the Museum.* With the eight-part (and continuing) Walker series; a companion internationally traveling stage play, *The Monk from Tang Dynasty*; the conversational documentary *Afternoon* (2016); the first Chinese-language long-form virtual reality film, *The Deserted* (2017); the documentary *Your Face* (2018); the short film *Light* (2019); the narrative feature *Days* (2020); and the short films *The Moon and the Tree* (2021) and *Night* (2021), Tsai's postretirement work finds mobility in a dialectical dance through institutional spaces for art, cinema, and theater.

This article adds to the growing interest in the transmedial and transnational possibilities of Tsai's work by foregrounding the rhythmic surprises of passivity between site and screen, between cinematic experience and philosophical experience, and between the isolated and the interrelational. Within the series, *Walker* is part of the omnibus, and *Beautiful 2012* (2012) and *No No Sleep* are part of Beautiful 2015. The Beautiful series was a joint initiative between the Hong Kong International Film Festival and the Beijing-based video hosting service Youku. The films were intended for festival circuits and release on Youku's online platform (Screendaily 2012). This mobility of cinema into and beyond institutional spaces forms part of the transformative potential of cinema. Focusing on *Visage* and *It's a Dream* (2007), Erik Bordeleau and Beth Tsai have written on Tsai's earlier relationship with museal spaces with the Louvre, the Venice Biennale, and the Taipei Fine Arts Museum (Bordeleau 2013; Tsai 2017). In the first Chinese monograph on Tsai's installations, Sing Song-yong (2014) proposes reading Tsai's transmedia career through the lens of "trans-art cinema." Paola Voci (2020) reads the Walker series in relation to postdigital possibilities explored across Chinese cinema, and Lim Song Hwee (2022) argues that the slow-moving figure in the Walker series illuminates the tempo of everyday life.

Cinematic time captured through celluloid or digital means incurs differences in cost and also practical possibilities because celluloid costs more and requires reel changes, which limits the length of a shot. Tsai's retirement from celluloid cinema allows for an intensification of slow cinema by a further emancipation from rhythmic conventions and what counts as cinematic action. Lee walking relentlessly on, or sleeping insouciantly, across multiple films produces a cinema of passivity that does less in order to bring the fleshly vulnerability of interrelated beings into focus. Jonathan Crary (2021, 27) argues for "powering down" in the face of "24/7 exploitation and exhaustion." Jenny Odell's (2019, ix) best-selling *How to Do Nothing: Resisting the Attention Economy* opens with the truism that "nothing is harder to do than nothing" and argues that doing what counts as nothing resists the optimization of life as capitalist productivity. Tung-Hui Hu (2017) argues for lethargy and withdrawal as acts of political (in)action within the affective negotiations of the everyday. Relatedly, there has been renewed attention on boredom studies (Richmond 2015; Gardiner and Haladyn 2017; Paasonen 2021). Theorists have argued for the transformative potential of a politics of refusal, of nonparticipation, of withdrawal, and for the performative efficacy of saying "I prefer not to" as a form of minimal action that interrupts the operations of unjust systems (Honig 2021; Simpson 2014; Agamben 1998). Following the footsteps of the Walker series leads to a fundamental questioning of the multiple ways in which cinema could be an ethicopolitical art of withdrawing from the accelerationist tendencies of capitalism.

Tsai's experiments with sleep are shared by other artist-filmmakers today. Shu Lea Cheang has collaborated with Matthew Fuller on investigations of the aesthetics of sleep in museums: *Sleep 48* (Linz, 2018), *Sleep 79* (Taipei, 2018), *Sleep 1237* (New York City, 2019), and *Sleep 5959* (Malmö, 2021). Apichatpong's *SLEEPCINEMAHOTEL* was held at the 2018 International Film Festival Rotterdam, and guests were invited to sleep in a hall while a projection screen showed Apichatpong's films. As with *No No Sleep*, *SLEEPCINEMAHOTEL* extends an invitation for guests to be with cinema, whether in attentiveness or soporific distraction.[5] Erika Balsom (2022) notes that the 1990s heyday of the love affair between cinema and art spaces has since settled into "something more routine, more predictable." Pamela L. Lee (2021, 54) positions lying down in museums and galleries as practices that "model new relationships between leisure and work, body and machine, gender and agency." The horizontal bent of the Walker's body and the invitation for the audience to participate by lying down are part of the queer invitation of the Walker series for the enactment of intimate vulnerability in public spaces. This is not Walter Benjamin's (1968, 197) nineteenth-century leisurely flaneur walking with a turtle in the crowd, protesting against the industriousness and specialization of the age, but its antithesis: the labor of walking becomes the focal point of the scene.

The Walker, Lee as the shaven-head monk-like figure in red robes, walks at an unendurably slow pace, rhythmically at odds with the sense of speed that is a cliché of cinematic portrayals of Hong Kong, as exemplified by the dizzying experiments with time in Wong Kar-Wai's *Chungking Express* (1994). *Walker* begins with Lee exiting a narrow set of concrete stairs in an old building as if emerging from an urban cave. Throughout the walk, his head is bent at a painful ninety degrees, and in his left hand, he carries a nondescript plastic bag, while in his right, he holds a ham and egg bun. As we see in Figure 2, on a pedestrian street, passersby steal glances or stare openly at the Walker, but his head remains bowed as he follows the lane markings on a crosswalk. Notably, a man pushing a cart full of black garbage bags enters and exits the scene at the edge of the frame, walking in the same direction as the Walker even as they pay no attention to each other. High in the background is a gleaming, royal-looking figure astride a majestic black horse. In this frame, the sovereign, the ascetic, the shoppers, workers, and passersby, coexist in the same space without, it seems, sharing the same world.

The journey of the monk comes to an end in the only close-up of the film, where we see the profile of the Walker against dark green security grills as he lifts the bun in slow motion and eats with closed eyes, while a 1974 song, "A Stream Divides the Land," accompanies the final image into the credits. The song is from Sam Hui's debut Cantonese album that accompanied *Games Gamblers Play* (1974), a comedy film directed by Michael Hui and celebrating the pursuit of wealth. Overlaying Tsai's image, the song takes on a melancholic tone. The journey's end leads not to otherworldly enlightenment but to the solemnly sensual consumption of the bun, with the prosaic visual and aural reminder that "Even bread costs a few pennies a piece." Sam Hui's song's bread-and-butter concerns link together the plastic of the disposable bag from the earlier scenes, the final image with the steel of the grills, the fabric of the robe, the softness of the bun, and Lee Kang-sheng's flushed face. These textures serve as reminders of fleshly materiality embedded in the global commodities trade that has become normalized in the visual fields of the hypercapitalist present.

How, then, could the processes and content of cinema—embedded within these globalized processes, heavy with the weight of inequity—reflect on the demands and dreams of the present? In its iterations, the Walker series vacillates between entertainment and drudgery, withdrawal

Figure 2. Screenshot of Lee in *Walker*.

and participation, passivity and activity. The Walker series' enactment of slow motion is an intensification of Tsai's earlier works that have been discussed as slow cinema (Lim 2014; Koepnick 2014). In this article, I highlight the polyphonic rhythms of what appears to be slowness such that even in scenes of slow-motion walking, we can often discern multiple temporalities at work. As a comparative rather than an absolute term, *slow* connotes desire. If the scene lingers on, and the audience is unclear what they are supposed to be looking at, the desire for more is thwarted and a film can be deemed "too slow." Proponents of slow cinema share affinities with those who have called for slowing down in a culture of speed and efficacy, such as the slow food movement (Petrini 2003) or *The Slow Professor* (Seeber and Berg 2016). Olivia Cosentino (2021, 64) proposes the term "slower cinema" to describe "a type of cinema that slows down spectators without lulling them to boredom or inattention." With the Walker series, what we see is the slowest cinema, with live-action slow-motion that is unafraid of soliciting the revelation of boredom.

In Tsai's cinema of passivity, slowing down does not necessarily lead to redemptive enlightenment but allows for a pause that lengthens the interval between movements and the creation of a quiet space within a tumultuous city. The aesthetics of passivity minimizes plot-based action, but it is not without action. In the giving of time to frames of minimal and slow-motion action, the audience is invited to be in synchrony with the unfolding of time on-screen. In its haunted relationship to time, cinema is a practice of asynchrony that reserves time for synchronized encounters. The cinematic possibility that someone else could be watching the same scene at the same time, or will experience the same rhythmic unfolding of scenes at another time and place, creates a synchrony-in-asynchrony. The solipsistic figure of the Walker on-screen, performing spectacles of amplified lassitude within the arrythmias of modern spaces, is thus never truly alone in its anticipation of an audience that the scene could gather.

A reconsideration of time in relation to the other is at the heart of Tsai's works that share Levinas's concerns. Levinas locates the arrival of the stranger in the time before time begins, and it is the possibility for sociality that allows the self to enter the passage of time prior to the process of individuation as a distinct entity. Even as Levinasian philosophy embraced the nonfigurable face of the other, when confronted in the political world with the face of the dog, the snake, the Palestinian, and what he called the "yellow peril," Levinas could not agree that nonhuman and racialized others could be considered to have faces marked by the relation to the transcendental that demands justice.[6] For Levinas, it is not the face in its corporeal manifestation that issues an ethical demand, but the face is a surface through which transcendental alterity can be discerned. In contrast, across Tsai's films, interrelationality is grounded in the tremulous vulnerability of physical flesh, as I will show in my analysis of *No No Sleep*. Across the series, the camera frequently dwells on the solitude of Lee Kang-sheng's body within trembling scenes of desire for queer connections that disrupt the anonymity and isolation of modern existence.

Like his retirement dreams, Tsai's work reaches toward renunciation yet remains tethered to the worldliness of everyday spectacles, from the allure of Hong Kong's colorful, polyphonic streets to the faint magic of Kuching's estates. The opening scene of *Walking on Water,* set in Tsai's birthplace of Kuching, Malaysia, invokes the religious mythology of walking on water with the contemplative, itinerant figure of the monk, whose halting steps on water gain no notice from anyone. *Walking on Water* is part of *Letters from the South* (2013), an omnibus of six short films produced by Tan Chui Mui, under the Malaysian New Wave company Da Huang Pictures. Figure 3 shows that as the Walker steps across a puddle of water by the side of a grimy wall, it is through their muddied reflections that we see indistinct aspects of the red-robed Walker, a mid-rise housing estate, and a strip of clear sky. Rather than placing religion on a vertical scale of height, with the foregrounding of bending down, lying down, and slowing down, the Walker series weighs down the body of the monk toward the horizontal. Despite the importance of terms like *fatigue,*

Figure 3. Screenshot of the opening scene of *Walking on Water.*

insomnia, and *exhaustion* in Levinas's work, terms that suggest horizontal relationality, Levinas's philosophy of ethical relations is predicated on the vertical relation to the divine, or in Levinas's (1979, 41) words, "the idea of infinity designates a height and a nobility." With Tsai's cinema, the iconography of the religious is inseparable from the mundane. Tsai's work shows that the encounter with the stranger is mediated through the materialities and temporalities of existence. The stranger is never just another human individual but also enmeshed within the environment. The subtly subversive use of inverted reflection in *Walking on Water* is repeated in a crowded scene in *Journey to the West.* In the next section, I discuss the ethicopolitical significance of Tsai's shift in orientation from the vertical to the horizontal and the subtle disorientation of the "West."

■ **THE INVERTED DISORIENTATION OF THE WEST**

The minimal movements of the bent body of the Walker in Taipei, Hong Kong, Tokyo, Kuching, and Marseille cast into question the globality of Asian cinema. In the slow steps of Lee on-screen meeting the carnivalesque of the museum as an exhibition venue, and in the interactions between the passivity of Lee's body and the series' location shooting across global cities, there is a collision of "the multiple, overlapping, and embedded contradictions" that Tina Chen (2018) has named the "structural incoherence of Global Asias." Thomas Lamarre (2017) argues that area studies and media studies have the tendency to treat their subject of study as stable categories. Lamarre engages with Ani Maitra's, Rey Chow's, and Arjun Appadurai's work that has sought to disaggregate the idea and understanding of what is called "Asia" (294). Through the Walker series, there is a chance to rethink the potential of the transnational from the emergence of the interrelational in a way that can trouble the concept of the international world as the multiplication of nations with internal units of distinct individuals.

Wu Cheng'en, the sixteenth-century writer of the classic *Journey to the West*, is given writing credits on Tsai's *Journey to the West*. Whereas Wu's classic novel was a literary account of Tang Dynasty Buddhist monk Xuanzang, who traveled to the "Western Regions," referring then to India, Tsai's *Journey to the West* shows the robed figure of Lee already in the so-called Western world of Marseille, France. In place of Xuanzang's disciples, the mythologized and beloved cast of folk religion–inspired Monkey, Pig, and Sand Monk, Lee is followed by Denis Lavant—a French actor from the mythological universe of art house cinema. In his perspicacious reading of *Journey to the West*, Song Hwee Lim (2022, 89) highlights the "ethnic difference within the body politic of the modern nation-state of France" in the postcolonial space of Marseille that is magnified by "the appearance of a pilgrim from the East in its cityscape." In reading the postcolonial encounter within his project on Taiwan cinema's soft power, Lim eschews lingua-centric or national-centric approaches and foregrounds how elements of the transnational "negotiate[] with the national on all levels" (7). Moreover, in situating the Walker series within what he calls Tsai's "medial turn," Lim questions the adequacy of the transnational in "capturing the new sites of Tsai's intermedial practices" (71), an insufficiency that Lim attributes to the deterritorializing potential of the films' online consumption and distribution. Following the footsteps of the Walker allows us to pursue the transgressive aspect of the transnational alongside the troubling of the figure of the individual.

Naoki Sakai (2019, 96) has challenged us to conceive of the transnational as "the foundational modality of sociality" and to understand that "nationality is a restrictive derivative of transnationality." Developing Stuart Hall's discourse on "the West and the Rest," Sakai (2022, 16) shows how the fiction of the "West" is tethered to epistemological and geographical fictions of where the "Rest" is and what the outside of the West encompasses. The "West" has persisted in its mythical hold over the political imagination despite its bloody colonial baggage and imprecision. Sara Ahmed (2006, 3) reminds us that "orientations shape not only how we inhabit space, but how we apprehend this world of shared inhabitance, as well as 'who' or 'what' we direct our energy and attention toward." In *Journey to the West*'s shifting of the referent of the "West" from India to Marseille, the signifier of the "West" also shifts, as it has in history. *Journey to the West* is composed of a nonteleological following of one actor by another. It begins with an awakening and ends in an inverted suspension, maintaining the possibility of an upside-down, arrhythmic sociality in a public square, which, for an extended moment, suspends the ossified orientations of East/West.

The first image of *Journey to the West* is a close-up of Lavant's face in a supine position. His expression is inscrutable and shadowy. He could be waking up or falling asleep. Though Levinas rarely writes on cinema, following a discussion of fatigue and the dialectical interiority of the existent, he raises the example of the close-up that pauses an action and "lets it exist apart" from the world. Levinas (1978, 55) compares the close-up to a painting's or sculptural form's ability to set aside "a piece of the universe and brings about, in an inwardness, the coexistence of worlds that are mutually alien and impenetrable." From this in-between state of consciousness between the withdrawal of sleep and the involvement of being in the sunlight of the world, the film continues to construct the asymmetrical relation between Lavant and Lee.

In the fifty-six-minute film, Lavant follows Lee across Marseille, but at a different pace. Recall that in the Levinasian model of time, it is with the interruption of the other that the gift of temporal existence begins. Before the contact with alterity screened by the face of the other, the existent is sunk in fatigue and alienated from time. Unlike the solipsistic ambulation shown in *Walker*, *Journey to the West* suggests the possibility of rhythmic sociality. However, though Lavant follows Lee, Lavant's presence is not acknowledged by Lee. It is the audience that completes the triangulation of faces. As the film loops for strangers, half asleep or half awake in the dim light of the MoNTUE, in the gallery space with throw pillows on the floor, some audience members mirror Lavant's initial horizontal position. Tsai's Walker series puts pressure on the habitual orientation of daily life and social interaction such that the walking body is weighed down by the horizontal line. In these passive, vulnerable postures that Tsai's work brings into public light, horizontal sociality gestures toward a temporary suspension of hierarchical and other presupposed differences.

In the film's disorientation of East/West, up/down, the final scene offers critical interpretive possibilities. As Figure 4 shows, the film ends

Figure 4. Screenshot of the ending of *Journey to the West*.

with a long take of an upside-down, reflected wide shot with people milling about a public square and the tiny, minimal figure of the Walker at the edge of the frame. In the long take and wide space of this inverted vision, the figures in the square are granted an opacity. Here there is a flicker of a utopic cobelonging in a busy, public, transitory space. The rhythmic slowness of the Walker invites contemplation of the rhythmic differences between bodies in transit. On-screen, the solipsistic walk accentuates the multitudinous colors and rhythms of public coexistence. Like his declarations of retirement, in Tsai's cinematic world, the acknowledgment of impermanence and solitude begets desires for queer, asynchronous rhythms of possibility.

■ HORIZONTAL PROXIMITY ACROSS THE FRAMES OF DESIRE

Of the films in the Walker series, the voluptuousness of queer desire is most pronounced in *No No Sleep*. It comprises a series of static shots scattered in the urban locations of Tokyo, Japan: a pedestrian crossing, an overhead bridge, trains, a bathhouse, and a capsule hotel. The film opens at Shibuya crossing, the world's busiest scramble intersection. We see pedestrians cross the intersection in every direction, but the Walker is nowhere in sight. He appears in the next shot on an overhead bridge, and his excruciatingly laborious steps are shown from various angles. The few passersby in the scene pay no attention to one another. This is the only scene of walking in *No No Sleep*. In the slowing down of steps, the

Figure 5. Silhouette of Tsai Ming-liang photographing a projection of *No No Sleep*. Photograph by Elizabeth Wijaya.

weight of the interval between movement and nonmovement becomes more pronounced. With each step, there is the anticipation of a possible future, of a social world to be entered. But within this perambulatory scene, the Walker finds no pardon from his solitary existence.

Even the static camera is restless, and before long, its attention leaves the Walker, as an audience might, attracted instead by the libidinal energy of the night. The camera, from the position of a train leaving the platform, brings the viewer for a night tour of the city, showing, in a blur of light and shadows, the passengers in another passing train and the restive energy of the phosphorescent nightscape. The sequence ends with overexposed, blown-out, obscure images of people and the city mixed with indistinct contours. A hard cut transports us to a long take showing a full-frontal nude shot of the actor Masanobu Ando soaping himself alone in a narrow communal shower. In the next scene, reminiscent of the homoerotic tension of the toilet scene in *Goodbye, Dragon Inn* (2003), Lee and Ando sit side by side in the waters of a public bathhouse, in silent, proximate distance. For this interval, the Walker is silently, rhythmically in sync with another body. Figure 5 shows the scene taking place both on a large screen and as a blown-out image on the screen of Tsai Ming-liang's phone. As we emerge from or persist in social distancing, this scene of being tremulously together, connected by the same body of water but without direct contact or dialogue, takes on a renewed pathos.

The aesthetics of passivity extends from content (scenes of queer proximity in isolation) to form (interrelationality mediated by cinematic possibilities). *No No Sleep* evokes what Judith Butler (2012b) discusses as the recognition of shared vulnerability as the foundation of hospitality in earthly cohabitation. Levinas (1978, 85) emphasizes that it is only through the relation with the other that there can be pardon from the solitude of existence:

> Reaching the other is not something justified of itself; it is not a matter of shaking me out of my boredom. It is, on the ontological level, the event of the most radical breakup of the very categories of the ego, for it is for me to be somewhere else than myself; it is to be pardoned, to not be a definite existence.

The intense moment of Lee and Ando being in proximate distance is followed by an image of Lee shown in close-up, sweating in a sauna. Levinas establishes ethics as first philosophy by positing the screen of the face as a passive resistance. For Levinas (1979, 254–55), the possibility of intertwined notions of justice, ethics, and hospitality rests not in the materiality of the face of the other but in the transcendence-in-immanence that shines through it, where "the face filters the obscure light coming from beyond the face, from what is not yet, from a future never future enough, more remote than the possible." Tsai is a consummate Levinasian, beyond even Levinas. No director has been more obsessed, not just with the face in general but with the body of one person—Lee Kang-sheng. For Tsai, interrelational ethics is underpinned not by the transcendental possibility of the face alone but by the porosity of a singular body in its horizontal vulnerability. Over the decades of their intertwined careers, in giving more rather than less cinematic time and space to the barest movements of Lee's body as it is weighed down by age and time, Tsai's cinematic oeuvre forms a rhythmic, longitudinal study of a specific body's transformation and transformative potential. In its passive modes of observing Lee's body, Tsai's cinema performs an ethical attachment that is queer in its refusal to discard an aging actor's body according to capitalist practices of consumption with expiry dates.

The film ends in a doubled supine suspension between sociality and

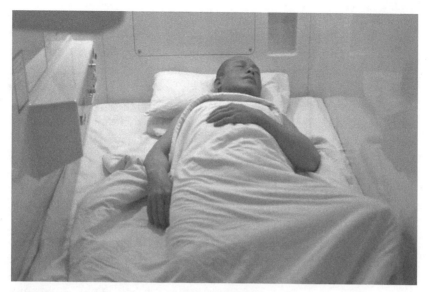

Figure 6. Screenshot of Lee in bed in *No No Sleep*.

withdrawal, as well as between insomnia and slumber. In the penultimate shot, from the point of view of a camera positioned at the end of the narrow bed, Ando sleeps (or does not sleep) alone, in a cubicle hotel room. As he tosses and turns, his nude lower body becomes intermittently visible beneath a narrow, thin sheet. Figure 6 shows the final shot, similar in camera positioning and angle: Lee with his eyes closed and most of his body covered by the sheets. In both shots, their bodies are partially doubled by their own images in the reflective surface of the wall. The concluding sequence of shots are Ando and Lee in proximity, Lee alone in close-up, Ando alone in a capsule hotel's bed, and Lee alone in a similar-looking space. These shots form a rhythmic, erotic slow dance of quivering, passive desire. Even though they are in isolated frames, this desirous sequence spotlights the ethical-erotic event marked by the vulnerabilities of the somnolent flesh that is at rest, or almost at rest. In the absence of physical touch between the two, the editing allows a proximity of touch across the cinematic frames. At the end of *No No Sleep,* what we are left with is not the sweaty textures of the face or the intervals of slow steps but an open vulnerability punctuated by soft breaths.

The intervals of breath from Ando and Lee disperse from the screen to the nocturnal exhibition site. Jean Ma (2021, 52) investigates spectatorial somnolence as a way of experiencing cinema across its "exhibitionary dispositive" and understanding "cinema's afterlives, relocations, and reincarnations." With Tsai's work, we never enter a world marked as a dream that is distinct from reality, but the dreamworld of cinema allows for queer encounters tangential to conventional rhythms and frames of existence. Tsai's wavering between cinema's impermanent light and its invocation of palpable desire was already present in his short film *It's a Dream* (2007), accompanied by Tsai Chin's nostalgic pop song "Shimeng shizhen" (Is this a dream, or is this reality?). To further explore the twinned desirous and renunciative modes of Tsai's aesthetics of passivity, I return to the scenes of the *No No Sleep* exhibition.

■ INSOMNIAC NIGHTS

The nights at the exhibition offered entertainment soaked in celebrity culture, a modality that is not often associated with Tsai Ming-liang's slow cinema. Taiwan's movie rating system precludes children from encountering many of Tsai's films within the cinema theater. Yet, the exhibition drew a disparate crowd of all ages, including children and crawling babies, who stayed overnight in blue tents. On Tuesdays, Tsai held late-night talks, mainly attracting students. On weekends, special guests were invited. The guests included the actors Masanobu Ando and Lee Kang-sheng, singers Fan Wei Qi and Zhu Tou Pi, and Professor Chang Hsiao-hung. Tsai's singing was the constant feature across the events. Tsai sang for hours, to live piano accompaniment, sometimes by himself and sometimes with his guest stars. He sang Mandarin songs from his films by Yao Li, Zhou Xuan, and Lee Xiang Lan; songs in Taiwanese; and children's songs for the gathered children.

Whether owing to the hypnotic allure of Lee Kang-sheng multiplied on two screens, the draw of the guest stars, or the amusement of a family camping night at the museum, hundreds of people packed the museum on weekend nights. Other than promotional appearances in universities around Taipei and the Eslite book chain, as he did with *Stray Dogs*, Tsai (awarded the Venice Golden Lion for *Vive L'Amour* [1994] and the Chevalier des Arts et Lettres in 2002) recounted to his captive night audience how he walked the streets during the day to hawk tickets to the public, a practice he began with the film *What Time Is It There?* (2001). From street canvassing to turning the museum into an insomniac space, Tsai's cinematic practice renegotiates the borders of high and low art, art house cinema and popular entertainment.

So much depended on the allure of the director as a charismatic figure. As he strolled through the seated audience in the museum, holding his mic, belting out a tune, and bantering with the audience, Tsai resembled a celebrity, reveling in the adulation of the audience. On the night of

Figure 7. Music video of Fan Wei Qi's song "Some Time After" plays as Tsai Ming-liang sings. Photograph by Elizabeth Wijaya.

Fan Wei Qi's guest appearance, Tsai switched the looping *No No Sleep* to a music video promoting a song by Fan, starring Lee Kang-sheng as her estranged lover. Figure 7 shows Tsai looking at the close-up of Lee Kang-sheng's face in the music video. After that and the customary duet between Tsai and his guest, *No No Sleep* was set to loop again for the faithful who were staying overnight. And thus mixed the sacred and the profane, the director as sage, entertainer, and salesman. Every night of his appearance, Tsai asked some version of the question "is this still a museum?" Just as he desacralized and eroticized Lee's embodiment of the legendary Xuanzang, so, too, did the desirous carnivalesque infiltrate the night at the museum. Yet, in the hours after the fanfare, when the films looped on in the quiet, the boundaries between the museum, the cinema, the audience, as either passive or active, were laid, even if only temporarily, to rest. The convivial atmosphere of the interactions between Tsai, the museumgoers, the films, the special guests, and the interplay of light and opacity between the screens, sleepy bodies, and the world beyond the glass windows melded into one another and into memory, as night turned to dawn and the screen appeared to dematerialize.

The existent has interiority and exteriority; the screen has entry and exit points. Tsai's work carries the experiential encounters of the cinematic into arenas outside the walls of the cinema. The pandemic brought about painful global closures and restrictions on spaces of collective appearance, including the cinema theater. During these years, the virtualization of the cinematic from the material basis of the elements of cinema, such as the theater, has become more apparent. One might even ask, if, as Francesco Casetti (1999, 316) suggests, cinema "no longer has its own place, because it is every-where, or at least everywhere where we are dealing with aesthetics and communication," does everywhere also become nowhere? Indeed, in *Cinema by Other Means*, Pavle Levi (2012, xiv) argues for an expanded notion of cinema as "a form of praxis" that can be freed from the cinematographic apparatus. Through the Walker series, we could consider the innermost possibility of cinema as rhythmic interruptions that offer possibilities of attunement to alternative modes of being together.

Some years later, when I read Alan Klima's (2019, 163–64) invocation of "silence that eased my mind and filled me with the bare and ordinary presence of the world," my self-in-isolation returned to the moment of the vanishing screen and the bodies of intimate strangers in a space no longer public or private. In passive postures of sleep, inertia, or insomnia, these bodies in horizontal assembly perform an ethicopolitical possibility of being together as vulnerable strangers mediated by windows and screens, holding in abeyance the questions of who the others are, where they come from, or what language they speak. As the mechanisms of the world slowed down during the Covid-19 pandemic and physical movements through the passages and networks of the world became restricted, and as the world reshapes itself in this aftermath, the urgency of retaining a place and time for an ethics and aesthetics of passivity should not be forgotten. The downward movements of slowing down and lying down offer rhythmic counterpoints to a future conceived of as accelerationist progress.

■ CONCLUSION: ANOTHER STEP, ANOTHER SLEEP

Beyond film and video, the Walker series is accompanied by a traveling stage play: *The Monk from Tang Dynasty*, which first traveled to art festivals in 2014. *The Monk from Tang Dynasty* showed in New Taipei City concurrently with the *No No Sleep* exhibition. Figure 8 shows the foyer, where another face of the economics of cinematic survival is visible—the sale

Figure 8. Merchandise and Tsaileelu coffee for sale at Cloud Gate Theater before the start of *The Monk from Tang Dynasty*. Photograph by Elizabeth Wijaya.

of Tsaileelu branded coffee and other merchandise. Indolence, fatigue, and weariness are refusals of the performances of social and economic life and a refusal of the imperatives of the day—of the numerous actions required in the pursuit of becoming or surviving. However, the fatigued figure, in refusing the performance of existence, also risks the future of its own existence. The twinned images of merchandising and of the Walker/ monk asleep serve as reminders that the cinematic is an attraction of contradictions: even the vanishing and mercurial drive of the cinematic cannot escape the need for capital in order to persist in some form.

How loud, and how soft, how palpable, and how imperceptible, can a minimal act with ethical force be? Globally, we are at a moment when sleeping, or lying flat, is a collective, political gesture. The horizontal inclinations of the Walker series anticipate the 2021 phenomenon of *tangping* (lying flat) in China that has caught on as a social protest movement against overwork in the pursuit of elusive, material goals. In an age of extractive capitalism that has been termed the Capitalocene to foreground the entwinement of capitalism with colonialism, rather than the Anthropocene, which attributes the ecological crisis to the human species as a whole, the exhaustion of humans and the earth is sometimes seen as a capitalist achievement (Moore 2015). Under the logic of maximal extraction from the body, where rest and sleep are deemed wasteful and unproductive, to be horizontally inclined is a passive act of refusal.

The Walker series is also a waiting series. The Walker series stages passivity in cinema, presenting waiting and momentary withdrawals from the world as more than evacuations of agency. Passivity, sleep, and the associated moods and acts of lassitude, such as boredom and distraction, can be sensuous, languid acts of protest within the excessive frame of extractive, accelerationist living promoted as consumable and consumerist lives. The evacuation of dynamic action on-screen shows the ethical and political power of moving as slowly as possible in a post–Industrial Revolution, post–Internet Revolution, networked world that offers little space for reserve and retreat. In the words of the poet William Wordsworth (1807), "the world is too much with us."

There are different stakes to waiting for daylight in an overnight museum exhibition, waiting for the unfolding scenes of film after film showing a slow-walking figure perambulating the world, and waiting for the time after a pandemic. The practice of waiting requires the training of passive action, which has collective, political potential. Passivity might seem like an abdication of responsibility, a selfish turning away from the possibility of political or social action. However, as my analysis of Tsai's works shows, the moods, postures, and practices of passivity do not necessarily signal a lack of action: lying down, insomnia, fatigue, refusal, sleep, waiting—these are all less perceptible practices of the will. Ethical spectatorship as radical passivity in the drawn-out time of slow cinema encourages dwelling on textural spaces. Tal S. Shamir (2016) writes on the cinema as a space of philosophical experience rather than cognition. This form of cinema, which creates space for the supine/distracted/soporific audience, acknowledges that bodily spectatorship is more than the presence of conscious attention. While our bodies are mirrored and multiplied by the sleeping body on-screen and the bodies asleep around us, the cinematic shows not a dream of another world existing on another reality but a dream of the contours of that world appearing luminously. In the entanglements between sites of cinematic form and the experience of cinematic time as the rupture of the entry of the other, the lone spectator, the public, the phantoms, may come together to create sites of appearance where ways of being together might be possible. These rhythms of soporific sociality transgress silhouettes of embodiment, whether marked by the lines of the body of the individual, the city, or the frames of a film.

On the last night of the *No No Sleep* exhibition, Tsai signed the pillows that were provided for the overnight visitors. Without quite knowing why, I, too, brought home a signed pillow. When I left Taipei, I left the pillow behind but carried with me the contrapuntal rhythms of those insistent steps, punctuated by the light of the city and the screen. Since then, this pandemic has highlighted our global, mutual interdependence even when it seems that we are living in individual silos. For some to be able to remain isolated, others had to continue in intensified or accelerated forms of labor. In a tired time, "to hope then is to hope for the reparation of the irreparable; it is to hope for the present" (Levinas 1978, 91). Exhortations of collective awakening abound in Thich Nhat Hanh's (2021) *Zen and the Art of Saving the Planet* on the urgency of recognizing interbeing and collective responsibility in the face of interrelated crises on the planetary scale: "We have to wake up together. And if we wake up together, then we have a chance" (4). But awakening to the mindful awareness of interconnected being and dwelling in fatigue need not be mutually exclusive states. In the twilight of sleep and sleeplessness, fatigue can be a symptom of the atomized individual who can barely persist, and it can be a force of emancipation from the "definite existence" of the individual self (Levinas 1978, 85). As scenes from the Walker series show, what appears to be slow is never monorhythmic.

Passivity proliferates. With another step (and perhaps another walking alongside), there is the possibility of another future, another form of collectivizing existences. And as Matthew Fuller (2018, 5) reminds us, "sleep persists." In the horizontal fall toward sleep, we, too, could persist.

Elizabeth Wijaya is an assistant professor of East Asian cinema at the University of Toronto.

■ **NOTES**
Thank you to Chan Cheow-thia, Sarah Woodstock, Conall Cash, the participants and mentors of the 2021 Summer Institute for East Asian Studies at the University of Pittsburgh, and the reviewers and editors of the journal. The first audience for an early version of this article was on a panel organized by Christopher Lupke at the 2017 Modern Language Association's annual convention. The field research for this article was funded by the Taiwan Fellowship.
1. On Levinas's engagement with Jewish philosophy, see Kleinberg

(2021) and Putnam (2008). See also Tsai's interview on Buddhism in Kramer (2015).

2. The preface to *Existence and Existents* notes Levinas's wartime captivity in a stalag.

3. Deleuze's volumes on cinematic time respond to Bergson on duration (see Deleuze 1986, 1989; Bergson 1988; Lundy 2018). King (2015) assesses Bergson and Deleuze on duration in relation to contemporary moving images.

4. See Gorfinkel (2019) on Tsai's late cinema after his announced retirement.

5. See Koepnick (2017) for a comparison of Apichatpong's and Tsai's cinema. See *Flowers of Taipei* (2014) for Apichatpong's comments on sleeping in the cinema. See also the sleeping soldiers in *Cemetery of Splendor* (2015) and Apichatpong's segment in the omnibus *Ten Years Thailand* (2018).

6. There has been much debate over the transcendental structure of Levinas's philosophy and its fraught encounters with human and nonhuman others. See Levinas (1989), where Levinas is unable to recognize ethical obligations to Palestinians, and Levinas (1988) on the (non)faces of animals. For a reparative reading of Levinas and animal friendship, see Guenther (2007). In "Dialectics and the Sino-Soviet Quarrel," first published in 1960, Levinas (2003) invokes the "yellow peril" as a spiritual threat against the West. See Caygill's (2002, 184) evaluation of Levinas's racism and its implications for Levinas's philosophy.

■ WORKS CITED

Agamben, Giorgio. 1998. *Homo Sacer: Sovereign Power and Bare Life*. Translated by Daniel Heller-Roazen. Stanford, Calif.: Stanford University Press.

Ahmed, Sara. 2006. *Queer Phenomenology*. Durham, N.C.: Duke University Press.

Balsom, Erika. 2022. "Between Art and Film: Revisiting the Exhibition Passages de l'image." *STILL: Studies on Moving Images* 4. https://still.inbetweenartfilm.com/en/between-art-and-film-revisiting-the-exhibition-passages-de-limage/.

Benjamin, Walter. 1968. "On Some Motifs in Baudelaire." In *Illuminations*, edited by Hannah Arendt, translated by Harry Zohn, 155–200. New York: Schocken Books.

Bergson, Henri. 1988. "Of the Survival of Images." In *Matter and Memory*, translated by Nancy Margaret Paul and W. Scott Palmer, 133–78. New York: Zone Books.

Bordeleau, Erik. 2013. "Soulful Sedentarity: Tsai Ming-Liang at Home at the Museum." *Studies in European Cinema* 10, no. 2–3: 179–94.

Butler, Judith. 2012a. *Parting Ways: Jewishness and the Critique of Zionism.* New York: Columbia University Press.

Butler, Judith. 2012b. "Precarious Life, Vulnerability and the Ethics of Cohabitation." *Journal of Speculative Philosophy* 26, no. 2: 134–51.

Casetti, Francesco. 1999. *Theories of Cinema, 1945–1995.* Translated by Francesca Chiostri et al. Austin: University of Texas Press.

Caygill, Howard. 2002. *Levinas and the Political.* New York: Routledge.

Chen, Tina. 2018. "Always Verging on the Impossible: The Structural Incoherence of Global Asias." *Social Text Online.* https://socialtext journal.org/periscope_article/always-verging-on-the-impossible-the -structural-incoherence-of-global-asias/.

Chen, Tina. 2021. "The Imaginable Ageography of Global Asias." *Verge: Studies in Global Asias* 7, no. 1: 39–48.

Cooper, Sarah. 2006. *Selfless Cinema? Ethics and French Documentary.* New York: Routledge.

Cooper, Sarah, ed. 2007. "The Occluded Relation: Levinas and Cinema." Special issue, *Film-Philosophy* 11, no. 2.

Cosentino, Olivia. 2021. "Slower Cinema: Violence, Affect, and Spectatorship in *Las elegidas.*" *Journal of Cinema and Media Studies* 60, no. 3: 62–82.

Crary, Jonathan. 2021. "Powering Down." *October* 176: 27–29.

Deleuze, Gilles. 1986. *Cinema 1: The Movement-Image.* Translated by Hugh Tomlinson and Barbara Habberjam. Minneapolis: University of Minnesota Press.

Deleuze, Gilles. 1989. *Cinema 2: The Time-Image.* Translated by Hugh Tomlinson and Robert Galeta. Minneapolis: University of Minnesota Press.

Fuhrmann, Arnika. 2016. *Ghostly Desires: Queer Sexuality and Vernacular Buddhism in Contemporary Thai Cinema.* Durham, N.C.: Duke University Press.

Fuller, Matthew. 2018. *How to Sleep: The Art, Biology and Culture of Unconsciousness.* London: Bloomsbury.

Gardiner, Michael, and Julian Jason Haladyn, eds. 2017. *Boredom Studies Reader: Frameworks and Perspectives.* New York: Routledge.

Girgus, Sam. 2010. *Levinas and the Cinema of Redemption: Time, Alterity, and the Feminine.* New York: Columbia University Press.

Gorfinkel, Elena. 2019. "To Extent into the Beyond: On Tsai Ming-liang's Digital Late Style." *Sight and Sound,* April 19. https://bfi.org.uk/news

-opinion/sight-sound-magazine/features/tsai-ming-liang-late-digital
-period-deserted-your-face.

Guenther, Lisa, 2007. "Le Flair Animal: Levinas and the Possibility of Animal Friendship." *PhaenEx* 2, no. 2: 216–38.

Honig, Bonnie. 2021. *A Feminist Theory of Refusal*. Cambridge, Mass.: Harvard University Press.

Hu, Tung-Hui. 2017. "Wait, Then Give Up: Lethargy and the Reticence of Digital Art." *Journal of Visual Culture* 16, no. 3: 337–54.

Irigary, Luce. 1991. "Questions to Emmanuel Levinas: On the Divinity of Love." In *Re-reading Levinas,* edited by Robert Bernasconi and Simon Critchley, 109–18. London: Bloomsbury.

King, Homay. 2015. *Virtual Memory: Time-Based Art and the Dream of Digitality*. Durham, N.C.: Duke University Press.

Kleinberg, Ethan. 2021. *Emmanuel Levinas's Talmudic Turn: Philosophy and Jewish Thought*. Stanford, Calif.: Stanford University Press.

Klima, Alan. 2019. *Ethnography #9*. Durham, N.C.: Duke University Press.

Koepnick, Lutz. 2014. *On Slowness: Toward an Aesthetic of the Contemporary*. New York: Columbia University Press.

Koepnick, Lutz. 2017. *The Long Take: Art Cinema and the Wondrous*. Minneapolis: University of Minnesota Press.

Kramer, Gary M. 2015. "Tsai Ming-liang: Creation, Bathrooms and Buddhism." *Bomb Magazine,* April 8. http://bombmagazine.org/article /916542/tsai-ming-liang/.

Lamarre, Thomas. 2017. "Platformativity: Media Studies, Area Studies." *Asiascape: Digital Asia* 4, no. 3: 285–305.

Lee, Pamela L. 2021. "Lying in the Gallery." *October* 176: 53–72.

Levi, Pavle. 2012. *Cinema by Other Means*. Oxford: Oxford University Press.

Levinas, Emmanuel. 1978. *Existence and Existents*. Translated by Alphonso Lingis. The Hague: Martinus Nijhoff.

Levinas, Emmanuel. 1979. *Totality and Infinity*. Translated by Alphonso Lingis. The Hague: Martinus Nijhoff.

Levinas, Emmanuel. 1988. "The Paradox of Morality: An Interview with Emmanuel Levinas." Conducted by Tamra Wright, Peter Hughes, and Alison Ainley. In *The Provocation of Levinas: Rethinking the Other,* edited by Robert Bernasconi and David Wood, 168–80. London: Routledge.

Levinas, Emmanuel. 1989. "Ethics and Politics." In *The Levinas Reader,* edited by Seán Hand, 289–97. Oxford: Blackwell.

Levinas, Emmanuel. 1997. *Difficult Freedom*. Translated by Seán Hand. Baltimore: Johns Hopkins University Press.

Levinas, Emmanuel. 1998. *Otherwise than Being*. Translated by Alphonso Lingis. Pittsburgh, Pa.: Duquesne University Press.

Levinas, Emmanuel. 2003. "Dialectics and the Sino-Soviet Quarrel." In *Unforeseen History*, translated by Nidra Poller, 107–9. Champaign: University of Illinois Press.

Lim, Song Hwee. 2014. *Tsai Ming-liang and a Cinema of Slowness*. Honolulu: University of Hawai'i Press.

Lim, Song Hwee. 2022. *Taiwan Cinema as Soft Power: Authorship, Transnationality, Historiography*. Oxford: Oxford University Press.

Lundy, Craig. 2018. *Deleuze's Bergsonism*. Edinburgh: Edinburgh University Press.

Ma, Jean. 2021. "Sleeping in the Cinema." *October* 176: 31–52.

Moore, Jason W. 2015. *Capitalism in the Web of Life: Ecology and the Accumulation of Capital*. London: Verso.

Ng, Teng Kuan. 2018. "Pedestrian Dharma: Slowness and Seeing in Tsai Ming-Liang's Walker." *Religions* 9, no. 7: 200.

Odell, Jenny. 2019. *How to Do Nothing: Resisting the Attention Economy*. New York: Melville House.

Paasonen, Susanna. 2021. *Dependent, Distracted, Bored: Affective Formations in Networked Media*. Cambridge, Mass.: MIT Press.

Petrini, Carlo. 2003. *Slow Food: The Case for Taste*. Translated by William McCuaig. New York: Columbia University Press.

Putnam, Hilary. 2008. *Jewish Philosophy as a Guide to Life: Rosenzweig, Buber, Levinas, Wittgenstein*. Bloomington: Indiana University Press.

Richmond, Scott. 2015. "Vulgar Boredom; or, What Andy Warhol Can Teach Us about Candy Crush." *Journal of Visual Culture* 14, no. 1: 21–39.

Sakai, Naoki. 2019. "Translation and Image: On the Schematism of Configuration." In *At Translation's Edge*, edited by Nataša Durovicova, Patrice Petro, and Lorena Terando, 79–97. New Brunswick, N.J.: Rutgers University Press.

Schoonover, Karl, and Rosalind Galt, eds. 2016. *Queer Cinema in the World*. Durham, N.C.: Duke University Press.

Screendaily. 2012. "Youku Launches Year-long Beautiful Programme." March 18. https://www.screendaily.com/youku-launches-year-long -beautiful-programme/5039385.article.

Seeber, Barbara K., and Maggie Berg. 2016. *The Slow Professor: Challenging the Culture of Speed in the Academy*. Toronto: University of Toronto Press.

Shamir, Tal S. 2016. *Cinematic Philosophy*. New York: Palgrave.

Simpson, Audra. 2014. *Mohawk Interruptus: Political Life across the Borders of Settler States*. Durham, N.C.: Duke University Press.

Sing, Song-yong. 2014. *Rujing chujing: Tsai Ming-liang de yingxiang yishu yu kuajie shijian* [Projecting Tsai Ming-liang: Towards trans art cinema]. Taipei: Wunan.

Thich Nhat Hanh. 2021. *Zen and the Art of Saving the Planet.* New York: HarperOne.

Tsai, Beth. 2017. "The Many Faces of Tsai Ming-liang: Cinephilia, the French Connection, and Cinema in the Gallery." *International Journal of Asia Pacific Studies* 13, no. 2: 141–60.

Tsai, Ming-liang. 2011. "On the Uses and Misuses of Cinema." *Senses of Cinema* 58. https://www.sensesofcinema.com/2011/feature-articles /on-the-uses-and-misuses-of-cinema/.

Voci, Paola. 2020. "Alternative Ways of Seeing: Post-digital Detours in Chinese Cinema." In *The Chinese Cinema Book,* edited by Song Hwee Lim and Julian Ward, 258–68. London: Bloomsbury.

Wordsworth, William. 1807. *Poems in Two Volumes.* Vol. 1. London: Longman, Hurst, Rees, and Orme.

SHANNON WELCH

Belonging beyond Borders: Japanese Brazilian Stories of Diasporic Return without a "Homecoming"

BECAUSE DIASPORIC COMMUNITY is often characterized by a desire to return to a shared homeland, one could argue that the more than three hundred thousand Japanese Brazilian "return migrants" now residing in Japan have lived out this dream of "homecoming." Their "return" was facilitated by the Japanese state's revision to the Immigration Control and Refugee Recognition Act in 1990,[1] which permitted "Nikkeijin,"[2] or persons with Japanese ancestry (to the third generation), to obtain renewable visas for temporary residence and work abroad. Though the state justified its restriction to Nikkeijin with the argument that their shared ethnicity with Japanese citizens would allow for easy assimilation into Japanese society, historians and social scientists, including Daniel Linger (2001), Joshua Hotaka Roth (2002), Jeffrey Lesser (2003), and Takeyuki Tsuda (2003), have challenged the essentialist presumption that ethnicity guarantees belonging by providing various examples of Japanese Brazilians struggling to feel at "home" in their ancestral homeland owing to Japanese and Brazilian cultural disparities. Yet the continued evocation of "home" as a model of belonging neglects to account for the *multiple* hegemonic ideologies animating this paradigm and who might confront exclusion because of other identity formations that *intersect* with cultural difference.

In this article, I explore two Japanese Brazilian literary texts preceding this generation of "return migrants" that grapple with the question of diasporic return in a way that draws attention to the intertwined dynamics of race, class, gender, and sexuality that shape this fantasy of "homecoming" and foreclose its actualization to certain subjects. Both works are narrated by first-generation Japanese immigrant women who migrated to Brazil after World War II and return to their hometowns for a temporary visit with their families in the 1970s. The first text, Japanese Brazilian writer Arai Chisato's 1974 short story "Homecoming," imagines a Japanese immigrant woman named Tomoko who returns to Japan to introduce her parents to their grandchildren. Despite her excited expectations, she discovers that her hometown has transformed under capitalist development and that her parents, too, appear unfamiliarly cold, which ultimately makes her regret the trip. The second work, "I Cannot Sing the National Anthem" (2007), is a chapter within a collection of memoirs by six Japanese immigrant women titled *Women's History of Immigration to Brazil (Onna tachi no burajiru ijūshi),* edited by Kusakano Yoshitake. Authored by Tsuchida Machie, the chapter comprises nineteen autobiographical vignettes that describe significant moments in Machie's life, from her migration to Brazil in 1957 to her eightieth birthday in 2005. In the middle of her memoir, Machie gives an account of her return "home" to visit her mother, a stay characterized by disorienting changes, state bureaucracy, and instances of social connection.

By juxtaposing "Homecoming" and "I Cannot Sing the National Anthem," I argue that the dialogue between the two texts renders visible the gendered, sexualized, racialized, and classed logics that underpin dominant imaginations of the Japanese national community and the Japanese diaspora in Brazil as putatively unified, stable entities. I utilize a mode of comparison that brings the two stories of "homecoming" into relation, while remaining attuned to the different insight that each offers from the narrator's individual perspective. Specifically, each text sheds light on the hegemonic dimensions of the paradigm of "home" and the related institution of the "family," which can (re)produce restrictive and hierarchal community formations when they become privileged models of collectivity. While Tomoko's account particularly questions the notion of diasporic return as a "homecoming," Machie's narrative explores the exclusion fomented by idealizations of "home" and "family" in both national and diasporic contexts and illuminates alternative possibilities for fostering belonging beyond their boundaried logics.

Because the dominant historical narrative surrounding the Japanese diaspora in Brazil has largely been composed by male voices, Tomoko's and Machie's perspectives as immigrant women disclose less familiar stories from the postwar generation. My reading of their accounts follows the work of historian Mieko Nishida (2018), who aims to "hear" the stories of Japanese Brazilian women and posits that a conceptual category like "diaspora" does not guarantee a shared sense of communal belonging.

In this article, I regard diaspora as an imagined community based on a departure from a common space (another imagined community) that is always already heterogeneous. I also approach it as what Stuart Hall (1998, 226) calls a "positioning," suggesting that diasporic identity formations are contingent and unstable even if they may be strategic for counterhegemonic movements.

Through investigating movements between Japan and Brazil, this article speaks to the field of transpacific studies and current scholarship working to extend its scope into Latin America to move beyond an overfocus on the United States.[3] While the transpacific as a geopolitical region between "Asia" and "America" has long been imagined as a site of capitalist development and conquest under names like the Pacific Rim, the field of transpacific studies has more recently been working to theorize the flows of capital, ideas, people, and so on across the space and critique their entanglements with multiple systems of power. Scholars including Lisa Yoneyama (2017) and Tina Chen (2020) have traced developments within the field genealogically and note a shift toward not simply recharting these circulations but utilizing the "transpacific" as a methodology for interrogating the purpose of mapping and its relationship to knowledge-power. My use of a transpacific optics continues this critical work and is further inspired by literary scholar Andrea Mendoza's (2022, 20) description of the transpacific as a "reorientation," which "moves beyond the inflections of area and nation-based scholarship and turns toward decolonial analyses of the effects created by the imagined boundaries of communities and bodies."

Specifically, this article engages in a reorientation between "Asia" and "Latin America" as a decolonial move to denaturalize the divisions between geopolitical regions and nation-states and rethink the ways these separations have shaped our understandings of the world and the everyday social relations happening in it. In doing so, it draws from Chiara Olivieri and Jordi Serrano-Muñoz's (2022, 2) theorization of transpacific studies in their newly edited volume, *East Asia, Latin America, and the Decolonization of Transpacific Studies*, which advocates for the field to acknowledge a plurality of perspectives by accommodating "analogous, tangential, and even contradicting approaches to the studies of our ideas." By exploring stories about migratory routes that do not transit through the so-called West, I interrogate how the texts represent diaspora, nation, gender, and race in ways often not commensurate with U.S. and Eurocentric paradigms. That is, while still accounting for the global force of white supremacy and the knowledge it has produced in line with the discourse of "the West" and "the Rest,"[4] I look at how modern/colonial[5] logics have been mediated, appropriated, and localized in ways that have created distinctive hegemonic formations across different time-spaces.

To remain attuned to epistemic pluralities, my comparative reading of "Homecoming" and "I Cannot Sing the National Anthem" engages a transnational feminist analytic that particularly utilizes the practice of border thinking. As decolonial and women of color feminists (see, e.g., Anzaldúa [1987] 2022; Lugones 2010) have elaborated, border thinking involves critical, collaborative reflection from the in-between, liminal spaces constructed by the intertwined forces of racialization, colonization, heterosexualism, and capitalist exploitation. It employs a multiplicity of ways of thinking, knowing, and doing, especially by listening to and learning from those most impacted by these modern/colonial systems of power. In this way, it overlaps with the concept of "relational nonalignment" in Global Asias scholarship, which brings together disciplines, methods, and critical perspectives without insisting on consolidation and resolution (Chen 2021, 1002–3). Both take incommensurability as a crucial condition of possibility for dialogue and coalitional work that can challenge hegemonic regimes of knowledge production.

By utilizing border thinking to analyze literary representations of the Japanese diaspora in Brazil, the article enters into conversation with scholars like Tina Campt and Deborah Thomas (2008), who have employed transnational feminist frameworks to scrutinize the hegemonic gender and racial formations *within* diasporic communities. Marianne Hirsch and Nancy Miller (2011, 4) have also taken a transnational feminist approach to studies of diasporic return to begin thinking through "a multifaceted paradigm of community that acknowledges longings to belong and to return while remaining critical of a politics of identity and nation." As Tomoko and Machie dwell within the borderlands of not only the Japanese diaspora in Brazil but also the Japanese and Brazilian nations, I utilize transnational feminist frameworks to look at how both narrators illuminate the exclusionary processes that demarcate the limits of these imagined communities and point us toward other ways that we might rethink relationality, community, and social connection.

To make my argument, I start with a summary of the history of the Japanese Brazilian community to contextualize the transpacific power entanglements that the literary texts bring into focus. I then elaborate on Arai's and Tsuchida's oeuvres and their relationship to the development of Japanese Brazilian literature. Following this contextualization, I read Tomoko's and Machie's accounts of traveling back to Japan and examine how they question the notion of a diasporic return "home" and expose the gendered, sexualized, racialized, and classed ideologies that condition their exclusion from the Japanese national community. Finally, I interrogate the extent to which these intersecting hegemonic ideologies continue to animate their attempt to imagine the Japanese diasporic community as a "home" in Brazil. The comparative dialogue between the two texts ultimately allows for a reflection on diaspora and community building that verges on critique, caution, and creativity. It inspires a critique of essentialized understandings of national culture believed to tie a diasporic community to its "homeland," caution against repeating nationalist practices of exclusion and dominance within diasporic formations, and creative imaginations of belonging based on embodied relationships of interdependence and care.

■ TRANSPACIFIC POWER ENTANGLEMENTS IN THE HISTORY OF THE JAPANESE DIASPORA IN BRAZIL

The process of Japanese immigration to Brazil emerged from negotiations between the Brazilian and Japanese governments that began in the late nineteenth century. Brazilian policy makers had originally advocated for white European immigrants to both replace its plantation workforce following the abolition of slavery in 1888 and "whiten" its population (Lesser 1999, 82–85). However, European immigrants frequently protested against their labor conditions, causing the Brazilian elite to seek a more docile workforce. Japanese immigrants then became a favorable option, with the suggestion made by Japanese diplomats that the Japanese were "the 'whites' of Asia" and a hardworking people. The Japanese state, too, found immigration to Brazil to be an attractive solution to address overpopulation and poverty in rural Japan, especially after the United States implemented restrictions on Japanese immigration with the 1907 Gentlemen's Agreement.

On June 18, 1908, the ship *Kasato Maru* brought the first immigrants from Japan to the state of São Paulo to work primarily as contract laborers on Brazilian-owned plantations. The Brazilian government required them to migrate in family units led by a male head of household, believing this would prevent unrest among workers (Nishida 2018, 24). Japanese state officials also supported family-based migration as they thought it would guarantee moral stability as a safeguard against Japanese exclusion (Azuma 2019, 130–35). Yet, similar to their European predecessors, many Japanese workers found their labor conditions to be unfavorable and broke their contracts. The Brazilian and Japanese governments then pivoted toward Japanese-run colonies that allowed Japanese migration companies to purchase land from the Brazilian state and oversee the agricultural settlements themselves (Lesser 1999, 88–91).

The Japanese government took on a more direct role in managing emigration in 1924 after the Great Kantō Earthquake (1923) exacerbated demographic crises in Japan and the United States further curbed immigration with the 1924 Immigration Act. Scholars Endoh Toake (2016), Eiichiro Azuma (2019), Sidney Xu Lu (2019), and Fujinami Kai (2020) argue that Japanese state-sponsored migration to Brazil at this moment should be understood as a practice of imperial expansionism continuous with Japanese colonization in East Asia and the Pacific. Azuma and Lu use the term "settler colonialism" to describe the migration system that appropriated local and/or Indigenous lands to build up an agricultural economy abroad. Reflecting on what is called *ishokumin,* or "migration-colonization," which took place first in Hokkaido, then in the Americas and Manchuria, Azuma (2019, 2) writes,

> Agrarian settler colonialism was always integral to modern Japanese imperialism, and it constituted one of the many ways in which state officials and social leaders adopted policies and initiated reforms that were intended to both defend the nation against being colonized by western powers and demonstrate that they were worthy imperialists as well in the Eurocentric international order of the time.

Various Japanese political actors, therefore, looked upon migration-colonization as not only an opportunity to support the empire's material and territorial growth but also a way for the nation to showcase its development capabilities as a modern power.

Japanese state-managed migration evinced several contradictions. Migration recruiters targeted their efforts toward the prefectures of Hiroshima, Kumamoto, Fukuoka, and Okinawa, claiming that they contained population "surpluses" responsible for Japan's demographic problems. However, these regions were also home to Japan's working class, the Burakumin caste, and indigenous Okinawans—peoples considered superfluous to the nation's central elite (Endoh 2016, 114–20). Additionally, these areas had a history of worker resistance that officials feared might threaten the nation's stability (Endoh 2016, 123–38; Fujinami 2020, 84–89).

Despite the insinuation that emigrants were "excess," state actors still recognized them as a necessary faction within Japan's expansionist enterprise. They sought to maintain the emigrants' loyalty to the nation through establishing predeparture education facilities to "instill a nationalist sense of 'duty' in the mind and heart of every imperial subject" (Azuma 2019, 131). For Okinawan immigrants in particular, the predeparture training wielded colonialist violence as it promoted assimilation that attempted to erase their indigenous languages and cultures.

From within Brazil, Japanese immigrants experienced racialization and assimilationist forces that conflicted with the Japanese state's imperialist pressure. During the 1930s, under the Getúlio Vargas regime, the Brazilian government banned foreign-language education and placed restrictions on immigration (Lesser 2013, 163–68). Then, with the establishment of the Estado Novo (New State) dictatorship in 1937, Vargas initiated the Brasilidade (Brazilianization) campaign, which enacted even harsher assimilationist measures, such as banning Japanese-language newspapers (see Schpun 2019). World War II escalated the policing of the Japanese Brazilian community—Brazilian authorities searched the homes of Japanese immigrants, forced thousands to relocate, and took control of Japanese agrarian operations in the interior of São Paulo (Rivas 2012, 111–13). The structural violence in addition to everyday discrimination pressured immigrants to decide whether to consent to assimilation or assert their Japanese identities against Brazilianization.

Some Japanese immigrants who resolutely affirmed their "Japaneseness" published underground newspapers in the 1940s that castigated immigrants "disloyal" to the empire (Lesser 2013, 168–75). Owing to the ban on foreign-language media, these publications managed to perpetuate rumors of Japan's victory in World War II, which took hold among a portion of Japanese Brazilians. Eventually, the community split into two factions: kachigumi (victorist), who believed Japan won the war, and makegumi (defeatist), who accepted Japan's loss. Some kachigumi members developed secret societies, such as the notorious Shindo Renmei, which engaged in assassinations and kidnappings to punish Japanese "traitors" from 1946 to 1950.

After its interruption during the war, Japanese immigration to Brazil resumed in 1952. Many of the same prewar Japanese migration agents took up similar leadership positions, while targeting emigration toward "surplus" populations associated not only with overpopulation but also with marginal class and racial identities. Lu (2019, 239) asserts that these consistencies are "crucial for our understanding of the trans-Pacific legacies of Japanese settler colonialism in the postwar era." One important difference was that Japanese discourses no longer portrayed the United States and Europe as competitors but rather embraced U.S. hegemony and the role of Japan as "a 'surrogate for the whites' in developing Latin America" (Endoh 2009, 193).

Yet, also at this time, large numbers of prewar immigrants and their descendants had migrated into major cities—especially São Paulo—

and actively integrated themselves into mainstream Brazilian society. Contrasting the "traditionalist," first-generation *kachigumi* immigrants, this group embraced a new postwar identity and referred to their community as *koronia,* or "a settlement of immigrants" (transliterated from the Portuguese *colônia*). The new generation, with limited knowledge of Brazilian culture and Portuguese, however, reignited discrimination and long-standing accusations that the Japanese were "unassimilable," which led some prewar immigrants to pressure these newcomers to quickly become "Brazilians" (Nishida 2018, 103–5).

The 1960s and 1970s became Brazil's "Diaspora Decades," in which Japanese Brazilians found opportunities to shape Brazil's international connections and renegotiate their identities (Lesser 2007, 1–24). With the start of Brazil's military dictatorship in 1964, many young Japanese Brazilians seized the chance to move up the social ladder through pursuing higher education and adhering to the political regime's promotion of discipline and conformity as paths to success. Japan's economic growth additionally influenced the perception of Japanese Brazilians as a "model minority," which exhibited a major change from the racialized oppression experienced by prewar immigrants.

Moreover, Japan and Brazil forged greater economic networks at this time, and Japan especially increased its investments in Brazil. These economic ties generated more commercial flights in the 1970s, which made travel between Japan and Brazil more convenient and affordable (Nishida 2018, 63), as we will see was the case for Tomoko and Machie. In the following sections, as I analyze "Homecoming" and "I Cannot Sing the National Anthem," I carefully read the works within this transpacific historical context to account for the multiple layers, directions, and entanglements of power with which the texts engage in their stories of diasporic return. This history especially helps clarify the positionalities of Tomoko and Machie that require the interdisciplinarity and epistemic plurality of border thinking to work through the gender, sexuality, race, and class dynamics of their experiences.

■ JAPANESE BRAZILIAN LITERARY PRODUCTION

Arai Chisato and Tsuchida Machie both belong to the postwar generation of Japanese immigrants, and their stories provide representations of the Japanese diaspora in Brazil primarily during the 1960s and 1970s. Tsuchida migrated from Kumamoto prefecture to Brazil in 1957 at age 33, and Arai arrived later in 1961 at age 23 from Nagano prefecture. Neither was a writer by profession, although Arai did write *tanka* and *haiku* poetry throughout her life and coauthored a book of memoirs with her husband titled *Kuni futatsu seoite* (Carrying two countries, 2011). Tsuchida, too, took lessons in writing poetry while in Brazil and composed *haiku* under the name Machijō.

Their works, "Homecoming" (1974) and "I Cannot Sing the National Anthem" (2007), made their appearances decades into the development of Japanese Brazilian literature, which can be traced back to poems written aboard the inaugural voyage of *Kasato Maru* (Arata 2008, 9). The prewar collection of texts was known as *shokumin bungaku*, or "colonial literature," as Japanese settlements in Brazil at the time were referred to as *shokuminchi* (colonies). These works—serialized short fiction and poetry—appeared mainly in literature columns printed as early as 1916 in Japanese-language newspapers and magazines in Brazil, such as *Burajiru Jihō* (Brazil times) and *Nōgyō no Burajiru* (Agricultural Brazil) (Hosokawa 2012, 36). Zelideth María Rivas (2015) identifies print media as an integral medium through which early Japanese communities scattered around Brazil shared each other's experiences and began to see themselves as a connected group. Yet these publications did not always guarantee unity, as Japanese-language newspapers divided into separate media networks alongside the community's split into the *kachigumi* and *makegumi* factions.

Arai's "Homecoming" emerged after these conflicts during an era that Hosokawa Shūhei (2013) and Arata Sumu (2008) refer to as the Golden Age of Koronia Bungaku—*Koronia Bungaku* being the new appellation of Japanese Brazilian literary texts in Japanese and Portuguese. The period coincides with the establishment of the Koronia Bungakukai (Koronia Literary Association) in 1966 and the publication of its literary journal, *Koronia Bungaku*, which ran until 1977. Amid the Diaspora Decades and the rise of internationalism in Brazil, the first director of the association, Suzuki Teiti, aimed to propel *koronia* prose fiction forward toward the international recognition that Japanese Brazilian informalist abstract painters like Tomie Ohtake, Tikashi Fukushima, and Manabu Mabe had earned (Hosokawa 2013, 265; Erber 2015).

During this period, anthropologist and literary enthusiast Maeyama Takashi (1975) also took on a leading role and urged writers to engage critically with their experiences as an ethnic minority group in Brazil. He emphasized the importance of preserving the history of *koronia* literature and worked with the Koronia Bungakukai to compose three anthologies of short stories in the 1970s (Hosokawa 2013, 266). Arai's "Homecoming" was republished in the third edition of this series after first being printed in the 1974 *Paurisuta Nenkan* (Paulista annual publication).

Tsuchida's chapter in *Women's History of Immigration to Brazil*, on the other hand, did not have an affiliation with the Koronia Bungakukai, which had renamed itself Burajiru Nikkei Bungakukai (Brazilian Nikkei Literary Association)[6] in 1999 to be more recognizable to readers outside Brazil. Rather, the book was published in Japan in 2007 by Mainichi Shinbun-sha with the help of Japanese journalist Kusano Yoshitake, who wanted to share the contributions of women to the history of Japanese immigration to Brazil. Though Tsuchida's writing has circulated in Japan, it does not quite reflect Suzuki's dream of international literary prestige, as the piece of creative nonfiction is categorized as historical journalism rather than a literary "masterpiece."

To date, only two Japanese Brazilian prose writers have earned such recognition in Japan as "professional" authors: Daigo Masao[7] and Matsui Tarō (Mack 2022, 232). In Brazil, Oscar Nakasato has received commendations after his win of the coveted Jabuti literary prize in 2012 for his novel *Nihonjin*. The acknowledgment of these men as exemplary writers coincides with the long-standing male dominance in the Japanese Brazilian literary community, in addition to male-centered frameworks within Japanese diasporic studies and Japanese-language literary studies. Hence Arai's and Tsuchida's writings bring to the surface traditionally marginalized voices that complicate how the history of the Japanese diaspora in Brazil is remembered.

Although both male and female Japanese Brazilian authors have engaged with a myriad of themes, such as worker exploitation, discrimination, dreams of returning to Japan, generational differences, troubled romances, and *mestiçagem* (miscegenation), female writers have often dealt with these questions with a sharper focus on the gender and sexuality dynamics entangled with them (López-Calvo 2019). Unlike modern Japanese women writers like Tamura Toshiko and Hayashi Fumiko, who depicted immigration to Canada and French Indochina, respectively, as an opportunity for working-class women to find some liberation from patriarchal structures in Japan,[8] Japanese Brazilian women have generally represented the perpetuation of male dominance in Brazil. For example, prewar female writers like Hayashi Ise[9] and Yanagisen Shinako wrote stories about the patriarchal structure of the Japanese family and the pressures it exerted on women in Japan and the Japanese diaspora in Brazil. In the postwar period, female immigrants have written in both Japanese and Portuguese with a continued accentuation on the everyday challenges of women within the diasporic community. Among these writers are Kitajima Fumiko, who wrote extensively for the journal *Yomimono* (Reading material), and Mitsuko Kawai and Laura Honda-Hasegawa, who wrote longer novels in Portuguese, drawing from their own experiences as Japanese Brazilian women.

Arai's and Tsuchida's texts also add their perspectives on the gendered dimensions of diasporic return for postwar Japanese immigrants prior to the "return migration" boom. As we will see, the narrators of their stories, Tomoko and Machie (Tsuchida's first name), travel back to Japan in the 1970s and experience disorienting changes to the culture of their hometowns that shed light on the instability of Japanese national identity and how shifting gendered, classed, and racialized ideologies work to construct and reconstruct it. Narrated from different decades, the two stories diverge in the ways they show Tomoko and Machie navigating these transformations. Because Tomoko gives her account shortly after her trip, she focuses on its immediate negative affect, in comparison to Machie, whose reflective distance allows her to weigh moments of connection in tension with feelings of "foreignness." Bringing the two texts into conversation thus permits both a critical reflection on nationalist exclusivity and a possibility for imagining communal connectivity beyond paradigms of a national "home."

◼ REEVALUATING DIASPORIC RETURN AS A "HOMECOMING"

The fantasy of a diasporic "homecoming" draws on an imagination of the community's coherence based on its members' relationship to a shared "origin," with which they long to reunite. In the case of Japan, as previously discussed, Japanese imperialist discourses largely shaped the construction of this essentialized connection between the diaspora and the nation to maintain the immigrants' loyalty to the metropole. At the same time, Japanese state officials contradictorily regarded these same imperial subjects to be "superfluous" populations, as most came from marginalized racial and class groups. Yet, as we will see, Tomoko and Machie unravel the legacies of these imperialist representations by illuminating their differences from the "homogeneous" national community.

When Tomoko and Machie return to their hometowns in Japan, they describe similar scenes of transformation. As Tomoko walks up to her parents' house in Shinshū, she finds that there are no longer the beautiful ponds, abundant mulberry fields, and copious peach trees from her memories. In their place now stand large, upscale houses—identical and orderly, aligned in a row (Arai [1974] 1978, 315).[10] Capitalist development has homogenized the space, destroying the once brightly colored variance of nature and replacing it with the strictly structured array of human-made houses. Machie, too, notices the drastic changes to her rural hometown in Kumamoto that have ushered in new infrastructure with wide roads and brick roofs (Tsuchida 2007, 225). She comments particularly on the house of her former employers, who, during the war, had experienced similar socioeconomic precarities to Machie but now live in an elegant, mixed Japanese- and European-style home in an affluent neighborhood. For both narrators, these palpable conversions from postwar economic recovery stimulate a sense of disorientation as the two women feel out of place in locations they believed to be "home."

The depictions of Tomoko's and Machie's hometowns break from dominant representations of the *furusato* (for examples, see Scheiner 1998; Dodd 2004), meaning "native place" or "hometown," which is a discursive construct that has functioned to define a "timeless" Japanese national identity and designate who belongs to its imagined space. Usually in the countryside, the *furusato* is characterized by warmth and familiarity—the comforts of "home"—which includes the mother as its central figure (Karlin 2014, 16; Yoda 2000). The construct emerged during modernization in the Meiji era that destroyed the environment in rural Japan, transformed ways of life, and sparked massive migration to the cities (Ivy 1995, 103–5). These changes fueled anxiety over the loss of Japan's unique identity and produced a nostalgic desire for the *furusato* and its "traditional" customs. However, in both prewar and postwar discourses, dominant representations of the *furusato* recuperated and spectacularized only partial aspects of the spaces to which they claimed to refer, while negating the more disruptive elements that might tarnish the image of a "pure" and "eternal" Japanese culture. Put simply, the discursive construct supported an exclusive imagining of a Japanese identity.

The *furusato* in these discourses functions as a point of "origin" that helps the nation to construct a smooth, linear narrative of the Japanese people's development since this moment in time. It also attempts to work out the contradictions within national time—between the forward-moving time of progress and the consistency of a Japanese cultural "essence"—by serving as a symbol of tradition that attests to the present existence of a Japanese culture inherited from the past. Marilyn Ivy (1995, 23, 105–7), however, sheds light on how this homogenizing process of narrating the nation and its cultural identity operates through a politics of repression by reading the *furusato* as "uncanny." The "uncanny" or "unhomelike" is a Freudian term (*das Unheimlich*) defined as something that is both terrifying and familiar—unsettling because what has been concealed returns to sight. The "uncanny," as Ivy posits, destabilizes the assumption of a singular national culture by pointing to what becomes repressed to construct an image of homogeneity.

Tomoko experiences the "uncanny," as illustrated in her description of her familiar home feeling strangely "unfamilial." Beyond the eeriness surrounding the uniformity of her neighborhood, she notes her mother's incessant coldness, which brings her to lament, "This is not my home, not my mother, I didn't return to uh . . . Japan" (Arai [1974] 1978, 318). Her exclamation illustrates a perception of change that troubles the assumption of an "eternal" culture and its unbroken tradition. In particular, she pictures her mother as a mediating figure whose connection to the comforts of "home" determines if the space will offer her belonging. Yet, as she shows, the signs of "home" and "mother" that point to an "origin" do not, in fact, add up to a return to Japan. Her remark, therefore, exhibits a logic of supplements that questions the *furusato*'s "originary" status altogether. For Tomoko, the understanding of the *furusato* as an origin came into being as an aftereffect of her migration to Brazil, which brought the *notion* of the origin into consciousness.[11] Her listing of "home" and "mother" within a chain of supplements, therefore, exposes the "originary" *furusato* as always deferred and displaced.

Tomoko further discloses the national narrative's dependency on exclusion through her own embodiment of the "uncanny." As a working-class, immigrant woman, Tomoko becomes marginalized within the Japanese national community as both "surplus" to the nation and subordinate within a heteropatriarchal society. Yet Tomoko does not perceive her repudiation from the national imaginary until she returns to Japan and comes to realize her difference. As her narrative underscores her alternative temporality from the nation's linearity, it brings to light the temporal dissonance within Japan that its national history attempts to smooth over.

For example, Tomoko initially indicates her perception of unity with Japan while she is working in Brazil through the numerous references she makes to counted units of time. Tomoko calls attention to the fact that ten years have passed since she left her home by mentioning this number twelve times in the narrative. Moreover, she repeats phrases like "every day, every day" and "days and days of working overtime, working overtime" (Arai [1974] 1978, 309–10) to relay her experience of a measured temporality in which units carry the same, meaningless value and pass by linearly. This comprehension of time resembles the idea of "homogeneous, empty time"—the time of the nation—as theorized by Benedict Anderson ([1983] 2006, 24) and is what permits Tomoko to picture her connection to the Japanese national community while in Brazil.

But Tomoko's move from the diasporic periphery to the center of the nation sparks a clash between various temporalities within the national community that exposes who and what have been occluded within the nation's telling of history. We see this when Tomoko's mother scorns her daughter for wearing a sweater that looks like it was sewn during the war, to which her father adds the label *"kōshinkoku"* (undeveloped country) (Arai [1974] 1978, 318). Their remarks relegate her to a time of the past, alienating her from the "homogenous" time of the nation. They engage in a gesture aligned with the modern/colonial logic of the Japanese empire, which often employed time as a tactic to distinguish Japan's exceptionalism through transposing difference "from the realm of space to the realm of time, so that 'foreignness' increasingly came to be reinterpreted as 'underdevelopment'" (Morris-Suzuki 1998, 28). Similarly, Tomoko's parents deny their daughter's coevalness by assigning her to a past temporality associated with the "underdeveloped" modes of production characterizing her lifestyle in Brazil.

The mix of temporalities within the nation that we witness here resonates with Harry Harootunian's (2019, 178–81) discussion of the "everyday" as a temporal category introduced by the masses and the subaltern that disrupts the nation's attempt to portray its history as a linear process experienced uniformly by its "people." According to Harootunian, through the contingent and frictional interactions that these marginalized individuals have with the totalizing forces of capitalism, "the past will be seen to break into and be gathered up in the seemingly eternal present . . . often acting as a revenant or ghostly specter of the past bent on haunting and destabilizing the present" (190). In "Homecoming," we witness Tomoko's return to her hometown as a return of the repressed. She inserts into the present the time of working-class, immigrant women, which brings to the surface the uneven temporalities within Japan that the national narrative tries to smooth over to appear homogeneous. Tomoko, therefore, challenges the stability of the Japanese national culture and its authority as a unifying force that binds the diaspora to the nation.

In comparison to Tomoko, Machie's reencounter with her hometown proves to be similarly disorienting and causes her, at times, to feel "foreign." Specifically, when she goes to visit her mother in the hospital, she does not have the proper documentation from the municipal government to enter her mother's ward (Tsuchida 2007, 228). The application process, she learns, takes half a year, which makes her acutely aware of her "temporary visitor" status. In other words, the bureaucracy of the state institution reminds her that she does not belong to the nation-state, as it bars her from seeing her mother.

Despite this sense of unbelonging, Machie does find some moments of genuine connection during her trip. When she visits her former employers, for instance, the three friends spend the evening reminiscing about when Machie was working at their post office during World War II. Machie recalls a woman in their community who asked her to help write a letter to her son in the war and then later repaid her with a small gift of food. The couple responds with an acknowledgment of the extra burdens they all had taken on to support their community. Machie, the narrator writing in 2007, then concludes with the reflection, "We overcame nearly thirty years since the war and the distance between Brazil and Japan, speaking continuously to one another as if it were yesterday" (227).

Her comment serves as an illustration of an alternative imagination of time and space that differs from the nation's linear timeline and closed borders. Machie pictures the possibility of transcending temporal and spatial distances through everyday embodied relations that carry the past into the present. In this encounter, time is multidirectional and works genealogically to facilitate connections between peoples through their shared lived experiences. Moreover, these past moments importantly speak to moments of intimate, intersubjective relations based on reciprocity and care. Machie and the couple's memories demonstrate how the precarious circumstances of the war necessitated that they rely on one another to sustain themselves. Unlike the capitalist structure that divides Tomoko from her family and the state institutions that separate Machie from her mother, this form of relationality brings people together. Machie's narrative, therefore, introduces the possibility of building community through embodied connections and thinking relationality beyond borders.

■ BELONGING BEYOND MODELS OF "HOME" AND "FAMILY"

The dislocation that Tomoko and Machie experience from their return trips to Japan prompts reflection about where and how they might better locate a sense of "belonging." Tomoko's story, as I will show, illustrates an idealization of "home" tied to the "family," which implies to its 1970s Japanese diasporic readership that they might build community with one another by upholding the values of these institutions. However, through juxtaposing her account with Machie's narrative, I demonstrate how "home" and "family" function as more than metaphors; they carry with them particular gendered, sexualized, and racialized logics that may and, in Machie's case, have created hegemonic formations within the Japanese diaspora in Brazil. Imagining the Japanese Brazilian community around these two models, therefore, risks repeating nationalist practices of exclusion to construct a collective identity.

At the beginning of "Homecoming," Tomoko describes the motivation for her trip to Japan based on a conversation she had with an elderly passenger on the boat she took to Brazil ten years earlier. The woman urged her to return home while her relatives are still alive, even if she is not "wearing a brocade" (Arai [1974] 1978, 309). The brocade *(nishiki)* refers to a myth commonly held by prewar Japanese immigrants who believed that they could immigrate to Brazil, become wealthy quickly, and repatriate wearing a "brocade" symbolizing their riches and success. By changing the purpose of return to focus on family instead of wealth, Tomoko hints at a change within the postwar diasporic community and its values. This recollection sets the tone for the rest of the story, which continually emphasizes Tomoko's cherishing of family and a "homelike" environment that appear antithetical to capitalist greed.

Yet, as she elaborates her romanticization of family values, she illustrates a complicity with Japanese heteropatriarchal ideologies. For example, as Tomoko notices her parents' egotism, it stirs up memories from her childhood when they taught her that "money is secondary" next to the well-being of others (311–12). She remembers her father's diligent work ethic undertaken to support their family so that her mother would not need to work outside the home and contrasts him with her lazy father-in-law, who expected his wife to labor on the family farm (311). Although Tomoko's father appears as the more admirable individual among the two men, both families operate with the father as the head of household. In other words, the contrast she makes serves as a critique, not necessarily of heteropatriarchy, but of certain ways that heteropatriarchy can be practiced.

Looking at the modern genealogies of "home" and "family" in Japan, we become further aware of what is risked by imagining a diasporic community around these ideas that hold ties to Japanese imperialist legacies and their residual gendered, sexualized, and racialized ideologies. The Meiji state created the family registry system in 1871 and then, under the 1898 Civil Code, redefined the traditional Japanese family or *ie* in a hierarchical way, with men as the heads of household (Kumagai 2014, 47). Women were expected to act as a "good wife, wise mother," meaning they should engage in reproduction and perform household duties but also support their husbands' work and raise Japan's next generation to be strong and loyal citizens (Koyama 2013, 48).

Around the same time, the word *hōmu* (home) was introduced to Japan by Protestant reformers but did not gain influence in Japanese domestic life until it was adapted into the localized concept of *katei* (home) in the 1880s (Sand 1998, 193–96). *Katei* alongside the Civil Code began to transform family relations into tighter units of solidarity and privacy, leading to increased consideration over the moral practices within the household. Women's magazines and political discourses designated women responsible for its upkeep, while the Meiji government further invested in *katei kyōiku* (home education) to ensure mothers would properly educate future national subjects.

These gendered expectations carried over into the realm of migration. Prewar Japanese migration planners sought to balance the male-to-female ratio of the family-based system and called for the recruitment of more women who would contribute to "building a new home for the Japanese in South America" (Lu 2017, 461). They believed that a stable home would not only strengthen the moral integrity of the immigrant communities in Brazil but also contribute to reproducing the community and its racial "purity." Predeparture education devoted specific attention to women so that they could properly fulfill the role of "good wife, wise mother" (Azuma 2019, 130–32). The metaphor of the "extended family," at this time, further functioned to justify settler colonialism in Brazil, with claims that the Amazonian Indigenous people were ancient Asiatic descendants who would welcome "their superior brethren" (Azuma 2019, 146).

Idealizations of "home" and "family" continued to shape the male-dominant relations within the postwar diaspora. Nishida (2018, 223–26) explains how many first-generation parents prioritized education for their children, yet they emphasized higher education for their sons and skill-based schooling for their daughters to prepare them for managing the "home." Moreover, postwar marriage norms among educated and elite Japanese immigrants set expectations for daughters to practice endogamy to preserve their family's Japanese identity, while accepting marriages between sons and white Brazilians (227). The responsibility placed on women to reproduce the racial community highlights the intersection of racialized and heteropatriarchal logics underlying the imagination of a Japanese diasporic family.

Although Tomoko's story suggests to its audience that the Japanese Brazilian community might work together to preserve the value of family and construct a space of belonging that feels like "home," the narration ends before showing the actual effects that these values have on the community's social structure. Therefore, from "Homecoming," we can only speculate what is risked from utilizing "family" and "home" as paradigms for community building. However, "I Cannot Sing the National Anthem" does offer a deeper look into how the hegemonic ideologies animating the two terms migrate with Machie and lead to hierarchical racial and gender formations within the Japanese diaspora in Brazil.

Across several vignettes in her memoirs, Machie engages with the "good wife, wise mother" ideology and draws attention to the pressure she feels to conform to these family-based norms in both Japan and Brazil. The first subsection in her chapter, "'Good Wife' and 'Wise Mother,'" starts in 1957 Japan, when food scarcity and poverty make it difficult for Machie to sustain herself and her five children, especially because her unfaithful and irresponsible husband does not adequately provide for their family. As she looks to her mother for sympathy, her mother merely quotes, "Be a good wife, wise mother" (201). Hearing these words, Machie thinks to herself that she understands the sacrifices she must make for her children to be a "wise mother" but struggles to conform to the role of "good wife." The Meiji ideology surfaces again in another segment, titled "Mother," that recounts a moment eleven years after Machie immigrated to Brazil. In this short section, she shares a letter she wrote to her mother that communicates how she has finally moved up into the middle class in Brazil and can better live out the ideals of the *katei* (home) (Tsuchida 2007, 224). She also mentions how her husband has grown into a diligent worker to whom she can be a "good wife," while at the same time, her children have become her teachers—mostly helping her with the Portuguese language—so she feels less adequate as a "wise mother" (225).

The repetition of the "good wife, wise mother" ideology and its connection to the *katei* speak to the persistence of "traditional" female roles from Japan to the Japanese diaspora in Brazil. In these two segments, Machie often places her mother's words in quotations when she repeats phrases outlining gendered expectations. In this regard, lines like "be a good wife, wise mother" (201) and "being a housewife is how women live well" (224) almost seem to call attention to themselves as reiterations of Japanese heteropatriarchal discourses that construct female subject positions. Machie does attempt to perform these gendered subjectivities even after migrating to Brazil, yet her struggle to do so further points to acting as a "wife" and "mother" as a constructed role rather than being "innate" female characteristics. In the process, she leaves her mark of mediation by separating "good wife" and "wise mother" both in the way she describes them and with the insertion of "and" between the two identities in the first section's title (normally, the expression is written as a four-kanji character compound: 良妻賢母, not 「良妻」と「賢母」). The division shows that the two roles are not naturally and seamlessly intertwined but rather performed with varying degrees of "success."

In addition to disclosing the heteropatriarchal structure internal to the diaspora, Machie provides a look at the racialized implications of the notions of "home" and "family" in her penultimate vignette, "The Birth of My Mixed-Race Grandchild." In this section, Machie's second eldest son, Kenji, reveals his marriage to a mixed-race Brazilian woman named Valquiria that he had kept secret from his parents for fear of their disapproval, especially since Valquiria's mother is Black. Although Machie does not disapprove of their marriage, she does understand Kenji's impulse to hide his relationship. She regrettably recalls having repeated to him growing up: "If possible, you should marry a *Nikkei* woman" (247). Similar to her mother's earlier platitudes, she writes this line as a quotation that creates a separation between the self present with Kenji and the self from the past seeming to speak in a voice that is not her own. While her past remark demonstrates a complicity with a racialized imagination of the Japanese diaspora, the heteroglossia in these lines produces a tension that brings into focus the hegemonic discourses that construct such a representation of an exclusionary Japanese Brazilian community.

At the same time, this vignette offers a glimpse into another way of enacting ties of belonging that does not depend on a "pure" racial community. Machie concludes the segment with a description of the birth of her two grandchildren and the frequent visits she makes to Valquiria and Kenji's house to help raise them. She outlines an image of Valquiria, Valquiria's mother, and the two children—all of whose first language is Portuguese—trying to speak and learn Japanese with Machie (250). The scene highlights the friendship that has developed between the three adult women as they reciprocate an openness toward one another and encourage their grandchildren to celebrate their different backgrounds.

This model of "family" departs from the racialized, heteropatriarchal institution in Japan through the way social connections are built, not through blood ties, but through embodied relations reminiscent of the ones Machie experienced in Japan. It can also be said to diverge from dominant imaginations of the Brazilian national family. This national imaginary, unlike the Japanese presumption of a homogeneous ethnos, evokes the concept of *mestiçagem,* or "racial mixture," to point to Brazil as a "racial democracy." Yet, despite claims to its inclusivity, *mestiçagem* depicts the Brazilian people as a harmonious blend of Portuguese, African, and Indigenous racial groups, while historically excluding immigrant groups like Japanese Brazilians from this national community.

Moreover, historians have evidenced that *mestiçagem* was not originally conceptualized as a balanced process of mixing but rather a phenomenon of whitening in which nonwhite races would be gradually absorbed into the dominant group (see Skidmore [1974] 1992; Lesser 1999; Alberto 2011). Around the turn of the century, during Brazil's First Republic, the white elite who endorsed globalized ideas of eugenics claimed that continued miscegenation would eventually whiten the population and remove the nation's stain of "blackness" (Lesser 2013, 11–14). We may also recall how the idea of "whitening" played out in Brazilian immigration policy when state officials prioritized white Europeans and then "honorary white" Japanese immigrants to fulfill its plantation labor shortages.

Rather than demonstrate an example of racial mixture in which her grandchildren become "whitened" by Valquiria's partially white European heritage, Machie shows how they learn linguistic and cultural practices from their Black and Japanese Brazilian grandmothers and build their own mixed identities. This practice resembles Machie's own relationship with language and the linguistic identity she develops within the text. Throughout the chapter, Machie (2007, 204, 244) inserts transliterated Portuguese words, such as パトロン (*patoron*, "employer") and パラベンス (*parabensu*, "happy birthday") into her Japanese-language narrative, a practice known as *koronia-go*. As Zelideth María Rivas (2015, 800) has delineated, *koronia-go* illustrates Japanese Brazilians' "everyday interactions with Portuguese language speakers" and the process of negotiating their own language community. Machie's repeated use of *kolonia-go*, thus, hints at her daily encounters with Portuguese speakers, who then have reciprocal influences on one another's linguistic identities. It accentuates the embodied relations involved in the process of transliteration and translation, which we see also characterize the way Machie's grandchildren form their identities. While such cross-cultural and cross-linguistic encounters are not always free of conflict, Machie sketches the possibility for them to yield open collaboration and the building of communal relations across difference.

Finally, Machie clarifies in the conclusion to her memoirs how this intersubjective process of linguistic and cultural negotiation works across the constructed boundaries of national and diasporic communities. In the last subsection, she reflects on her life as she celebrates her eightieth birthday and expresses her sense of "rootedness" in Brazil as she watches her daughter repeat the same journey back to Japan that she made thirty years earlier. She then closes the chapter with two *haiku* poems:

> 節約は 移民の性や 木の葉髪
> ブラジルの 国歌唱へず 秋昏るる
> Saving money is
> The nature of immigrants
> Hairs falling like leaves
> While I cannot sing
> Brazil's national anthem,
> Fall comes to a close (255)

The poems clarify that the space of belonging that Machie has constructed in Brazil does not have a national affiliation, as singing the national anthem would imply. In other words, even though Machie does not feel a desire to return to Japan, she also does not wish to claim a Brazilian national identity. Rather, as time passes with the seasons and she enters into the final stage of her life, she demonstrates a contentment with her humble way of life that she will continue to pursue in her final years on earth.

Additionally, in the second poem, the modern Japanese spelling of "Brazil" (she uses ブラジル instead of the older 伯剌西爾) in katakana—the Japanese alphabet used mostly for transliterated foreign words—stands out within a poem that utilizes more antiquated Japanese grammar and kanji characters, such as 唱へず (cannot sing) and 昏るる (comes to a close). This mix of old and new, "foreign" and "native," once again reminds us of Machie's own process navigating linguistic and cultural changes over time through her lived encounters with the persons she meets moving between Japan and Brazil. In this way, she concludes her narrative with a look into the everyday moments that have helped her to find belonging in Brazil by keeping herself open to the experiences that will come next.

■ CONCLUSION

Through putting into conversation Tomoko's and Machie's stories of diasporic return, I have reflected on what their experiences suggest about feelings of belonging within and across the boundaries of national and diasporic communities. In particular, I have focused on how they show the concepts of "home" and "family" to function as models of community that can create structures of exclusion and domination as much as offer spaces of safety and inclusion. Tomoko's "uncanny" visit to Japan especially works to question the conceptualization of diasporic return as a "homecoming" by exposing how the construction of a national "home" depends on an essentialized Japanese cultural identity constructed through the repression of raced, classed, gendered "others" like Tomoko. Machie's account adds to the critique of national identity construction yet also provides a deeper interrogation of the paradigms of "home" and "family" within the context of the Japanese diaspora in Brazil and how they have shaped heteropatriarchal and racialized formations in the community.

In conclusion, "Homecoming" and "I Cannot Sing the National Anthem" bring into focus multiple, intersecting forces of power that circulate across the transpacific, which Tomoko and Machie negotiate in ways specific to their positionalities as working-class Japanese Brazilian women. Looking at how idealizations of national or diasporic "homes" do not fit with their experiences, their stories inspire reflection on where else to locate belonging. Machie's memoir offers us moments that picture relationality beyond constructed borders. She portrays community building through an ongoing collaborative and embodied process in which bonds are formed coalitionally between differently situated beings. Reflecting on her example as one instance of connection, what other ways of being together in the world might be possible if we start rethinking ways of belonging by first leaving "home" behind?

Shannon Welch, PhD, is a project researcher at the Tokyo College research institute at the University of Tokyo. She recently completed her doctoral degree in literature with a specialization in critical gender studies from the University of California, San Diego (December 2022).

■ NOTES

I thank Kobe College Corporation–Japan Education Exchange (KCC-JEE) for its generous Graduate Fellowship that enabled me to conduct research for this article in Japan.

1. This law went into effect in 1990, but Japanese Brazilians had started migrating to Japan since the mid-1980s through dual citizenship, having a spouse with citizenship, or overstaying their visas (see Linger 2001, 23).

2. *Nikkeijin* refers to people of Japanese descent. However, I use "Japanese Brazilian" rather than "Nikkei Brazilian" when discussing the Japanese diasporic community in Brazil following Jessica A. Fernández de Lara Harada (2021), who notes that not all persons with Japanese ancestry identify themselves as Nikkei, especially given the presumption of many elite self-identified Nikkeijin to exclude "mixed-race" and working-class persons from the ethnic categorization.

3. The fall 2017 special edition of *Verge: Studies in Global Asias,* edited by Andrea Bachner and Pedro Erber, especially engages in these critical dialogues.

4. I am referring here to Stuart Hall's ([1992] 2018, 143) assertion that the idea of "the West" "produced knowledge. It became *both* the organizing factor in a system of global power relations *and* the organizing concept of term in a whole way of thinking and speaking."

5. I use the term *modern/colonial* in line with decolonial theorists like María Lugones (2010) and Walter Mignolo and Catherine Walsh (2018), who assert that modernity and coloniality are inextricably intertwined, meaning "coloniality is constitutive, not derivative, of modernity" (Mignolo and Walsh 2018, 4).

6. The Burajiru Nikkei Bungakukai, also known in Portuguese as Associação Cultural e Literária Nikkei Bungaku do Brasil, remains active today and still prints a bilingual journal titled *Burajiru Nikkei Bungaku.*

7. Masao's accolades include the "Ginza and Southern Cross" Newcomer Award (1974), candidacy for the Naoki Prize (1976), and an honorable mention for the Suntory Mystery Award (1991).

8. For an in-depth examination of these authors, see Horiguchi (2012).

9. She is the younger sister of prominent Japanese author Tanizaki Jun'ichirō.

10. All translations of "Homecoming" and "I Cannot Sing the National Anthem" are mine.

11. This follows Ivy's (1995, 22) argument about the *furusato*.

■ **WORKS CITED**

Alberto, Paulina L. 2011. *Terms of Inclusion: Black Intellectuals in Twentieth-Century Brazil*. Chapel Hill: University of North Carolina Press.

Anderson, Benedict. (1983) 2006. *Imagined Communities: Reflections on the Origin and Spread of Nationalism*. London: Verso.

Anzaldúa, Gloria. (1987) 2022. *Borderlands: The New Mestiza*. 5th ed. San Francisco: Aunt Lute Books.

Arai, Chisato. (1974) 1978. "Kikyō." In *Koronia shōsetsu senshū*, 3: 308–18. Sao Paulo: Koronia bungakukai.

Arata, Sumu. 2008. *Burajiru Nikkei koronia bungei: gekan*. São Paulo: Centro de Estudos Nipo-Brasileiros.

Azuma, Eichiro. 2019. *In Search of Our Frontier: Japanese America and Settler Colonialism in the Construction of Japan's Borderless Empire*. Oakland: University of California Press.

Bachner, Andrea, and Pedro Erber, eds. 2017. "Remapping the Transpacific: Critical Approaches between Asia and Latin America." Special issue, *Verge: Studies in Global Asias* 3, no. 2.

Campt, Tina, and Deborah Thomas. 2008. "Gendering Diaspora: Transnational Feminism, Diaspora, and Its Hegemonies." *Feminist Review* 90, no. 1: 1–8.

Chen, Tina. 2020. "(The) Transpacific Turns." In *Oxford Research Encyclopedia of Literature*. https://oxfordre.com/literature/view/10.1093/acrefore/9780190201098.001.0001/acrefore-9780190201098-e-782.

Chen, Tina. 2021. "Global Asias: Method, Architecture, Praxis." *Journal of Asian Studies* 80, no. 4: 997–1009.

Dodd, Stephen. 2004. *Writing Home: Representations of the Native Place in Modern Japanese Literature*. Cambridge, Mass.: Harvard University Press.

Endoh, Toake. 2009. *Exporting Japan: Politics of Emigration to Latin America*. Urbana: University of Illinois Press.

Endoh, Toake. 2016. *Nanbei "kimin" seisaku no jisō*. Tokyo: Iwanami Shoten.

Erber, Pedro. 2015. *Breaching the Frame: The Rise of Contemporary Art in Brazil and Japan*. Oakland: University of California Press.

Fernández de Lara Harada, Jessica A. 2021 "Unstable Identities in Search of Home: Introduction." *ASAP/Journal*, June 28. https://asapjournal.com/tag/unstable-identities-in-search-of-home/.

Fujinami Kai. 2020. *Okinawa diasupora nettowāku: gurōbaru-ka no naka de kaikō o hatasu Uchinānchu*. Tokyo: Akashi Shoten.

Hall, Stuart. (1992) 2018. "The West and the Rest: Discourse and Power." In *Essential Essays: Vol. 2. Diaspora and Identity*, edited by David Morley, 141–84. Durham, N.C.: Duke University Press.

Hall, Stuart. 1998. "Cultural Identity and Diaspora." In *Identity: Community, Culture, Difference*, edited by Jonathan Rutherford, 222–37. London: Lawrence and Wishart.

Harootunian, Harry. 2019. *Uneven Moments: Reflections on Japan's Modern History*. New York: Columbia University Press.

Hirsch, Marianne, and Nancy K. Miller, eds. 2011. *Rites of Return: Diaspora Poetics and the Politics of Memory*. New York: Columbia University Press.

Horiguchi, Noriko J. 2012. *Women Adrift: The Literature of Japan's Imperial Body*. Minneapolis: University of Minnesota Press.

Hosokawa, Shūhei. 2012. *Nikkei burajiru imin bungaku 1: nihongo no nagai tabi[rekishi]*. Tokyo: Misuzu Shobo.

Hosokawa, Shūhei. 2013. *Nikkei burajiru imin bungaku 2: nihongo no nagai tabi[hyōron]*. Tokyo: Misuzu Shobo.

Ivy, Marilyn. 1995. *Discourses of the Vanishing: Modernity, Phantasm, Japan*. Chicago: University of Chicago Press.

Karlin, Jason G. 2014. *Gender and Nation in Meiji Japan: Modernity, Loss, and the Doing of History*. Honolulu: University of Hawai'i Press.

Koyama Shizuko. 2013. *Ryōsai Kenbo: The Educational Ideal of "Good Wife, Wise Mother."* Translated by Stephen Filler. Boston: Brill.

Kumagai, Fumie. 2014. *Family Issues on Marriage, Divorce, and Older Adults in Japan: With Special Attention to Regional Variations*. Singapore: Springer.

Lesser, Jeffrey. 1999. *Negotiating National Identity: Immigrants, Minorities, and the Struggle for Ethnicity in Brazil*. Durham, N.C.: Duke University Press.

Lesser, Jeffrey, ed. 2003. *Searching for Home Abroad: Japanese Brazilians and Transnationalism*. Durham, N.C.: Duke University Press.

Lesser, Jeffrey. 2007. *A Discontented Diaspora: Japanese Brazilians and the Meanings of Ethnic Militancy, 1960–1980*. Durham, N.C.: Duke University Press.

Lesser, Jeffrey. 2013. *Immigration, Ethnicity, and National Identity in Brazil, 1808 to the Present*. Cambridge: Cambridge University Press.

Linger, Daniel Touro. 2001. *No One Home: Brazilian Selves Remade in Japan*. Stanford, Calif.: Stanford University Press.

López-Calvo, Ignacio. 2019. *Japanese Brazilian Saudades: Diasporic Identities and Cultural Production*. Boulder: University of Colorado Press.

Lu, Sidney Xu. 2017. "Japanese American Migration and the Making of Model Women for Japanese Expansion in Brazil and Manchuria, 1871–1945." *Journal of History* 28, no. 3/4: 437–67.

Lu, Sidney Xu. 2019. *The Making of Japanese Settler Colonialism: Malthusianism and Trans-Pacific Migration, 1868–1961*. Cambridge: Cambridge University Press.

Lugones, Maria. 2010. "Toward a Decolonial Feminism." *Hypatia* 25, no. 4: 742–59.

Mack, Edward. 2022. *Acquired Alterity: Migration, Identity, and Literary Nationalism*. Oakland: University of California Press.

Maeyama, Takashi. 1975. "Imin bungaku kara mainoritī bungaku he." In *Koronia shōsetsu senshū: paurisuta bungakushō izen*, 1: 306–20. Sao Paulo: Koronia bungakukai.

Mendoza, Andrea. 2022. "Confronting 'the Ends' of Area: Murmurs toward a Transpacific Phenomenology." In *East Asia, Latin America, and the Decolonization of Transpacific Studies*, edited by Chiara Olivieri and Jordi Serrano-Muñoz, 19–41. Cham, Switzerland: Palgrave Macmillan.

Mignolo, Walter D., and Catherine E. Walsh. 2018. *On Decoloniality: Concepts, Analytics, Praxis*. Durham, N.C.: Duke University Press.

Morris-Suzuki, Tessa. 1998. *Re-inventing Japan: Time Space Nation*. New York: M. E. Sharpe.

Nishida, Mieko. 2018. *Diaspora and Identity: Japanese Brazilians in Brazil and Japan*. Durham, N.C.: Duke University Press.

Olivieri, Chiara, and Jordi Serrano-Muñoz, eds. 2022. *East Asia, Latin America, and the Decolonization of Transpacific Studies*. Cham, Switzerland: Palgrave Macmillan.

Rivas, Zelideth María. 2012. "Narrating Japaneseness through World War II: The Brazilianization, Peruvianization, and U.S. Americanization of Immigrants." In *Expanding Latinidad: An Inter-American Perspective*, edited by Luz Angélica Kirschner, 109–22. Trier, Germany: WVT Wissenschaftlicher.

Rivas, Zelideth María. 2015. "Songs from the Land of Eternal Summer: Beyond Duality in Japanese Brazilian Publication and Colonia Man'yōshū." *Comparative Literature Studies* 53, no. 4: 787–817.

Roth, Joshua Hotaka. 2012. *Brokered Homeland: Japanese Brazilian Migrants in Japan*. Ithaca, N.Y.: Cornell University Press.

Sand, Jordan. 1998. "At Home in the Meiji Period: Inventing Japanese Domesticity." In *Mirror of Modernity: Invented Traditions of Modern*

Japan, edited by Stephen Vlastos, 192–208. Oakland: University of California Press.

Scheiner, Irwin. 1998. "The Japanese Village Imagined, Real, Contested." In *Mirror of Modernity: Invented Traditions of Modern Japan,* edited by Stephen Vlastos, 68–79. Oakland: University of California Press.

Schpun, Mônica Raisa. 2019. "The Japanese Community of São Paulo, Liberdade, and Brazilian State Persecution (1937–45)." *Verge: Studies in Global Asias* 5, no. 1: 209–36.

Skidmore, Thomas E. (1974) 1992. *Black into White: Race and Nationality in Brazilian Thought.* Durham, N.C.: Duke University Press.

Tsuchida Machie. 2007. "Kokka tonaheru." In *Onna no burajiru ijū-shi,* edited by Kusakano Yoshitake, 199–255. Tokyo: Mainichi Shinbun-sha.

Tsuda, Takeyuki. 2003. *Strangers in the Ethnic Homeland: Japanese Brazilian Return Migration in Transnational Perspective.* New York: Columbia University Press.

Yoda, Toshiko. 2000. "The Rise and Fall of Maternal Society: Gender, Labor, and Capital in Contemporary Japan." *South Atlantic Quarterly* 99, no. 4: 865–902.

Yoneyama, Lisa. 2017. "Toward a Decolonial Genealogy of the Transpacific." *American Quarterly* 69, no. 3: 471–82.

RYAN BUYCO

"Finding New Routes": Visualizing an Oceanic Okinawa in Laura Kina's *Holding On* (2019)

■ VISUALIZING AN OCEANIC OKINAWA

On October 18, 2019, mixed-race Okinawan American artist Laura Kina opened her art show titled *Holding On* in Chicago, Illinois.[1] This exhibition comprised a series of landscape paintings that were inspired by the artist's travels to Okinawa and observing "prop roots from banyan trees and how they keep holding on, regenerating, finding new routes to persist and reclaim the land around them" (Kina 2019, "Artist Statement"). The painting *Ufushu Gajumaru* depicts a giant banyan tree in the Valley of Gangala—now a tourist spot in Okinawa known for its café inside a large cavern (Figure 1). The viewer is drawn to the large banyan tree, which functions as the image's central object, jutting out beyond the open cavity of a cave. Shades of darkness and lightness color the banyan tree as its prop roots descend from the upper branches to support the main trunk. The prop roots themselves are not located in but outside the ground and are rendered in red and blue—evocative of veins that move blood to the heart. They transfer nutrients from unexpected places to ensure the overall survival of the tree.

This painting, and Laura Kina's *Holding On* series in general, is significant for its ability to awaken a particularized meaning of Okinawan culture that unsettles the geographical rootedness of Okinawa in the context of diaspora.[2] While the notion of roots signifies connections deeply buried into the land, the exposed roots of the banyan tree—which can grow in seemingly unexpected places—function as a visual record of a remapping of Okinawan cultural politics that is happening today, a cultural politics that reaches out beyond the context of Okinawa prefecture and toward

Figure 1. *Ufushu Gajumaru (giant banyan tree), Valley of Gangala, Okinawa, Japan.*
Courtesy of the artist.

the diaspora and the greater Pacific. Indeed, while *Holding On* centers on images that represent daily life in Okinawa—daily life where the prefecture carries the uneven burden of hosting approximately 70 percent of all U.S. military bases in Japan—the series also includes an image that connects Okinawa to another Indigenous struggle across the Pacific: this being Mauna Kea on the Big Island of Hawai'i (Figure 2).

Representations that reimagine Okinawa beyond the immediate context of the Japanese nation-state are significant, not only as they challenge the persisting myth of Japanese cultural homogeneity but also because they offer potential strategies to rethink Okinawa's colonial relationship with Japan and the United States. As the Okinawan studies scholar Annmaria Shimabuku (2012, 134) has pointed out, the concentration of U.S. military bases in Okinawa is a result of the co-constitution of U.S. and Japanese colonialism: the United States enjoys its military dominance in East Asia, while Japan enjoys America's protection without the negative effects of U.S. military bases, which include instances of sexual violence and other crimes committed by U.S. military personnel. Furthermore, because Okinawa is a prefecture of Japan and not its own nation-state, Okinawans are unable to bring their grievances to the United States

Figure 2. *Mauna Kea*. Courtesy of the artist.

directly, because the United States will only entertain discussions with Japan (Shimabuku 2012, 136). Given this limiting geopolitical context, expressions of Okinawa beyond the United States–Japan relationship have become important sites of political, as well as artistic, intervention.

In the diaspora, Laura Kina and other cultural producers have been drawing from their experiences in the Pacific to contribute to discussions of Okinawan indigeneity, which have emerged in recent years as part of a larger, global Indigenous movement (Chibana 2013, 2018; Yokota 2015). As Megumi Chibana (2013, 136) observes, Indigenous identification, although a new component within the political ideology for Okinawans, draws on a historical understanding of their communities' connections to lands, cultures, and spiritualities. It is important to note that although these discussions are about personal or communal identity, they are inextricably linked to debates about the presence of U.S. military bases and protecting sacred land (Kina 2020, 60–61). For Kina and other cultural producers in the diaspora, their expressions of Okinawan indigeneity have been shaped by their experiences in Hawaiʻi, a major site of the Okinawan diaspora.[3] This is especially reflected in such works as *Okinawan Princess: Da Legend of Hajichi Tattoos* (2019), a children's book that was written in Pidgin

English, standard Japanese, and the Okinawan Indigenous language of Uchināguchi.[4] As Kina (2019, 378) notes, *Okinawan Princess* was a collaborative project between herself, Okinawan linguist Masashi Sakihara, and Okinawan American writer Lee A. Tonouchi, who were all "inspired by the Native Hawaiian movement to remember, reclaim, and relearn about *Shimanchu* (person of the island) Okinawan culture."[5] Considering the Native Hawaiian influence on Okinawan diasporic cultural productions in recent years, *Holding On* offers an important perspective from which to view how representations from the diaspora can help nourish ongoing movements against Japan and the United States today.

■ LOOKING TOWARD THE PACIFIC

In this article, I argue that Kina's *Holding On* makes visible an "oceanic Okinawa"—that is, a discourse in the Okinawan diaspora that draws from Indigenous critiques in the Pacific to challenge the marginalization of Okinawa within the United States–Japan relationship. My reference to the oceanic in this essay is informed by Native Pacific studies scholars who have forged key conceptual tools to reject the dominant narratives that have marginalized, if not erased, Pacific Islander worldviews from discussions of the Pacific. In his essay "Our Sea of Islands," Epeli Hauʻofa (2008, 31) reimagined the idea of the Pacific Islands from "islands in a far sea" to "a sea of islands" to express the ocean's capacity to connect instead of to separate. In his view, the Pacific Islands are not small, isolated, and marginal to larger landmasses; rather, they are interconnected to each other and the greater world through the movements and interactions of Pacific Islanders across the sea. In line with Hauʻofa's expansive vision, I suggest that *Holding On* critiques the view that limits Okinawa to its status as a small island prefecture in southern Japan and, instead, looks toward the movements and interactions of its diaspora in the Pacific.

This articulation of an oceanic Okinawa that surfaces from the images of *Holding On* dislocates Okinawa conceptually from a fixed, marginal position in the Japanese nation-state by connecting Okinawa to other Indigenous peoples. As Demiliza Saramosing, Katherine Achacoso, and Roderick Labrador (2021) theorize, one of the primary meanings of the oceanic is "a practice and metaphor/analytic for flow, movement, specificity and expansiveness, relationality, mobility, nonlinearity, and congruence."[6] In this series, such oceanic connections are expressed through the parallels that are made between Okinawa and other islands in the Pacific, especially Hawaiʻi, as they concern their common histories of colonization and movements against ongoing occupation.[7] Such Indigenous affiliations that are made in the diaspora assert a rethinking of Okinawa's inclusion within the Japanese nation-state and, thus, the legitimacy of the United States–Japan relationship that enables the continuing presence of U.S. military bases in Okinawa. Put in this way, *Holding On* can be read as a diasporic work that affiliates itself with the Pacific not only to articulate the collective agency of Okinawans and Indigenous peoples everywhere but also to disrupt the colonial processes that continue to marginalize Okinawans from their lands and waters.

Despite this, I am not advocating that Okinawa be included in the area category of the "Pacific Islands." Rather, I use the term *oceanic* to describe the movement of the Okinawan diaspora and to acknowledge Okinawa's location within larger, interconnected struggles of which it is a part. For instance, as the Chamorro activist, lawyer, and writer Julian Aguon (2021, 8) notes, upcoming plans to relocate the U.S. Marines from Okinawa to Guam will result in the destruction of Guam's northern coastline for a massive firing range. Although the immediate removal or reduction of U.S. military bases is of utmost importance in Okinawa, the circumstances of U.S. militarization in the Pacific require analyses that connect seemingly disparate places together. Thus the methodological approach that I deploy in this essay is one that analyzes *Holding On* in relation to the larger oceanic context that this series embraces. At the same time, to analyze Kina's work this way requires an engagement with Asian American studies' discussions of Asian settler colonialism, given its influence in framing Indigenous and Asian relations in recent years. As I suggest later, this discussion of an oceanic Okinawa challenges a rigid binary of Indigenous and Asian settler relations by its articulation of Indigenous connections across the ocean, which links antibase activisms in Okinawa with the Native Hawaiian sovereignty movement. It is important to note, however, that although *Holding On* does give expression to such Indigenous connections, the idea of an oceanic Okinawa must also take into account Kina's contradictory positionality as an Indigenous Okinawan in the diaspora, an Asian settler who resides in the continental United States, and a tourist who travels to Okinawa and Hawai'i. Ultimately, given *Holding On*'s reorientation of Okinawa away from the enclosed borders of Japan and toward Oceania, this essay contributes to Global Asias scholarship as well as related conversations that examine the interconnections between Asia, the Pacific Islands, and the United States (see Shigematsu and Camacho 2010; Dvorak and Tanji 2015; Fujikane 2008; Yoneyama 2017; Kim and Sharma 2021).

Asian American and Asian diaspora studies' engagement with settler colonial critique and indigeneity has largely taken place within discourses of Asian settler colonialism in Hawai'i and Native North America.[8] Since the 2000 special issue of *Amerasia Journal,* and its subsequent edited volume in 2008, the framework of Asian settler colonialism has been and continues to be a major intervention in the field that has provided a language to address the complicity of Asians and Asian Americans within ongoing structures of Indigenous dispossession under the context of U.S. colonialism. In Hawai'i, where the intervention of Asian settler colonialism first emerged in the field of Asian American studies, the Native Hawaiian nationalist leader, scholar, and poet Haunani-Kay Trask (2008, 46) has asserted that the self-identifications of Asians as "local" operates within a settler colonial logic that denies the genealogical histories that connect Native Hawaiians to the land. This marginalization, as Candace Fujikane (2000, 158) has rightly pointed out, is one that performs a depopulation that opens Hawai'i to settler claims of belonging. This works in conjunction with the myth of Hawai'i as a harmonious multicultural state, which erases Native Hawaiians' struggles for self-determination (Fujikane 2008, 3). Although the question of Asian complicity has been central within these discussions, it is important to appreciate that scholars have also used the space of Asian settler colonial critique in Hawai'i to theorize alternatives beyond the limitations of the settler state, acknowledging the agency of Asian settlers and their capacity to support decolonial movements in Hawai'i, as well as other Indigenous struggles in the world.[9]

Such engagements in Asian American studies with settler colonial critique, I suggest, have not only been crucial in rethinking Indigenous and Asian relations in the United States but also generative in imagining settler formations that inform articulations of Indigenous Asias in the diaspora.[10] In "Writing Settlement: Locating Asian-Indigenous Relations in the Pacific," Yu-ting Huang (2018, 31) observes that there is an assumption within the context of Asian American studies that separates "Asian" and "Indigenous," particularly pertaining to the groups of people who may identify or be identified as Indigenous in Asia. Indeed, within the context of Asian settler colonialism, Indigenous–Asian relations are mediated by the U.S. settler state, in which settlers—racialized as Asian— are complicit in structures of dispossession. Kina's *Holding On,* and the idea of an oceanic Okinawa that her series conveys, invites us to expand the geographical reference point through which Indigenous–Asian relations are largely framed and to consider the Okinawan context where the U.S. state is not the only colonizer. It is important to clarify that although this does not undermine or minimize the urgency for Asian accountability within Indigenous space, it does move the conversation beyond an enclosed frame of complicity—whether Asians are complicit with the settler state—and toward a reading that does not preclude the ways that Indigenous histories in Asia may inform Asian and Indigenous relations in the United States.

Indeed, for Kina, her interactions in the Pacific and with Pacific Island-ers have been influential to her own understandings of Okinawan indi-geneity. For instance, in her article "Ancestral Cartography," Kina (2020, 50) acknowledges her position as an Asian settler but also recognizes how the resurgence of Okinawan Indigenous identity today is influenced by what she credits as the transpacific interchanges between Okinawans and other Indigenous peoples. Indeed, her own Okinawan identity as Indigenous has been a relational process where the first time she heard of Okinawans claiming Indigenous identity was when she was challenged by the American Samoan artist and poet Dan Taulapapa McMullen to think in a more oceanic perspective, where waterways and horizontal histories connect island peoples (Kina 2020, 59). Considering the influence of the Pacific on Kina's thinking about Okinawa, *Holding On* opens us up to view such connections across the ocean.

■ GROWING IN A DIFFERENT SOIL

Kina's positionality as a cultural producer who resides on the lands of other people, and not on Okinawa itself, speaks to the potential and pos-sibilities of taking root and growing in a different soil.[11] Kina traces her genealogy to her father's maternal side, who immigrated to the Big Island of Hawai'i from Yonabaru, Okinawa, in the beginning of the twentieth century to work as sugarcane workers, in addition to her mother, who is Basque/Spanish, French, English, Irish, Scottish, and Dutch (Kina 2020, 59). She was born in Riverside, California, grew up in Poulsbo, Wash-ington, and currently resides in Chicago, Illinois. In his article "Making Sense of Diasporic Okinawan Identity within U.S. Global Militarisation," Wesley Ueunten (2015, 8) argues that although Okinawans in the diaspora live physically away from the shores of Okinawa, they are nevertheless a part of the struggle over the control of their homeland. This has become especially pressing given the celebratory discourses about the Okinawan diaspora in recent decades, in particular, the trope of Okinawan immigrant success, which involves achieving upward mobility in foreign lands while retaining Okinawan identity and culture. Such discourses in the diaspora, according to Ueunten (2015, 28–31), have worked to divert attention away from the problem of U.S. bases in Okinawa, which fits squarely with Japan's needs and desires to keep the large military base presence there.[12] Drawing from her experiences in the Pacific, Kina, with *Holding On*, moves away from such discourses of the diaspora, and instead questions the legitimacy of the U.S. military base presence by evoking local folktales, ancestors, and even the dead who continue to dwell within Okinawa's militarized landscape.

At the same time, although *Holding On* evokes Okinawan indigeneity to contest Okinawa's marginalization, it is important to acknowledge that the series itself was informed by Kina's trips to Okinawa and Hawai'i, sites to which she traveled as a tourist. As scholars in Hawai'i and Okinawa have noted, the tourism industries in both places cannot be understood separately from their colonial contexts. Hōkūlani K. Aikau and Vernadette Vicuña Gonzalez (2019, 3) indicate that the infrastructures that make Hawai'i an ideal tourist destination are built on the historical and present-day dispossession of Kānaka 'Ōiwi. Likewise, Ayano Ginoza (2012, 14) contends that popular representations of Okinawa in Japan render the landscape as an exotic "Native" to be consumed by Japanese tourists. While Kina occupies the contradictory positions of Asian settler, Indigenous Okinawan, and tourist, they are nevertheless a reflection of her experiences as a mixed-race Okinawan American in the diaspora, which greatly informs her work. Therefore *Holding On* can also be read as an implicit disclosure of Kina's positionality that includes not only her genealogical connections to Okinawa but also her settler status and participation in the tourism industries in Okinawa and Hawai'i, all of which can be seen in the series.

For example, *Holding On* is a series of landscape paintings, itself a type of artwork in the United States associated with the colonial project or, as Karen Ohnesorge (2008, 44) describes, "a stage for fantasies of racialized white manifest destiny." The surface depictions of Okinawa in *Holding On* render the landscape as being absent of Okinawan people, who are replaced by infrastructures of the U.S. military, which continue to desecrate the land, air, and water. At the same time, this work challenges the inevitability of U.S. military occupation and the tourism industry by gesturing to the ways that Okinawans have persisted despite U.S. and Japanese colonialisms: such as the references to the ongoing protest movement in Henoko against further U.S. military construction (Figure 3), the collective wartime memories that fuel the antibase movement (*Chibi Chiri Gama, Yomitan, Okinawa, Japan*), and sacred landscapes that even today are deeply associated with ancestral practices (*Islands of the Gods, Cape Kaberu, Kudaka-jima, Okinawa, Japan*). Put in another way, the

Figure 3. *No Base Henoko*. Courtesy of the artist.

aesthetic decision not to include human figures in the series is significant, as it gestures toward the logics of settler colonialism and the tourism industry, on one hand, and the continuing persistence of Indigenous peoples, on the other.[13] This tension that is depicted throughout *Holding On* functions to convey Kina's positionality as an Indigenous Okinawan without downplaying her status as an Asian settler and tourist. This implicit acknowledgment of Kina's positionality thus becomes crucial to the idea of an oceanic Okinawa as it helps us to imagine Indigenous and Asian settler relations in more expansive ways when considering such Pacific connections.

Reading Kina's work this way motivates me to disclose my own positionality, especially because I, too, have grown on different soils. Given that I am neither Native Hawaiian nor Okinawan, I would like to engage in what Malissa Phung (2019, 20) describes as genealogical disclosure: "a practice of both vulnerability and accountability, a public detailing of family migration narratives to reveal to whom we are related, to whom we live among, and to whom we remain indebted." I am a Filipino American settler born on Yokuts land who grew up on the traditional territories of the Dakota and who has worked for, or attended, universities on the lands of the Piscataway and Anacostan peoples, Kānaka Maoli,

Haudenosaunee, and the Ute. I currently reside on the land of the yak tityu tityu yak tiłhini, Northern Chumash Tribe, where I also work. The reading practice that I employ is shaped by my experience as a second-generation settler from parents from the Philippines, as well as my experience assimilating into American mainstream culture, and the cultural and linguistic loss that it entails. I began to reconnect myself to a larger Pacific community since attending graduate school at the University of Hawai'i at Mānoa and, subsequently, doing research in Okinawa and in my father's hometown in the Western Visayas, Philippines. While being an uninvited visitor in these places and benefiting from their colonial histories as a tourist and a scholar, I wanted to rethink how I could move beyond being only a consumer and producer of area-based knowledge, as a rearticulation of the West and Rest binary (Sakai 2016). Reading works by Okinawan cultural producers was a way for me to think about my position in a different way, by relating to forms of resistance and resurgence from a context different from my own. Like the influence of the Native Hawaiian movement on cultural producers like Kina, reading and learning about Okinawa prompted me to reimagine my own scholarly practices away from exclusively producing area-based research and toward an oceanic practice of relationality and solidarity. In this way, my essay's consideration of an oceanic Okinawa must also entail acts of genealogical disclosure as a beginning point to making such connections across the Pacific, which not only insists on acknowledging our complicities in settler colonialism and tourism but also leaves room to reimagine our scholarly practices in the process of working collectively toward a decolonial future.

■ "HOLDING ON" TO OKINAWA ACROSS THE OCEAN

My discussion of an oceanic Okinawa in this essay emerges from Kina's images, which work to critique the marginalization of Okinawa within the United States–Japan relationship through the Indigenous connections that it makes. At the same time, it is important to note that although the sovereignty movement in Hawai'i has influenced diasporic cultural producers like Kina, the political deployment of indigeneity by Okinawan activists in Okinawa has been used since the 1990s (Yokota 2015, 59).[14] Furthermore, Okinawans are not recognized as Indigenous people by the Japanese government, unlike the Ainu of Hokkaido, who were formally recognized in 2008 (Chibana 2018, 154). Nevertheless, despite the lack of formal recognition by Japan—and as I mentioned previously—the assertion of indigeneity works to challenge the fixity of Okinawa's inclusion into the Japanese nation-state and its marginalized position within the United States–Japan security arrangement, which enables the continuing presence of U.S. military bases in the islands. Considering this, the articulation of an oceanic Okinawa in *Holding On* contributes to activist movements in Okinawa by disrupting the naturalization of Okinawa as part of Japan (a minority against a majority), as well as positioning Okinawa within a larger frame of Indigenous resistance in the Pacific.

Put in this way, the ability of Okinawa and the Okinawan people to "hold on" despite Japanese and American colonialism is celebrated in Kina's series, which is expressed in the figure of the banyan tree, which grows even in the most difficult circumstances. In an Okinawan folktale, the banyan was one of the last trees to arrive on the islands of Yaeyama, where it was met by an angry god. As punishment for arriving later than other trees, the god condemned the banyan to live off the remaining land, forcing it to rely on its prop roots to grab ahold of rocks "as if it was the last choice left to them" (Endo 1996, 24). Though it seemed that the tree had nowhere left to grow, the banyan's prop roots used what was available, finding a way to survive. The resiliency of the banyan tree is thus highlighted in *Ufushu Gajumaru*, whose prop roots not only maintain its connection to the land but also show how the tree can thrive even in a limited cavernous space (Figure 1). Indeed, the viewer of the image must look up at the banyan tree in admiration of its persistence. The vibrant images that compose this series were influenced by the light and colors of New Orleans, where Kina served as a Joan Mitchell Artist-in-Residence in 2019 while painting this series (Kina, interview with the author, August 25, 2020). Kina's interest in banyan trees, which inspired *Holding On*, began while she was a tourist visiting family members in Hawai'i and was impressed with their perseverance, sparking her own thinking about banyans in Okinawa.[15] Not unlike prop roots, which help the main trunk, the Okinawan community in the diaspora helps Okinawa to survive (Kina, interview with author, August 25, 2020).[16]

In this way, *Holding On* should be read as a work that makes connections to the greater Pacific to express the perseverance of Okinawa against Japanese and American colonialisms today. For example, as Vicente Diaz and J. Kēhaulani Kauanui (2001, 318) remind us, the land and sea constitute Pacific Islanders' genealogies and lie at the heart of the varied movements to restore Native sovereignty and self-determinations. In the same way, one of the major arguments that *Holding On* makes is the assertion that Okinawans are inseparable from their islands, even in instances when the U.S. military base presence seems insurmountable. In particular, *Henoko Flight Path* (Figure 4) depicts the contentious base reclamation site of Ōura Bay in Henoko, located in the northern area of Okinawa's main island. This reclamation site is part of the larger relocation plan to move the Futenma Marine Corps Air Station from the densely

Figure 4. *Henoko Flight Path*. Courtesy of the artist.

populated area of Ginowan to Henoko, which entails reclaiming parts of
Ōura Bay for base construction. This plan was originally a Japanese and
American response to quell the protests that emerged from the 1995 rape
case of an Okinawan schoolgirl by three U.S. soldiers but, since then, has
become a site of resistance for Okinawan activists and allies worldwide.[17]

Henoko Flight Path depicts two bright yellow lines cutting through the
center of the image, which is made against the blue and green shades of
Ōura Bay, representing the disruption of the Okinawan landscape by the
U.S. military. The orange outline in the water is a depiction of the above-
water fence that not only works to keep Okinawan activists away but also
outlines the construction project, which requires twenty-one million cubic
meters of dirt and sand to be poured into the water (Letman 2019). A dripping effect can be seen throughout the image, suggesting blood, sweat, or
tears, which emanate from the land and sea. While the dripping effect can
be read as the landscape's response to the continuing desecration caused
by the Japanese and American governments, it also evokes the words of
Pacific poet and scholar Teresia Teaiwa—"we sweat and cry salt water, so

we know that the ocean is really in our blood" (quoted in Hauʻofa 2008, 41)—insisting on the inseparability of Okinawans to their landscapes.

This inseparability becomes especially important considering that the series lacks direct depictions of Okinawan people, as I mentioned earlier. Nevertheless, visible and nonvisible references of Okinawan presence course through Kina's imaginative renderings of Okinawan landscapes. In *Henoko Flight Path,* what is present beneath the surface of the water are the dangers of the military base construction site on the dugong, or *zan,* who inhabit the bay. In local myths, the dugong are seen as the messengers of the gods of Nirai Kanai, the Okinawan afterlife across the ocean where the ancestors and gods are believed to live (Inoue 2007, 177). In "Looking towards Nirai Kanai," the poet and historian Urashima Etsuko (2016) discusses how the U.S. military construction in Henoko hinders the spirits from going to the afterlife. Urashima explains that Okinawan tombs face the sea so that the spirits of the dead can travel to Nirai Kanai beyond the horizon. However, the widespread reclamation project in Henoko will block the spirits' path toward Nirai Kanai, where they are in danger of becoming lost, with nowhere to go. It is important to note that at the time of this writing, the Japanese Defense Ministry and the U.S. Department of Defense are currently trying to use soil from Itoman in the southern area of the island for this reclamation project, which means they will be using soil that contains the remains of the war dead from the Battle of Okinawa (Hibbit 2021). The presence of ancestral and guardian spirits, practices, and people is felt throughout the series of *Holding On* even when they are not directly referenced. These implicit depictions of Okinawan presence thus unsettle the inevitability of the U.S. military as a completely done deal, by insisting on the continuing connections that the Okinawan people have to their lands and waters.

Additionally, *Holding On*'s assertion that Okinawans maintain connections to their islands despite U.S. and Japanese colonialism also extends to the diaspora. This can be seen especially in *Mabuni (suicide cliff)* (Figure 5), which depicts a site associated with the Battle of Okinawa, one of the most traumatic events in Okinawan history.[18] It is important to note that this image, though seemingly empty, is imbued with a history that not only galvanizes the antibase movement today but also disrupts the touristic gaze of Okinawa as Japan's Hawaiʻi, which was developed after Okinawa's reversion to Japan in 1972.[19] This painting depicts the area of Mabuni Hill in the southern region of Okinawa's main island, where much of the fighting took place during the war. Americans referred to this area as "Suicide Cliff," where the Japanese Thirty-Second Army made its last stand among civilian refugees during the Battle of Okinawa (Figal 2007, 88). The word "suicide" also has a particular meaning in the context of the battle, insofar as Okinawans were forced to commit suicide to prove their status as good Japanese subjects.[20] Today, Mabuni Hill is the location of the Okinawa Prefectural Peace Memorial Museum and the Cornerstone of Peace, which memorializes the battle—more than 140,000 people, or about one-third of the population in Okinawa at the time, died in the course of the war and its aftermath (Ōta 2014, xvii).

Mabuni (suicide cliff) is depicted from the perspective of the viewer standing on top of a cliff, overlooking the ocean. Darkness can be seen on the horizon, which meets dark, overcast clouds. There is a dripping effect that moves from the central image down a frayed, tan canvas that is pinned up against a white wall. The white wall and the tan canvas function together as a framing device in the foreground that works to distance the viewer from the central image—and the traumatic event that the central image references. This distance suggests the intergenerational and diasporic space between those who experienced the Battle of Okinawa and their descendants. This is indicative of Kina's location in the diaspora, given her own family's history during the war, in which four members perished during the battle (Kina 2015). The collective wartime memories that this painting conjures—and the atrocities committed by the Japanese government during it, such as forcing Okinawan civilians to commit suicide—root the diaspora back to this experience in Okinawa and inform the notion of *nuchi du takara,* or "life is precious," where the protection of life, including those that were lost during World War II, energizes the antibase movement today.

While *Holding On* advocates the connections that Okinawans have to their islands, this view is bolstered by the series' explicit connections it makes with Hawai'i. As I mentioned at the beginning of this essay, the inclusion of *Mauna Kea* (Figure 2) moves the viewer from Okinawa to a larger, Pacific context, bringing the political struggles in Okinawa into relation with the current movement against the Thirty Meter Telescope on the Big Island of Hawai'i. This image depicts an *ahu,* a Native Hawaiian altar, in the foreground and three telescopes in the background, sitting on top of Mauna Kea, which is a sacred site tied to Hawaiian genealogies (Casumbal-Salazar 2019, 208–9). This image was inspired by Kina's visit to Mauna Kea in 2017, where she visited as a tourist with members of her family who live on the Big Island. According to her, seeing and feeling the presence of telescopes on the sacred mountain was a surprising and stunning experience. She took a photo of this altar with the telescopes during this 2017 trip and painted this image in 2019 as she was reflecting

Figure 5. *Mabuni (suicide cliff), Itoman, Okinawa, Japan.* Courtesy of the artist.

on the parallel struggles between Henoko and Mauna Kea (Kina, interview with the author).[21]

Indeed, Mauna Kea is a sacred site tied to Native Hawaiian genealogies, and the current movement to protect it from the construction of the Thirty Meter Telescope should be understood as a practice of *aloha 'āina*, a Native Hawaiian concept that describes their love for the land. As the Native Hawaiian scholar Iokepa Casumbaal-Salazaar notes, Native Hawaiian understandings of their very beings are inextricably linked to the places they and their ancestors inhabit, the activities they practice, the ceremonies they conduct, and the intimacies they develop. The very term for the ground on which they walk—*'āina*, which translates to "that which feeds"—is a recognition of the island as a provider of food, as kin, and as a relation, instilling a sense of humility, responsibility, and respect for the natural world. The commitment to defend Mauna Kea from the Thirty Meter Telescope is thus an expression of *kuleana*: a *responsibility* and *privilege* to care for the land (Casumbal-Salazaar 2019, 208).

Considering this, my discussion of an oceanic Okinawa in this essay helps us to read *Mauna Kea* in ways that emphasize Indigenous connections while also taking into account settler colonialism and tourism. Like other images in *Holding On, Mauna Kea* is a reflection of Kina's positionality as an Indigenous Okinawan, an Asian settler, and a tourist. This Asian settler and tourist positionality can be seen in the representation of Mauna Kea as being absent of Native Hawaiian people, which can be read as opening the land to white and Asian settler appropriation. At the same time, however, reading *Mauna Kea* exclusively this way would have to overlook how this series challenges Okinawa's fixity within the Japanese nation-state and how the inclusion of Hawai'i represented here functions as a geographical reference point beyond Japan. By including *Mauna Kea,* the series makes an explicit connection with the Native Hawaiian movement and, with it, critical concepts that bring Hawaiian resistance politics today in line with the ongoing struggle in Henoko. Such an explicit connection dislocates Okinawa from the enclosed borders of Japan and repositions Okinawa within a greater Pacific context.

For example, the concept of *aloha 'āina* resonates with the Okinawan expression of *nuchi du takara,* or "life is precious," that I referenced previously. This phrase is attributed to the last king of the Ryukyu Kingdom, who, facing war with Japan, gave up his throne to save the lives of his fellow Okinawans (Ikehara 2016, 6) as they faced Japanese colonization, where they became a prefecture of Japan in 1879.[22] The phrase *nuchi du takara* animates the continuing protest movement today and can be seen in political spaces, such as rallies and sit-ins in front of U.S. military bases (Ikehara 2016, 6). Indeed, the assertion that "life is precious" can be read as an intervention in the continuing militarization of the islands, in which the land, and not the people, is deemed important only because of Okinawa's "strategic" location in the Asian and Pacific regions. *Nuchi du takara,* which asserts the inherent value of all life, goes against the logic of militarization that sustains the U.S. military base presence and recognizes the ways in which the land has been and continues to be used for violence against Okinawans and other people in the world. It is important to clarify that *aloha 'āina* and *nuchi du takara* are not terms that directly translate into each other—which is to say, they are not equivalent—but rather, they epitomize a larger discourse of Indigenous survival, agency, and resistance, one that juxtaposes Okinawa and Hawai'i in ways that support each other's movements. In this way, my articulation of an oceanic Okinawa not only works to critique Okinawa's marginalization within Japan but also insists on a rethinking of a rigid binary of Indigenous and Asian relations in the United States, especially as they concern Indigenous Asias and the cultural productions that emerge from their diaspora.

■ CONCLUSION

Thus far, I have argued that *Holding On* makes visible an oceanic Okinawa that challenges the limited position of Okinawa within the United States–Japan relationship though the Indigenous connections that the series makes. In particular, drawing from Indigenous critiques in the Pacific, Kina's *Holding On* asserts the inseparability of Okinawans from their islands and affiliates Okinawa with other Indigenous struggles. I end this essay by turning to the work of Lee A. Tonouchi, who is a yonsei Okinawan American writer from Oahu who writes primarily in Pidgin English. My discussion of an oceanic Okinawa in this essay can offer a reading into his work as it can be read problematically within an Asian American studies context, particularly as it reinscribes the logic of Asian settlement. However, given my earlier discussion, I argue for an additional reading, one that locates his work within a context of an oceanic Okinawa and not solely as local literature in Hawai'i.[23] In particular, Tonouchi's (2011) semiautobiographical collection of poetry, *Significant Moments in the Life of Oriental Faddah and Son,* is a work that expresses a continuing connection to Okinawa despite its location in the diaspora and the histories of Japanese and American colonialisms in the prefecture.

For example, "Okinawan Proverb" is about the loss of the Okinawan Indigenous language of Uchināguchi. This poem begins by noting that the word *Okinawa* (沖縄) has a literal meaning of "rope in the open sea." This is because all the islands of the Ryukyu archipelago look like a long rope cast out in the open water. The narrator describes how his family history in the United States is one of assimilation, where the Indigenous Okinawan language faded with each passing generation. When the narrator's great-grandparents migrated to Hawai'i, the only language they knew was Uchināguchi. They passed some of this language to his grandparents, who passed even less to his parents, which left the narrator not knowing any of it. Doing research on his own, the narrator finds this old Okinawan proverb: "*Nmarijima nu kutuba wasshī nē* / *kuni n wasshīn.* / If you forget your native tongue, / das means your forget your native country" (Tonouchi 2011, 104). Learning this proverb inspired the narrator to want to visit Okinawa, but he soon learned that people were speaking less and less Uchināguchi. The poem ends with the narrator lamenting that if everyone lets go of the rope, the rope will fall into the ocean, becoming lost at sea (105). While the poem conveys a sense of loss due to the realization that the language is vanishing, the very act of recording this loss—by citing an Okinawan proverb—can be read as an expression of Okinawan indigeneity that *holds on,* despite his family's experience assimilating in the United States and the historical attempts by the Japanese government to entirely erase the language in Okinawa.

This sentiment about the loss of language is shared by other Okinawan writers. For instance, this loss is conveyed in the bilingual poem "Morena Maiden—For Nini" by Okinawan poet Takara Ben. This poem is included in his poetry collection *Koeru (Beyond)*, which was written in 1994. "Morena Maiden" is a poem that is written in standard Japanese alongside English. In one part of the poem, Takara Ben expresses his feelings over the loss of Okinawan language through his admiration of Nini—a Filipina to whom he dedicates this poem. In particular, Takara Ben mentions that Nini can speak four languages, which prompts him to reflect on his use of the Japanese language in his poetry. He admits that expressing himself in Japanese brings him farther away from the languages and spirits of Okinawa, which fade with each passing day. Given Tonouchi's poem that I mentioned earlier, the loss of language is an experience that is shared by Okinawans across the Pacific. In the Japanese section of Takara's poem, there is a gap between the narrator and Okinawa, which is represented by the following: "私は 島の母たちの／言葉と魂から遠ざかり" (Takara 1994, 129), which in English corresponds to "I go away from ／ my motherland's words and spirits" (Takara 1994, 129). The space between "私は" and "島の母たちの" articulates the history of what has been lost since the beginning of Japanese colonization and the violent processes of assimilation that have made Okinawans Japanese subjects. This sense of loss is shared by other Indigenous peoples as well. For example, the Native Hawaiian scholar Brandy Nālani McDougall (2010, 51) argues that the knowledge of loss is what compels Native Hawaiians to continue the struggle of recovering what was and maintaining cultural traditions that have continued despite colonization. The grief that comes from this loss, according to her, is what Native Hawaiians find in their will to resist.

In his discussion of Okinawan diasporic literature in English, Ishihara Masahide (2013, 206) points out that the use of Japanese and Okinawan language in diasporic works like Tonouchi's represents the pride that Okinawan diasporic writers have toward Okinawa. Thus the narrative decision to use any Uchināguchi, such as Tonouchi's inclusion of an Okinawan proverb, can be seen as an act of resistance against the history of Japanese colonization, showing how the Indigenous language of Uchināguchi has not been totally erased. Including Indigenous Okinawan culture—no matter how little—centers the narrative not on how Okinawans have been marginalized in the past but on how they continue to survive today, even in the diaspora.[24]

To end, through the representation of an oceanic Okinawa in *Holding On,* Kina's work functions as a visual archive that not only expands Asian settler and Indigenous relations in Asian American studies but also reimagines Okinawa beyond the enclosed borders of Japan. Not unlike the prop roots of the banyan tree—which grow in unexpected places—the images of *Holding On* that I have analyzed in this essay were made in the diaspora yet remain tethered to Okinawa, drawing inspiration from Hawai'i to imagine an oceanic Okinawa for these times.

Ryan Buyco is an assistant professor of ethnic studies at Cal Poly, San Luis Obispo.

■ **NOTES**

I thank Tina Chen, reviewers 1 and 2, Chang Tan, Laura Kina, the participants of the 2020 Global Asias Summer Institute, and Yu-ting Huang for their insights and generous comments on this essay. I especially thank Laura Kina for her time and for allowing me to interview her in August 2020 to discuss this art series. Any errors in this essay are my own.

1. Laura Kina is a mixed-race Okinawan American artist-scholar and Vincent de Paul Professor at DePaul University in Chicago, Illinois. She was born in California and raised in Washington State. Her solo art exhibitions include *Champaru* (2018), *Uchinanchu: The Art of Laura Kina* (2016), and *Blue Hawai'i* (2015). She is also a cofounder of the Critical Mixed Race Studies conference, journal, and association. More information about her work can be found on her website: http://www.laurakina.com/.

2. It is important to clarify that "Okinawa" in this essay refers to the islands of Okinawa prefecture and not just the main island of Okinawa. Furthermore, the former Ryukyu Kingdom (now Okinawa prefecture) also included the Amami Islands, which are a part of present-day Kagoshima prefecture. See Yokota (2015, 70–71) for a discussion on the terms *Ryukyuan, Okinawan,* and *Uchinānchu.*

3. Hawai'i was one of the first destinations of overseas Okinawan migration, where "twenty-six men arrived in Hawai'i in January of 1900 to work on the sugar plantations" (Maehara 2007, 4).

4. This book can be read as part of the larger project to revitalize the Indigenous languages in Okinawa (see Ishihara 2016).

5. I use the term *Native Hawaiian* throughout this essay to refer to individuals with Hawaiian ancestry. However, it is important to note that *Kānaka Maoli, Kānaka 'Oiwi,* and *Kānaka* can also be used to refer to Native Hawaiians (Fujikane 2021, xii).

6. See "Call for Papers" in an upcoming special issue on "Towards an Oceanic Filipinx Studies" of *Alon: Journal for Filipinx American and Diasporic Studies*: https://escholarship.org/uc/alonfilipinxjournal.

7. Such parallels between Okinawa and Hawai'i are made by other diasporic Okinawan cultural producers as well. For example, Norman Kaneshiro, a leader of Ukwanshin Kabudan, an Okinawan performing arts troupe in Hawai'i, sees a parallel between Ukwanshin Kabudan's efforts to preserve Okinawan culture with comparable initiatives among Native Hawaiians to preserve their culture that began with the Hawaiian cultural renaissance in the 1970s (Okamura 2014, 196–97).

8. For an overview of Asian American studies' engagement with settler colonial critique, see Tiongson (2019) and Day et al. (2019).

9. For example, in his reading of Haunani-Kay Trask, Saranillio reminds us that in Trask's theorization, "settler colonialism goes beyond exposing complicity, offering instead new pedagogies—different ways of knowing, being, and responding to—of the living force of the colonial past in the present" (as cited in Day et al. 2019, 33). This invitation to reflect on the agency of Asian settlers resonates with recent formulations that imagine alternatives to Asian complicity, such as Fujikane's "settler ally" and "settler aloha 'āina." As Fujikane (2021, 14) notes, these terms "grapple with settler colonialism and cultivate the seeds of a decolonial future."

10. My reference to "Indigenous Asias" refers to the 2015 volume of the *Amerasia Journal* and the 2018 volume of *Verge* (see Dvorak and Tanji 2015; Eubanks and Sherba 2018).

11. In her discussion of off-island Hawaiians, Kauanui (1998, 689) suggests that there are "possibilities in taking root and growing in a different soil while maintaining an originary location and emphasizing Indigeneity as a central form of identification." She also observes that solidarity work of some off-island Hawaiians has entailed recognizing off-island sites as the "home" of another people (691).

12. Ueunten (2015, 27) makes this assertion in reference to the Worldwide Okinawan Festival held every five years in Okinawa, where thousands of Okinawans from the diaspora go to the homeland to participate in ceremonies, cultural performances, exchange visits, tours, and so on. Though he does argue that the discourse of the festival directs attention away from the presence of U.S. military bases, he acknowledges that the festival is a product of the tenacious efforts of both overseas Okinawans and people in Okinawa (29–30), which cannot be downplayed.

13. The tension between the settler colonial logic of elimination and Indigenous persistence in Kina's series resonates with Kauanui's (2016) discussion of "Enduring Indigeneity": while the operative logic of settler

colonialism may be to "eliminate the native," Indigeneity itself is enduring, and Indigenous peoples exist, resist, and persist. It is important to note that although analyses of colonialism in Okinawa have not engaged the question of settler colonialism, Iwama (2021, 97) has observed that the harms associated with the military bases in Okinawa—which include water system and noise pollution, motor vehicle and aircraft accidents, and sexual violence—display the traits of settler colonialism.

14. For example, Yokota (2015, 59) notes that Uchinānchu (Okinawan) "assertions of indigenousness at a supra-national level largely began with delegations to the UN Working Group on Indigenous Populations (WGIP) starting in 1996."

15. *Roots* is an image of a banyan tree in the tourist area of Waikiki in Honolulu (Kina, interview with the author). Banyan trees in Okinawa are also known dwelling places of the *kijimuna* spirits.

16. There is a history of the Okinawan diaspora in Hawai'i assisting their homeland, especially after the Battle of Okinawa. For example, Kina recounts how, in the post–World War II years, her great-grandmother would send "care packages back to her family in Okinawa—smuggling U.S. dollars by sewing money in the hems of clothes and filling canning jars with homemade caramel candy and hiding money in the tops of the lids" (Kina 2015).

17. For a recent overview of U.S. militarism in Okinawa, see Sakuma (2021).

18. *Holding On* also has other images relating to the Battle of Okinawa, such as *Chibi Chiri Gama, Yomitan, Okinawa, Japan* and *Thousand Origami Cranes, Himeyuri Monument, Itoman, Okinawa, Japan*. For more information regarding the battle, see Hein and Selden (2003, 2–13).

19. Tada (2015) explains that after Reversion in 1972, Okinawa developed as a major tourist destination for mainland Japanese tourists.

20. For a discussion about group suicide during the war, see Fields (1993, 61). For a discussion about Kina's series in relation to group suicide, see Yokota (2019).

21. It is important to note that Kina has turned to the context of Hawai'i before in previous projects, such as in her *Sugar* series (2010–11) and *Blue Hawai'i* (2012–13), which were informed by her family's immigrant history (Takezawa 2016, 67–71).

22. In his discussion of *nuchi du takara* and *aloha āina*, Kyle Kajihiro (2015) cautions against romanticizing the "golden age" of Ryukyu. Like the "unification" of the Hawaiian Kingdom by Kamehameha I was accomplished by violent conquest, the formation of Ryukyu in 1429 also entailed violent subjugation of neighboring kingdoms. While the "myth"

of an essential Okinawan pacifism and the nostalgia for the Ryukyu Kingdom may reflect elite interests as well as activist and tourist narratives, Okinawan pacifism—represented in the phrase *nuchi du takara*—has nevertheless become a real contemporary political and cultural phenomenon (Kajihiro 2015).

23. Considering Tonouchi's work within the context of an oceanic Okinawa and not solely as local literature in Hawai'i is significant given local literature's proximity to settler colonialism. For example, ho'omanawanui (2008, 119) asserts that Kanaka Maoli literature is often incorporated into the broader category of local literature, which is oppressive because it erases the centuries-long Native literary tradition.

24. This resonates with McDougall's (2010, 53) assertion that contemporary Native Hawaiian literature emphasizes how Native Hawaiians have survived, how their connections to their kūpuna have remained strong, and how they may recover what they have lost. In this way, Native Hawaiian literature represents a powerful site of resistance that resists racist stereotypes and colonially imposed narratives of their history that have been used to justify the ongoing occupation of Hawai'i.

■ WORKS CITED

Aguon, Julian. 2021. *The Properties of Perpetual Light*. Mangilao: University of Guam Press.

Aikau, Hōkūlani K., and Vernadette Vicuña Gonzalez. 2019. Introduction to *Detours: A Decolonial Guide to Hawai'i*, edited by Hōkūlani K. Aikau and Vernadette Vicuña Gonzalez, 1–13. Durham, N.C.: Duke University Press.

Casumbal-Salazar, Iokepa. 2019. "'Where Are Your Sacred Temples?': Notes on the Struggle for Mauna a Wākea." In *Detours: A Decolonial Guide to Hawai'i*, edited by Hōkūlani K. Aikau and Vernadette Vicuña Gonzalez, 200–210. Durham, N.C.: Duke University Press.

Chibana, Megumi. 2013. "Striving for Land, Sea, and Life: The Okinawan Demilitarization Movement." *Pacific Asia Inquiry* 4, no. 1: 136–54.

Chibana, Megumi. 2018. "An Artful Way of Making Indigenous Space." *Verge: Studies in Global Asias* 4, no. 2: 135–62.

Day, Iyko, Juliana Hu Pegues, Melissa Phung, Dean Itsuji Saranillio, and Danika Medak-Saltzman. 2019. "Settler Colonial Studies, Asian Diasporic Questions." *Verge: Studies in Global Asias* 5, no. 1: 1–45.

Diaz, Vicente M., and J. Kēhaulani Kauanui. 2001. "Native Pacific Cultural Studies on the Edge." *The Contemporary Pacific* 13, no. 2: 315–41.

Dvorak, Greg, and Miyume Tanji. 2015. "Indigenous Asias." *Amerasia Journal* 41, no. 1: ix–xxvi.

Endo, Shoji. 1996. *Folktales of Okinawa*. Naha, Okinawa: Bank of the Ryukyus International Foundation.

Eubanks, Charlotte, and Pasang Yangjee Sherba. 2018. "We Are (Are We?) All Indigenous Here, and Other Claims about Space, Place, and Belonging in Asia." *Verge: Studies in Global Asias* 4, no. 2: vi–xiv.

Fields, Norma. 1993. *In the Realm of a Dying Emperor*. New York: Vintage Press.

Figal, Gerald. 2007. "Bones of Contention: The Geopolitics of 'Sacred Ground' in Postwar Okinawa." *Diplomatic History* 31, no. 1: 81–109.

Fujikane, Candace. 2000. "Sweeping Racism under the Rug of 'Censorship': The Controversy over Lois-Ann Yamanaka's *Blu's Hanging*." *Amerasia Journal* 26, no. 2: 158–94.

Fujikane, Candace. 2008. "Introduction: Asian Settler Colonialism in the U.S. Colony of Hawai'i." In *Asian Settler Colonialism: From Local Governance to the Habits of Everyday Life in Hawai'i*, edited by Candace Fujikane and Jonathan Y. Okamura, 1–42. Honolulu: University of Hawai'i Press.

Fujikane, Candace. 2021. *Mapping Abundance for a Planetary Future: Kanaka Maoli and Critical Settler Cartographies of Hawai'i*. Durham, N.C.: Duke University Press.

Ginoza, Ayano. 2012. "Space of 'Militourism': Intimacies of U.S. and Japanese Empires and Indigenous Sovereignty in Okinawa." *International Journal of Okinawan Studies* 3, no. 1: 7–23.

Hau'ofa, Epeli. 2008. "Our Sea of Islands." In *We Are the Ocean*, 27–40. Honolulu: University of Hawai'i Press.

Hein, Laura, and Mark Selden. 2003. "Culture, Power, Identity in Contemporary Okinawa." In *Islands of Discontent: Okinawan Responses to Japanese and American Power*, 1–38. Lanham, Md.: Rowman and Littlefield.

Hibbit, Maia. 2021. "In Okinawa, the US Military Seeks a Base Built on the Bones of the War Dead." *The Nation*, February 18. https://www.thenation.com/article/world/japan-okinawa-henoko/.

ho'omanawanui, ku'ualoha. 2008. "'This Land Is Your Land, This Land Was My Land': Kanaka Maoli versus Settler Representations of 'Āina in Contemporary Literature of Hawai'i." In *Asian Settler Colonialism: From Local Governance to the Habits of Everyday Life in Hawai'i*, edited by Candace Fujikane and Jonathan Y. Okamura, 116–54. Honolulu: University of Hawai'i Press.

Huang, Yu-ting. 2018. "Locating Asian-Indigenous Relations in the Pacific." *Verge: Studies in Global Asias* 4, no. 2 (2018): 25–36.

Ikehara, Ariko. 2016. "Third Space as Decolonial Con/Text: Okinawa's

American Champurū." *Transnational Asia: An Online Interdisciplinary Journal* 1, no. 1: 1–40.

Inoue, Masamichi. 2007. *Okinawa and the U.S. Military: Identity Making in the Age of Globalization*. New York: Columbia University Press.

Ishihara, Masahide. 2013. "Hito no idō to bungaku no gengo." In <*Okinawa*> *hito no idō, bungaku,diasupora*, 203–7. Tokyo: Sairyusha.

Ishihara, Masahide. 2016. "Language Revitalization Efforts in the Ryukyus." In *Self-Determinable Development of Small Islands*, edited by Masahide Ishihara, Eiichi Hoshino, and Yoko Fujita, 67–82. Singapore: Springer.

Iwama, Daniel. 2021. "Tides of Dispossession: Property in Militarized Land and the Coloniality of Military Base Conversion in Okinawa." *Okinawan Journal of Island Studies* 2: 93–114.

Kajihiro, Kyle. 2015. "Life Comes from the Sea." *Ke Ka'upu Hehi 'Ale*, September 28. https://hehiale.com/2015/09/28/life-comes-from-the -sea-part-1/.

Kauanui, J. Kēhaulani. 1998. "Off-Island Hawaiians 'Making' Ourselves at 'Home': A [Gendered] Contradiction in Terms?" *Women's Studies International Form* 21, no. 6: 681–93.

Kauanui, J. Kēhaulani. 2016. "'A Structure, Not an Event': Settler Colonialism and Enduring Indigeneity." *Lateral* 5, no. 1. http://csalateral .org/issue/5-1/forum-alt-humanities-settler-colonialism-enduring -indigeneity-kauanui/.

Kim, Jinah, and Nitasha Tamar Sharma. 2021. "Center-to-Center Relationalities: At the Nexus of Pacific Island Studies and Trans-Pacific Studies." *Critical Ethnic Studies Journal* 7, no. 2. https://manifold.umn .edu/read/ces0702-01/section/858422f6-6b03-42ec-a888-cf70fdad61fc.

Kina, Laura. 2015. "From Okinawa to Hawaii and Back Again: A Pointer Follows the Currents of Her Family History." *Zócalo Public Square*, August 31. https://www.zocalopublicsquare.org/2015/08/31/from -okinawa-to-hawaii-and-back-again/chronicles/the-voyage-home/.

Kina, Laura. 2019. "Ancestral Cartography: Trans-Pacific Interchanges and Okinawan Indigeneity." *Asian Diasporic Visual Cultures and the Americas* 6: 48–70.

Kina, Laura. 2020. "Reflections on Encountering Minor-Transnationalism." *Amerasia Journal* 45, no. 3: 377–80.

Letman, Jon. 2019. "US Military Base Threatens Biodiversity in Okinawa." *Truthout*, April 15. https://truthout.org/articles/us-military-base -threatens-biodiversity-in-okinawa/.

Maehara, Shinichi. 2007. "Sekai no Uchinaanchu Okinawans around the World." In *Uchinaanchu Diaspora: Memories, Continuities, Constructions*, edited by Joyce N. Chinen, 3–14. Honolulu: Department of Sociology, University of Hawaiʻi at Mānoa.

McDougall, Brandy Nālani. 2010. "From Uē to Kūʻē: Loss and Resistance in Haunani-Kay Trask's *Night Is a Shark Skin Drum* and Mathew Kaopio's *Written in the Sky.*" *Anglistica* 14, no. 2: 51–62.

Ohnesorge, Karen. 2008. "Uneasy Terrain: Image, Text, Landscape, and Contemporary Indigenous Artists in the United States." *American Indian Quarterly* 32, no. 1: 43–69.

Okamura, Jonathan Y. 2014. *From Race to Ethnicity: Interpreting Japanese American Experiences in Hawaiʻi.* Honolulu: University of Hawaiʻi Press.

Ōta, Masahide. 2014 "The Battle of Okinawa." In *Descent into Hell: Civilian Memories of the Battle of Okinawa,* translated by Mark Ealey and Alastair McLauchlan, xv–xix. Portland, Oreg.: MerwinAsia.

Phung, Malissa. 2019. "Indigenous and Asian Relation Making." *Verge: Studies in Global Asias* 5, no. 1: 18–29.

Sakai, Naoki. 2016. "The West and the Tropics of Area Studies." *Asian Diasporic Visual Cultures and the Americas* 2: 19–31.

Sakuma, Sayaka. 2021. "Souvenirs of Solidarity: Toward an Okinawa-Centered Politics of Demilitarization." *The Asia-Pacific Journal* 8, no. 2. https://apjjf.org/2021/8/Sakuma.html.

Saramosing, Demiliza, Katherine Achacoso, and Roderick N. Labrador. 2021. "Call for Papers." *Alon: Journal for Filipinx American and Diasporic Studies.* https://escholarship.org/uc/alonfilipinxjournal/callPapers.

Shigematsu, Setsu, and Keith Camacho. 2010. "Introduction: Militarized Currents, Decolonizing Futures." In *Militarized Currents: Toward a Decolonized Future in Asia and the Pacific,* edited by Setsu Shigematsu and Keith Camacho, xv–xlviii. Minneapolis: University of Minnesota Press.

Shimabuku, Annmaria. 2012. "Transpacific Colonialism: An Intimate View of Transnational Activism in Okinawa." *CR: The New Centennial Review* 12, no. 1: 131–58.

Tada, Osamu. 2015. "Constructing Okinawa as Japan's Hawaiʻi: From Honeymoon Boom to Resort Paradise." *Japanese Studies* 35, no. 3: 287–302.

Takara, Ben. 1994. *Koeru Waga kami uta shishū.* Naha, Japan: Niraisha.

Takezawa, Yasuko. 2016. "Negotiating Categories and Transgressing (Mixed-) Race Identities." In *Trans-Pacific Japanese American Studies: Conversations on Race and Racializations,* edited by Yasuko Takezawa and Gary Y. Okihiro, 60–82. Honolulu: University of Hawaiʻi Press.

Tiongson, Antonio T., Jr. 2019. "Asian American Studies, Comparative Racialization, and Settler Colonial Critique." *Journal of Asian American Studies* 22, no. 3: 419–43.

Tonouchi, Lee A. 2011. *Significant Moments in da Life of Oriental Faddah and Son: One Hawai'i Okinawan Journal.* Honolulu: Bess Press.

Trask, Haunani-Kay. 2008. "Settlers of Color and 'Immigrant' Hegemony: 'Locals' in Hawai'i." In *Asian Settler Colonialism: From Local Governance to the Habits of Everyday Life in Hawai'i,* edited by Candace Fujikane and Jonathan Y. Okamura, 45–65. Honolulu: University of Hawai'i Press.

Ueunten, Wesley. 2015. "Making Sense of Diasporic Okinawan Identity within U.S. Global Militarisation." *Intersections: Gender and Sexuality in Asia and the Pacific* 37. http://intersections.anu.edu.au/issue37/ueunten1.htm.

Urashima, Etsuko. 2016. "Looking towards Nirai Kanai." Translated by Gavan McCormack. *The Asia-Pacific Journal* 21, no. 3. https://apjjf.org/2016/21/Urashima.html.

Yokota, Ryan Masaaki. 2015. "The Okinawan (Uchinānchu) Indigenous Movement and Its Implications for Intentional/International Action." *Amerasia Journal* 41, no. 1: 55–73.

Yokota, Ryan Masaaki. 2019. "On *Holding On* in Okinawa." In *Holding On,* by Laura Kina. Chicago: Flxst Contemporary.

Yoneyama, Lisa. 2017. "Toward a Decolonial Genealogy of the Transpacific." *American Quarterly* 69, no. 3: 471–82.

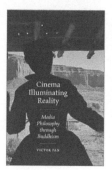